2   12-4-73

Elsa Annelea
fall, 1973

THE ANGUISH
OF CHANGE

THE
ANGUISH
OF CHANGE

Louis Harris

W·W·NORTON & COMPANY·INC·
NEW YORK

Library of Congress Cataloging in Publication Data

Harris, Louis, 1921–
  The anguish of change.

  Includes bibliographical references.
  1. United States—Social conditions—1960–
2. Social problems. I. Title.
HN65.H37   309.1′73′092   73–11473
ISBN 0–393–05505–1

Printed in the United States of America
1 2 3 4 5 6 7 8 9 0

FOR *Philip L. Graham*
whose initial faith in 1963
made much of this book possible

CONTENTS

FOREWORD

This book has been in the making for many years and represents a sizable portion of the professional work that has absorbed this writer much of his adult life. It is an effort to set right the record of American public opinion in the period from 1960 to 1973, as measured through some 436 separate surveys. The sponsors of these studies have been many, among them the Harris Survey, appearing twice weekly in over 250 newspapers during election periods and in fewer during the off season; *Newsweek,* with whom I spent a most enjoyable five years collaborating on the Newsweek Poll; Time, Inc., during the trying years of 1969–71; and numerous foundations, government agencies, and other sponsors of the research.

The book draws heavily from the literally thousands of questions asked of cross-sections of the American people over the past decade. In order to make the substance of the writing palatable to the reader, question wordings have not been included, although wherever a projective question has been used, the wording has been included in quotes. In all cases, the design and structure of Harris surveys is intended to pursue a policy of scrupulously balanced questioning to allow every conceivable point of view a chance to surface. However, there are basically three different types of questions used in our field: (1) Those which pose alternatives in a pro or con manner; (2) those which ask the respondent to answer in his own words without any choices; and (3) those which are projective or suggestive to the respondent, in all cases followed by an opposite point of view which can be agreed to. All three types of questions have been utilized in this book.

Every question asked and each result reported on is readily available to any reader who might inquire at the offices of Louis Harris and Associates, 1270 Avenue of the Americas, New York 10020. Our information services department stands ready to handle any and all inquiries about the material contained herein. On the dates and places of conversations reported on in the book, I have tried to go back over my own appointment books and voluminous notes from the past to document each as accurately as possible.

The major conclusion of this book is that American public opinion is quite different from what most leaders of the establishment have judged it to be. For this obviously sorry plight of the state of information dissemination among the leadership of the country, I must blame mostly myself and my colleagues in the polling and journalistic professions. Somehow, the leadership of the country has consistently underestimated the public's intelligence, its openness to change, its willingness to abide a pluralistic set of values, and its growing affluence. But, then, if the leadership were more atuned to the underlying mood and feelings of the people, then there would have been no central thrust to this book. For, in it, I have drawn upon my own privileged exposure to presidents and other leading public and private men, to contrast their own perceptions with the actual facts as we have found them through perhaps the most exhaustive body of public opinion collected during any period.

Obviously, I have read the facts as I have seen them. Unfortunately, there is a tendency on the part of many to seize upon one set of figures and to make sweeping generalizations based upon that single, slender fact. This method of ad hoc analysis is our bitterest enemy, for it leads otherwise intelligent men to grossly inaccurate conclusions. Trend data, identical questions asked over a period of time, is most valuable. The next most valuable method is to ask a whole cluster of questions dealing with a single subject, which then will yield a kind of level of public opinion. The voter or the citizen simply does not give you his opinions concisely. His actual views must be drawn out in long and probing interviews, many of which often last as much as an hour and a half. The sampling is painstakingly pursued, so that by 1973, we can say confidently that any national sample we construct will be accurate to within 3 percentage points on a sample of 1,500 or over in 95 out of 100 cases. Sampling, however, is by far the surest part of the craft of modern polling.

The technique of analysis used has been to assemble a body of evidence and then to determine what the people surveyed have been trying to say to us. No major or minor conclusion in the book is without proof from adequate and sound data. To remain within the parameters of the data and yet to be able to draw definite conclusions has always been the challenge in empirical research and always will be. My own personal philosophy has been that it is much more difficult to go the full route of saying precisely what people are trying to say than it is to hedge and to shift from the foot of "on the one hand" to the other foot of "on the other." Such analyses are usually not worthy of the time and energy wasted upon them. They mean either that the research on which they were based was not designed properly in the first place or that the analyst is lacking in proper discipline or proper courage or both. For better or worse, however, the conclusions reached are my own.

Throughout most of my adult life, I have been in and around the center of national politics, as well as in the mainstream of American business, labor unions, voluntary organizations, government at all levels, and even the arts in recent years. I have drawn upon this experience extensively in this book. If some individuals feel that I have misrepresented them or been unduly unkind to their cause or their point of view, I am not prepared to apologize, but to stand by my conclusions. I did not write this book necessarily to make friends, but instead to be true to my mission: to report where America has been, where it is, and where it is going, without fear or favor.

The public opinion analyst has two great advantages over other social observers. First, he can save himself embarrassment by learning his craft and remaining within the bounds of his data, thereby at least keeping himself in constant touch with reality. Second, he can make important observations and have a body of data to back him up. This book does not represent,

therefore, my opinions about this country and its people. Instead, it represents my conclusions as a professional analyst on
that subject, a distinction that is particularly critical in this day
of the so-called new journalism.

Behind the hundreds of surveys drawn upon is an organization, Louis Harris and Associates, which I founded in 1956. The
people who make up this organization are my close colleagues,
and must share any professional credits resulting from this effort. It is easy for me to enjoy my work with them, not only because they are rewarding people to be with, but because I can
do the best part of a survey, the survey design, writing the ques-
tionnaires, and then relishing those long hours of poring over
the computer print-outs to write the analysis, and then to report
to newspaper or magazine readers what it all adds up to. But
others have to do the really tough jobs, involving long hours of
organizing a field staff of over 3,000 supervisors and interviewers who struggle through foul weather and adverse conditions
and sometimes a public who wants to be interviewed these days
through peepholes or front doors with chains on them. Others
do inside work, such as the long and laborious task of statistical
typing, where numbers must be accurate. Others do the painstaking job of sampling; while still others spend their working
lives sorting out answers people give in their own words, trying
to find patterns in them in what we call the coding department.
Finally, there are those who work the computers, which are no
more than giant addition and subtraction machines, but without
which modern survey analysis would be impossible. I have
never hesitated to ask for impossible deadlines or to demand
backbreaking performance from these gallant people on our
staff, partly because I am willing to give back the best I have in
response, and partly because I know they share with me the ex-
citement of the creative process of finding out what people
really think. We have an unwritten rule that has been followed
for years to actively disagree with any design, questionnaire,
procedure, or finding which might emerge from our studies.
Rank helps no one in this process of staring down each other's
work.

The writing of this book itself has been made possible

through the patience and the persistence of my editor and publisher, Evan Thomas, who was clever enough to offer me an advance which then compelled me to do it; through the help and encouragement given me by one of my oldest friends, the author, Joseph P. Lash, who has kindly read the manuscript; the all-night typing under dreadful conditions imposed on my secretary, Marlise Kummer; and the painstaking checking of references to surveys and other facts of consequence used in the book by Graham Bright of our organization. My family has been equally enduring, with my wife, Florence, my sons, Peter and Richard, and my daughter, Susan, being prevailed upon to listen to portions at various times, for I have an incurable habit of wanting to show passages to people after writing them. I am also grateful to both my partners at Donaldson, Lufkin, & Jenrette, who now own the Harris firm, and to those at Louis Harris and Associates for allowing me the time to write it.

My earnest hope is that I have done right by the American people, whom I believe are the most underreported and most fascinating moving body in perhaps all the world's history. The message of this book, I trust, is their message, for it is the lives of all of them, as well as all of us, which hang in the balance for the rest of this century. And I hope, too, that at least a few of the men and women who will shape that future will read this book and come out with a better understanding of the ultimate constituencies they will be called upon to lead. I deeply believe the public desperately deserves leadership, and we have come up pitifully short in recent times.

LOUIS HARRIS

May 1973

O I see flashing that this America is only you and me,
Its power, weapons, testimony, are you and me,
Its crimes, lies, thefts, defections, are you and me,
Its Congress is you and me, the officers, capitols, armies, ships,
   are you and me,
Its endless gestation of new states are you and me,
The war (that war so bloody and grim, the war I will henceforth
   forget), was you and me,
Natural and artificial are you and me,
Freedom, language, poems, employments, are you and me,
Past present, future, are you and me.

I dare not shirk any part of myself,
Not any part of America good or bad. . . .
                    Walt Whitman, "By Blue Ontario's Shore"

I

JOY IS DEAD

The sad and tragic war in Vietnam was over, but the streets were empty. The protests were now a searing memory; the celebrants never even existed. For, after over fifty thousand American lives were lost, this was the first American war of which 72% of our people had said it was a "mistake" and 63% had said it was "morally wrong."

The economy was producing at record rates again. Employment was rising briskly. Yet there was little jubilation, nor even much enjoyment of the spate of new cars, refrigerators, washing machines, or color television sets filling the homes of the American people. A massive thirty-three million people felt largely bored by their jobs and 56% thought the quality of products and services now was worse than ten years ago. [1]

Richard Nixon finally received a massive 61% [1] of the vote in his lifetime quest for approval from the American people. Yet only five months later, in the wake of the disclosures of the Watergate scandals, no more than 24% of those same people could bring themselves to say their president "inspired confidence personally in the White House."

The law of the land proclaimed that it was now illegal to discriminate against blacks in jobs, education, and housing. At the same time, 66% of blacks felt they were still discriminated against in housing, 68% in white collar jobs, 53% in education. Most of all, a majority of blacks felt they were not "even treated as human beings" by most in the dominant white society.

The campus revolts of the late sixties were largely a thing of the past. Rock music and long hair for men had captured the taste of a generation. By now, even construction workers had frizzy wisps of hair sticking out the backs of their hard hats, and burly, 260-pound tackles in pro football had locks appearing beneath their helmets. Yet, at the same time, 61% of the people 50 years of age or older said they were still "bothered by the manners, hairstyles, and dress of young people."

The City of Brotherly Love, Philadelphia, as well as Minneapolis, an eminently enlightened city in Middle America, both had tough ex-cops for mayors. Only a generation before, reform mayors Joseph Clark and Hubert Humphrey had held out so much promise for urban progress in these same cities. A frightening 62% of all women in big-city America said they were afraid to walk the streets. An even higher 81% of all people thought "law and order had broken down" in the country. The chances were by now better than even that any house you visited had a gun in the closet.

Yet 71% of the people favored strict gun registration and control laws, that Congress somehow could not pass. A substantial 64% expressed a willingness to "set up programs of rehabilitation for criminals, so that they could return from prison and take their place as normal, law-abiding citizens." But no massive rehabilitation program for offenders was in sight.

The spread of the use of illegal drugs was alarming to 3 out of 4 people in the country. Even a majority of the young, fertile ground for the spread of illicit drugs, expressed deep concern about drug abuse. Yet, at the same moment, close to 4 in 10 adult Americans also reported using perfectly legal pep-up pills to keep them awake, tranquilizers to calm them down, or sleeping pills to put them to sleep. When asked if the use of these legal drugs was "dangerous," a majority of users acknowledged it was.

Just about as many Americans were distressed by the spreading use of soft and hard drugs as were upset by what they viewed as growing alcoholism. The sale of alcoholic beverages not only was legal almost everywhere, but liquor was even sold in state stores in many places, with liquor taxes a major source of governmental revenues. At the same time, 1 in 3 homes [2] reported a member of the family had chronic drinking problems.

A substantial 83% of the people were covered by some health insurance plan. Yet a third of the breadwinners of the country reported they "could be wiped out financially" in the event of a major illness. Most Americans favored a compulsory, comprehensive, federal health insurance program covering all possible medical problems from surgery to psychiatry, from hospital care to prescriptions, from checkups to eye glasses. Yet by 1973, Congress had not passed such a program and the president was opposed to it. The bitter fruit of unrelieved suffering from the system of health delivery and virtually no system of preventive medicine could be found in the 3 million Chicanos, 6 million blacks, and 11 million poor rural whites who said the state of their health could be described on a daily basis as "the living sick."

Women could count on living seven years longer than men; [3] the bare-bone facts might be pointed to as proof that America in the last third of the twentieth century obviously treated women better than men. Yet a growing number of women did not see it that way at all. On the contrary, most women gave their support to "efforts to give women a more equal status to men." The heart of the newly articulated female complaint was a sense of being sick and tired of being taken for granted from the neck up and of being forced into forever winning concessions through cajolery and exploitation of dominant male whims.

The singular mark of women was that they cared about human life. Most women opposed capital punishment, while a majority of men favored it. A solid majority of women opposed the bombings of Hanoi during the Vietnam War, while a majority of men favored them. The day had permanently passed when the man of the house could deliver the vote of his wife on election day. But the day had not arrived by any stretch of the imagination when women had an equal voice in running the country. At best, 66% reported, it would be at least fifty years before a woman might be considered seriously for president.

American mobility reached unheard-of heights by the 1970s for any nation in the history of the world. An estimated 1 in 8 families were moving to another place of residence every year. Theoretically, this meant that everybody could be expected to pick up roots every 8 years. It would be reasonable to assume that people would be increasingly pleased with the new neighborhoods they moved to. Yet a majority say where they live has become worse rather than better in the past 5 years. And, despite the fact that a sizable majority [4] now live in urban America and expect to be there 10 years from now, more than half of the young [5] would like to live in smaller towns and the wide open spaces. As a nation, we feel trapped by having to live more in places we like less.

Owning an automobile in America was almost as common as owning a pair of shoes. The day when possession of a new car was a prime status symbol had just about passed. Over half the country annually took a family holiday in the family car. Again, mobility seemed a yard wide. Yet for the crowded urban centers, the auto had become a multiple curse: the cause of interminable and constant traffic jams at rush hours and the leading cause of stifling air pollution.

Ralph Nader had become one of the few authentic folk heroes, with 65% [6] voicing the view that "new auto safety laws never would have been passed without his crusade for auto safety." At the same time, a majority of car drivers any day of the week will readily admit it is "too much bother" to use their auto safety belts. Majority support for mass transit as a substitute for getting to work in cars was nowhere in sight, although 86% expressed a desire to see the "pressures of day-to-day living relieved." It was obvious America was experiencing massive current shock in coping with its wondrous transportation mobility.

The spirit of enterprise, along with a willingness to work and virtually limitless material resources, was largely believed by most Americans to account for our rise to the most impressive industrial power on earth. In turn, this stunning industrial growth had led to a deep-seated mythology summed up as "American know-how." In World War II, the height of the adu-

lation of what know-how could do was reached. Almost overnight, millions of young Americans were taught to fly planes in
combat, sail ships around the world, master the operation of
sonar and radar, build airstrips and bases with lightning speed.
That war was won with American know-how.

A generation later, public service radio commercials wailed
forth the sad comment, "The lake is dead, the river is red." And
73% of the American people said they were deeply disturbed
that the environment had been raped by American know-how.
Air and water pollution became prime areas of national worry.
Consistently, leaders of industry, government, and the media labeled this concern fadism—the concern would fade in a trade-
off for more industrial growth and more jobs. Yet, when asked if
they would prefer to see 50% less air and water pollution in
their own community or a 50% cut in unemployment, by 54%
to 38% the public opted for curbing pollution. And in 1972 environmental bond issues, authorizing literally billions of dollars
to be spent on improving the quality of life, were passed from
one end of the country to the other.

After the resounding landslide victory of Richard Nixon in
1972, the American people were optimistic that many of the
roots of frustration could be eradicated. The war was finally
over. The prisoners of war had come home. A large majority felt
that a president elected by so heavy a margin could now build
the peace abroad and help resolve the searing and divisive
problems at home.

But none of these high hopes were soon to be in the offing.
The climactic aftermath of the 1972 election was not joy at the
end of the Vietnam War, a feeling shared by no more than 8 out
of every 100 Americans. Rather, the second Nixon term began
with the crashing disclosures of widespread political spying and
misuse of the apparatus of law and order by high officials in the
Nixon Administration, resulting in the resignations of the two
most important aides of the president in the White House and
the indictment of two former cabinet officers, including the attorney general.

It took the public a long time to become aroused by the Watergate affair, because the break-in at Democratic National head-

quarters was viewed as the kind of nefarious activity most politicians engaged in. Even as late as April 1973, a significant 73% of the people agreed with the claim that "dirty campaign tactics exist among both Republicans and Democrats, and the Nixon people were no worse than the Democrats, except they got caught at it." At the same time, 72% also felt that political bugging was "a violation of basic civil liberties" and "an invasion of the right to privacy."

As long as the Watergate affair involved low-level political operatives, the public was prepared to write it off as an unpleasant campaign memory. But when it enveloped the Department of Justice, then the attorney general himself, then the White House and top men on the president's staff, the credibility and the integrity of the president were cast in doubt. A sizable 63% of the people simply did not believe the integrity of the White House in the Watergate affair. More important, by 63% to 23%, a majority of the public agreed that "it is hard to believe that, with his closest associates involved in Watergate, President Nixon did not know about the planning and later cover up of the affair."

Almost overnight, the Watergate disclosures shattered the short-lived flicker of hope that a second Nixon term would be marked by new efforts to improve the quality of life and to elevate the standards of national leadership. By 53% to 33%, most Americans felt the president did not "inspire confidence personally in the White House." By 60% to 25%, a majority came to the conclusion that "President Nixon has lost so much credibility, it will be hard for him to be an effective president again."

The Watergate scandals would leave scars on the American presidency and the faith of the young in the constitutional system for many years to come. Already at a low level, faith in political leaders would be bound to sink to new failures of confidence. Young children watching the Watergate hearings on television would find it hard in later life to associate the highest morality with the office of the presidency.

The daily life of America was changed beyond recognition by the advent of the television set as the family hearth. In one fell swoop the tube became the source of instant, free entertainment;

of on-the-spot, flash news; a built-in tranquilizer for the young; and, with color, literally a way to travel to far-off, wondrous places. Yet by the 1970s, the hot medium of television had nearly devoured itself. The public was largely disenchanted with the fare of crime and spy programs, talk shows, quiz shows, and soap operas, the staples on which the commercial medium was built. A majority was delighted when Vice-President Spiro Agnew took on the television news establishment with charges of bias, even though Walter Cronkite, David Brinkley, and Howard K. Smith were still looked on as nightly celebrity friends, fixtures of American family life.

Television's troubles could be laid partly to familiarity breeding contempt. What was successful was instantly multiplied. The multiplied product became boring. The entertainment was no longer very entertaining. It became stylish for the rapidly increasing affluent to brag about not watching any more. A new age of selectivity in taste, of pluralism in style was taking over, but the insatiable commercial appetite to produce mass programs for ever-larger mass audiences produced the phenomenon by the early 1970s of television committing professional suicide.

Even the most golden escape of the era, live sports on television, appeared to be heading for trouble. With the revolt of the young against the establishment, one of the safest bets fifteen years ago might have been to predict the demise of spectator sports, as being a passive, uninvolving opiate to take the minds of the masses off real-life experiences. Yet, the number of sports fans in the country grew from 62% in 1966 to 82% [7] by 1973, with the young leading the pack in enthusiasm. The earliest televised sport, baseball, lost its luster quickly, partly because of overexposure on the tube, partly because it seemed slow and dragging, filled with inert moments that didn't fit the hot medium of TV. Faster-moving sports such as pro basketball and hockey moved to new and impressive fortunes. Pro football became king, with its fast and visible action on the tube, with all the suspense of a last-minute 60-yard pass that could pull a game out or the brutality of two huge linemen hitting an already crippled Joe Namath before he could get the pass off. Yet the demands for more and more exposure on television were beginning to threaten even pro football. The ultimate commercial trap had yet to be faced: to give the public all the live sports it wanted could produce so many competing sports shows that no one would be able to attain the viable mass commercial audience necessary to pay huge salaries to athletes and the high cost of producing the shows.

The litany of real and imagined frustrations and signs of current shock could be extended to many parts of our national life. But there were really only two kinds of resulting conditions that sum up much of the American scene today: the quality of life and the quality of leadership.

All of the foregoing had soured more Americans over the quality of life than at any other time since public opinion polls began to measure public moods in the 1930s. More people nationwide [8] believed America was a worse rather than better place to live in than it had been 10 years ago. The gulf between those with power and the rest of the people had rarely been so wide. As the middle of the 1970s approached, alienation had grown to accurately describe as much as 48% of the population 18 years of age and over, up substantially from 31% back in 1966. For example, the number who feel "what I think doesn't really count" rose from 39% to 50%. The proposition that "people running the country don't care about people like me" expanded to 45% and "people with power are out to take advantage of people like me" rose to 43%.

This sense of suspicion and powerlessness had reopened some of the old economic wounds of the depression days. The old saw that "the rich get richer and the poor get poorer" rose from 48% to 66% of the public in seven years. Cries to "soak the rich" were revived and found solid backing in the 64% who said "the tax system is designed to help the rich and not average people" and in the nearly unanimous 71% who agreed with the proposition that "tax laws should be rewritten to raise the taxes of the rich and corporations and to bring some tax relief to people with lower incomes."

The tax revolt stemmed from two deeply felt injustices. First, by over 5 to 1, the people were convinced that the so-called graduated federal tax system was not working that way at all.

They believed those in high income brackets had found porous holes in the tax laws to largely escape paying normal taxes, through devices ranging from oil and cattle investments to real estate and other tax shelters. Second, a substantial 58% of the people felt they simply "were not getting good value for the tax money they were paying."

In a word, the public had become convinced that the big, monied interests had found a way to beat the system, while the rank and file were stuck paying taxes to support a government that was performing poorly. This phenomenon was quite new. In the past, causes which sought to crack down on the rich and the privileged had turned to government as the protector and even savior of the people, of the "little man."

Not so in the 1970s, when the government was every bit as much the target of people's wrath as any private, selfish interests. In a period of severe inflation, the major cause for high prices, 82% of the public believed, was "federal spending," higher than "business raising prices" or "unions demanding wage increases."

By 1973, although there was deep alienation toward the private establishment, by the same token, people no longer looked to the federal government, or government at any level for that matter, for a way out. There were distinct signs of a revival of populist fervor against the rich, but no sign of equally popular fervor to mandate a big government to represent the disenchanted and disinherited.

Two insights illustrate the crux of the alienation. When asked if the bankrupt Penn Central Railroad should be taken over and run by the government, public opinion opted 61% to 20% against such a take-over. The main reason: "As bad as the Penn Central has been run, the government would run it worse." Still another fascinating finding emerged when people were asked if they would welcome their state and local governments monitoring industrial air polluters. A majority of the people were opposed. How about the federal government carrying out such environmental monitoring? By a small 43% to 41% margin, the public favored it.

But when asked about consumer advocate groups monitoring air polluters, by a thumping 57% to 33% margin, the public favored that. It is patently obvious that there must be laws governing air pollution, which ought to have real teeth such as fines and other stiff penalties for the law to work. But distrust and disenchantment with government had reached such endemic proportions that the public obviously trusted the integrity of voluntary consumerist groups more than government itself.

These findings are crucial and pivotal to understanding the deep frustrations of life in America in the 1970s. For they point up an essential American faith in finding solutions in the private sector rather than at the federal governmental level, a deep hostility to socialism or a government take-over of much of anything more, but an angry desire, nevertheless, to replace those not producing at the helm of the establishment—whether in the public or private sector. Thus, across the board, leadership in the established institutions was in deep trouble. The following table illustrates the responses to questions asked both in 1966 and in 1973 about how much confidence people had in those running key institutions:

Drop in Confidence for
Establishment Leadership [9]

Have "Great Deal" of Confidence in:	1973	1966	CHANGE
	%	%	%
Doctors	48	72	− 24
Financial leaders	39	67	− 28
Scientists	37	56	− 19
Military leaders	35	62	− 27
Educators	33	61	− 28
Psychiatrists	31	51	− 20
Religious leaders	30	41	− 11
Retail store operators	28	48	− 20
U.S. Supreme Court	28	51	− 23
Executive branch of government	27	41	− 14
Business leaders	27	55	− 28
Congress	21	42	− 21
Press leaders	18	29	− 11
People running TV	17	25	− 8
Labor leaders	15	22	− 7
Advertising leaders	12	21	− 9

The incredible part of these results is that of sixteen major areas of establishment pursuit, not a single one can evoke a majority of the public which can accord it "a great deal of confidence." Not only is this a massive failure of leadership, but it brings into sharp focus the target of the alienation: the heart of the entrenched establishment itself.

Doctors were widely criticized for not being available for house calls when people needed them. Financial leaders were viewed as having produced high-risk opportunities which then failed to deliver. Scientists were saddled with the charge of being culprits who advanced know-how that did not necessarily benefit mankind. Military leaders were widely associated with, not simply an unpopular war in Vietnam, but with waste and inefficiency, and tolerance of corruption. They were also suspect of preferring to prolong rather than to end U.S. involvement in Vietnam. Educators were believed to have let the educational system grow out of control, to have been passive and ineffectual administrators rather than leaders in a crisis.

Government leaders were viewed as heading an inert structure, more interested in perpetuating an overstaffed bureaucracy than in providing an institution with dedication and integrity, servicing a public constituency. The U.S. Supreme Court was in trouble over its controversial decisions in the criminal area, and the federal court system on the school busing issue. The media leadership was looked on with skepticism; the decided preference of the public was that news columns or electronic media provide news coverage straight, plus an open forum for divergent views instead of a vehicle for expression of a publisher's exhortations.

Business leaders were widely criticized for failure to deliver product and service quality, for lacking in humanity toward employees, and for not assuming responsibility for helping solve society's problems. Labor leaders were viewed as being inside manipulators running an essentially undemocratic establishment, rather than identifying labor's interests with the larger public weal. Advertising leaders were seen as the con men of the system, with 86% of the opinion that most advertising claims were pure "exaggeration."

The common strain running through the failure of confidence of leadership was that it had not been attuned to the needs of a changing America. People were less critical of the key institutions than they were of the men who were at their helm. It is almost as though the public felt that, if it took a man 15 to 20 years to rise to an important position of leadership, he had been so busy clawing his way to the top, that when he finally arrived his understanding of the public he was serving and his values might be 15 to 20 years out of date.

There was also a kind of ultimate assessment involved here. Because the system has failed to deliver on most of the problems, because the quality of life was felt to have deteriorated, because leadership itself had become at best a bland gray or even invisible, the American people felt it was fair game to take aim at the leadership itself. While a majority of over 9 in 10 wanted to work within the system, there were few sacred cows left.

So change was imminent in almost all areas of life. But, before change can be examined in detail, it is critical that the disenchantment, alienation, and failure of confidence be documented and understood.

II

THREE VIEWS
FROM THE TOP

Each of the last three presidents in the White House demonstrated a keen and abiding fascination with public opinion and particularly with polls. Yet each saw them in different lights and used the information in ways fitting his peculiar style. All shared, however, a common trouble that seems to haunt the office of the most powerful position in the world: a sense of isolation from the rank and file of the people themselves. "Sooner or later," the late John F. Kennedy mused one August afternoon in 1963,[1] "it seems that every problem mankind is faced with gets dumped into the lap of the president right here in the center of it all. But by the time it reaches here, the problem has been dissected, sanitized, and cast into a series of options—almost as though they were engraved in stone. What is missing is the heart behind them, what they mean in human terms."

Kennedy was reflecting about the issue of civil rights and it was the day before the March on Washington, led by Martin Luther King, Jr. As was characteristic, he was remarkably frank in private. "You know," he admitted, "I never dreamed that the central issue of this decade, of my time in the White House, would be the race question. [Clark] Clifford and others had

15

wisely pointed out the importance of not ignoring the race question during the campaign. I guess the Negro was the margin we won by in the '60 election. And I stood with Martin Luther King when he was jailed. But the electric quality of this movement, the depth of despair of those people, their incredible guts to face the dogs and hoses in Birmingham, to walk in Montgomery every day—and to do so much of it without resort to violence. All this was something I just didn't figure would happen at all."

The nature of the presidential office is that it is event-oriented. Each of the last three chief executives has had very different styles and tastes. But what seems to move the operation is the impact of outside events or the impact of presidential initiative on the outside world. Presidents tend to think in a "we" and "they" context, rooted in most cases to a specific meaning or future event.

The late Lyndon Johnson was easily the most subjective and he was always prone to react to events in a most personalized way. In the early evening of June 6, 1968, he reacted for approximately three hours to the tragic death of Robert Kennedy earlier that day. Throughout the conversation, three television sets blinked and blared in the Oval Office, carrying assorted commentaries, tributes, and reconstructions of the assassination of the second Kennedy brother to try for the White House.

At one point, Johnson exclaimed, "How could the Kennedys do this to me? Can you imagine, one getting killed at the beginning and another at the end of my term." Johnson estimated that evening that with the death of Bobby Kennedy, Hubert Humphrey, his self-selected heir apparent, would go on to win the Democratic nomination easily at the Chicago convention the following month. He speculated as to whether Humphrey was up-to-date enough in his thinking or too much wedded to "the old New Deal ideas."

Then, Johnson as Kennedy before him went on to puzzle over the strange, new tides that seemed to be sweeping over the country's and, most particularly his own, destiny. "It's hard to figure out what's going on out there. I'd have thought the young people would have liked all we did on civil rights and even medicare for their old folks and all the help for education. But they seem to have forgotten it all now, if you judge from the McCarthy and Bobby campaigns. But, then, maybe I'd be the last man to hear about it, stuck right here in the White House."

In the end, of course, events interact with the emotional make up of the man in the White House. Kennedy possessed an ability to look at himself reflected in what he liked to call "the unvarnished truth," and could seem clinically remote in discussing public reaction to himself, his stands, or his record. His emotions were hardly outpouring with affection in his personal relations. This quality led Walter Lippmann to observe critically in private that Kennedy suffered from "emotional constipation."

President Nixon obviously is not devoid of emotion, but he is strikingly depersonalized, especially in contrast to his immediate predecessor, Lyndon Johnson. In fact, on an October afternoon in 1971 in the Oval Office, Nixon pondered out loud just how important it might be for a president, himself particularly, to have to demonstrate charismatic personal qualities in order to get people to support his policies. By asking the question, Nixon was suggesting that, much as Johnson, he would be judged by what he accomplished rather than by his personal charm or appeal. Later that afternoon, he would come back to that point and admit with remarkable frankness that he well understood how the public did not rate him well on personal warmth and color.

Therefore, Nixon seemed to conclude, success in governing came down to a matter of properly reading the word and temper of the times and getting the president's activities into the mainstream of public consent. He was particularly interested in a recent Harris Survey that showed alienation was on the rise and confidence in leadership (including the executive branch of government) had fallen precipitously since 1966. He posed a most startling question to the effect of whether, given the state of public upset, the country was really governable or not.

Of the past three presidents, Nixon is most inclined to accept the findings of public opinion polls as events in their own rights. When the American people reported in a Harris Survey in May 1971 [2] that they were prepared to accept admission of the People's Republic of China to the UN and at least de facto recognition of the Peking regime by this country, following the visit of the U.S. Ping-pong team to China, Richard Nixon indicated, in retrospect, that the public was ready for his new breakthrough. Similarly, when the Nixon job rating in "keeping down the cost of living" went to an all-time low of 82% to 14% negative, the president believed it. Reports from the early August meetings at Camp David indicated that the trouble Nixon was in with the public for his failure to control inflation or rising unemployment contributed heavily to the final decision to impose a wage-price freeze on August 14. When similar Harris polls showed that 81% of the public favored an arms limitation agreement with the Russians, it was evident to Nixon that in consummating an initial SALT treaty he would meet with wide public support. Those three decisions, all well documented in heavy majorities in the polls before the fact, were to provide the cornerstones of the Nixon landslide victory in the 1972 election.

Kennedy was an extensive user of polls, but he had his reservations about them. He did not doubt the authenticity of public opinion measured through attitude surveys, but he had two major reservations about them, one pragmatic and one a matter of principle. The pragmatic doubt, often stated in private, was that opinions articulated by the public in a poll might emerge in somewhat different form and shape—and even in different proportions—than shown in the original poll. He would look back to the West Virginia primary of 1960, where he held a 70% to 30% [3] lead *before* the religious issue was drawn. But, *after* the anti-Catholic sentiment had surfaced, he was no better than even up with Hubert Humphrey (41% to 41%) with two weeks to go in the primary. He broke open that historic primary by following advice drawn from his polls that he could shame West Virginia voters for voting like bigots; he won going away 61% to 39%, as compared with our final estimate given to Senator Kennedy that he would win 58% to 42%.

The principle Kennedy felt deeply about was summed up in his own paraphrase of the Harold Laski doctrine that leaders in a democracy had to perform "within the jaws of consent of the governed." Kennedy would add, "You must come down on the merits of the issue, regardless of public opinion. But if you find yourself outside those jaws of consent of the governed, then you'd better *look around fast*. You can educate the public to extend those jaws. But if you're outside them too often, then you can get voted out of office."

An example of this Kennedy principle in operation was the case of Laos in 1961, when the U.S. agreed to a neutralist government there. One day that spring, President Kennedy asked this writer a cryptic question: "Do the American people care what happens to Laos [always pronounced 'Lay-oss']?"

The answer: "Mr. President, most never heard of Laos, let alone have great concern about it."

Came back a Kennedy retort, "Well, Laos just went down the drain. The Communists will have it before long." In the next ten years, the Communist Pathet Lao would occupy as much as three-quarters of Laos, but officially the neutralist government was still in power. Back in 1961, Kennedy had made his decision on Laos and was "looking around fast," to find out the parameters of public consent.

When years later, this writer asked a Russian diplomat why Laos had not gone Communist and suggested perhaps that the U.S. CIA had operated effectively there, the Soviet official replied, "You must never underestimate the power and resources of the Russian CIA. Maybe we didn't want Laos to go Communist."

A prime example of the Kennedy wariness about public opinion, especially as measured through polls, occurred in the early summer of 1963. The nuclear test-ban treaty with the Russians had been signed that May. Surveys before the agreement showed that a substantial 71% [4] of the public favored such a step to control nuclear testing in the atmosphere. After the agreement had been consummated, public support for the treaty rose to 81%.

Upon publication of the 71% support number, Kennedy expressed pleasure at the level of backing, but he also seemed far from convinced that people really felt that way. He would say, "I hope your findings are right."

It was not until he took off on a cross-country "nonpolitical" trip early that summer that he became convinced. He had decided to stump the country on a theme of conservation of natural resources, an issue he had long admired Gifford Pinchot, the Pennsylvania Republican, for advocating. But after a few stops on the tour, it was evident he was ahead of his time. (It would not be until later in the decade and in the 1970s that environment would rise to a moving and major issue with the people.) In midpassage of the tour, he decided he would talk about the nuclear test-ban treaty.

He privately expressed surprise when he received a very positive response. When he reached Salt Lake City, Kennedy bit the bullet on the test-ban treaty. At the Salt Lake Tabernacle, the seat of Mormon power, he decided to make the entire speech on it. For Kennedy, it was an acid test. On religious grounds, Mormon leaders had not looked with favor, to say the least, on a Catholic occupant in the White House. Utah had not spawned a notable group of internationalist U.S. senators, let alone men likely to become exultant politically over an agreement with the Communist regime in Moscow. After the speech at the Mormon Tabernacle, the presidential party spent the night in Yosemite National Park. About midmorning that Sunday, a call came from the president himself, "Well, I have to hand it to you. That nuclear test-ban treaty *is* popular. That was the goddamnedest response a president ever got when I delivered that test-ban speech at the Mormon Tabernacle."

A singular mark of Kennedy in politics was his ability to lay out a problem, ask for a creative idea, then seize it and exploit it. An episode during the 1960 presidential campaign which took place in early August of that year illustrated how Kennedy approached a key political decision.

The senator had had a discussion with Joseph Alsop and they thought it would be helpful if this writer came to Washington "to see if some basic campaign ideas could not be worked out." As in most campaigns, the elaborate research apparatus headed by Law Professor Archibald Cox of Harvard had come up with a "mountain of facts and very little focus to run a campaign on," as Kennedy himself put it. The senator was in a particularly frustrating situation, since he had to remain in Washington during a rump session of Congress called between the Democratic and Republican conventions. He was the nominee for president, but his leader of the Senate, Lyndon Johnson, the man who ran the upper branch with an iron hand, was also his nominee for vice-president.

Kennedy was given a suite of offices just off the Senate floor where Mrs. Evelyn Lincoln, his secretary, and other aides took temporary stations. He was like a caged tiger. He felt he was being trapped by hostile colleagues who might embarrass him into a voting stand that would prove harmful in the campaign ahead, or, worse, that the unlikelihood of the session to produce any legislation of significance might point up to the public that Kennedy could not produce much as the new leader of his party, after all.

Each evening with the Senate business done, Kennedy would come over to Joe Alsop's Georgetown house for dinner and talk. Each night, he would start out the same, proclaiming, "Time is overdue for us to close this awful sideshow down here and get this show on the road. The votes are everywhere in the country except here in Washington, D.C." (which did not yet have the right to vote in presidential elections). He was then running behind in the nationally published polls and this undoubtedly was on his mind.

Kennedy's campaign problem was that normally as the "out" candidate he could make political capital out of the eight-year record of the incumbent Republican Administration. Yet, in this case, he had to be extremely careful not to frontally criticize President Eisenhower, who remained enormously more popular than either Kennedy or his opponent, Richard Nixon. What is more, there was reason to believe that Ike did not care very deeply whether his successor were a Republican, and he was not running himself. The hunch that President Eisenhower was not going to get too deeply involved in the campaign was borne out shortly afterward when a reporter asked him to name a few contributions Nixon had made as vice-president. Eisenhower said, "Well, maybe I could, if I had a few weeks to think about it."

The problem was discussed incessantly that week—how to go on the attack, how to be positive about the future, but always

not to attack the president. The days went by and nothing
seemed to crystallize. It was impossible to say that the Eisenhower tenure had been "bad," even though there had been 3 re-
cessions in 8 years. To say they were "bad" would be to imply
that the president was "bad," and our own polls showed end-
lessly that the automatic, knee-jerk reaction of most Americans
to the mention of General Eisenhower was, "He's a good man."
It was obvious that Nixon would run on a pledge to continue
the Eisenhower years, for they had been by far the best the minority Republican party had seen in two long decades out of
power. Yet Nixon wasn't Ike. And, most important, the revered
general would not be in the White House during the next four
years. Therefore, while people did not want to reject Eisenhower, these would be new times and if Nixon could be painted
into the corner of simply wanting to continue the Eisenhower
era, but without Ike, perhaps it would work.

The key words that I scribbled down on a yellow pad late
one night were, "As a nation we can't stand still. We must move
ahead." Under this umbrella, then, Kennedy could project the
entire campaign into the next four years, make many sharp criticisms of the previous eight years, but all would be softened and
depersonalized by labeling them part of the "stand-still" policies
Nixon, not Eisenhower, would pursue. By the same token, the
"we must move ahead" part of the idea could incorporate all
kinds of hopes for the future, could capture the sense of hope
needed to give the Kennedy drive inspiration.

The next morning I took the one page of notes to Kennedy's
office off the Senate floor. I told him I thought I might have
something here and read them to him. He immediately ordered
me to sit down at Mrs. Lincoln's typewriter and put them into a
form he could read. He tried out the theme that night in a
speech in Alexandria and afterward made the simple cryptic
comment to me, "Lou, I think that will do." Of course, he repeated the theme over and over again throughout the campaign
until reporters stuffed cotton in their ears. Then he repeated it
again. Those original notes on lined yellow paper are among my
choice possessions and, along with the carbon of the memo

typed on Evelyn Lincoln's typewriter, are the only records I have ever preserved in permanent form.

Lyndon Johnson was something else again. He would become the truest believer of polls, but only when they tended to support what he was doing. For a considerable period from 1963 to 1966, he greeted many a visitor to the White House with a recital from a card with the latest results on the job the American people thought he was doing as president. He would proudly rattle off the numbers, much as a miser would count his gold aloud. The use of public opinion survey results, of course, fell off sharply as President Johnson's standing dramatically dropped in the polls in 1967. By 1968, he was prone to carry around with him another set of statistics, citing all the good works he had done in the social area and the numbers of people who had benefited from the flood of Great Society legislation he had pushed through in those historic days of 1964–65.

In an election situation, of course, all three were different— Lyndon Johnson not excepted. In 1964, a startled public opinion researcher received a call from a Johnson aide on the eve of the election. He said that the president, Dean Rusk, and Robert NcNamara were all meeting in the Oval Office, discussing the raid on the U.S. Air Force base at Bien Hoa in Vietnam, in which a number of American planes had been destroyed. The question from Bill Moyers was, "The president would like to know if a failure to respond to this attack immediately will be taken by the voters as a sign of weakness by the Administration." The answer: "That is the sort of thing people would expect from Barry Goldwater and probably the main reason they are voting against him." No immediate response to the attack was made before the election.

Other than on the eve of an election, however, Johnson was singularly his own man on major policy decisions. To this writer's knowledge, he did not seek out prevailing public opinion before making a decision, nor did he "look around fast" after he made a major move. He liked approbation from the people more than either Nixon or Kennedy. He literally thrived on such approval. But it was far more a kind of gestalt experience, a collective coming together in appreciation for all the good things he had done.

Lyndon Johnson simply was not a reader of public opinion. His main task, as he would say many times, was viewed as "doing right by the people, especially those who can't help themselves," and "taking it on the head" when he had to carry out an unpopular act he thought was right.

This may have fitted the notions of those who feel a leader must at all costs do what he feels he should. Indeed, it was a singular mark of Johnson's abundant supply of raw courage. But, had Johnson been a more sensitive student of the substance of public opinion, instead of simply basking in a high overall popularity rating when he had it, content to accept symptomatic praise from poll results when things were going well, he might have allowed additional insight into that Oval Office, which he once described "as the busiest, loneliest place in the world."

In fairness to Lyndon Johnson, of the past three presidents he was far from alone in finding religion in the substance of public opinion around election time.

While he was never in the position of running as an incumbent, John Kennedy was shown to be slipping in the final ten days of the 1960 campaign, after picking up a clear lead as a result of the first debate with Richard Nixon. The signs were unmistakable in his late slippage. Anti-Catholic feeling among white Protestants was mounting again and Catholics had become overconfident of his impending victory, so that the more affluent among his coreligionists could feel the luxury of voting their higher income self-interest and/or their conservative political philosophy and desert Kennedy.

Kennedy's credo in running for office always was to go "all-out, flat out," as he said many times. Thus he had no reserve the last ten days, except to go on a nonstop campaign schedule that left him totally exhausted by election day.

A key question in the final week was whether Kennedy should once again surface the religious issue by facing it the way he had in the final days of West Virginia in the primaries: to pledge if elected that if he allowed his church to influence him, he should be impeached. The decision to avoid the religious issue in the final week was not made by John but by his brother Robert and his father, Ambassador Joseph P. Kennedy. The ambassador was embarrassed by the attacks on his son John for "using the Catholic issue," and, in fact, privately had expressed real regrets the issue had had to surface frontally earlier in West Virginia and in September in a meeting before Protestant ministers in Houston.

Instead of a final climax, the 1960 Kennedy campaign backed across the finish line, barely a hairbreadth ahead of Nixon. Later, President Kennedy was to admit privately that he had foolishly ignored the warning signals in the closing days of the campaign. He hadn't come back to his most personal and dramatic campaign appeal in the end, and he was sorry he had not.

In 1972, Richard Nixon was similarly beset by a dilemma on his key issue: his record in "working for peace in the world," on which he was praised by 67% of the electorate with only sixteen days to go. But, by mid-October, the Vietnam issue was going soft for Nixon. People's hopes for peace had been buoyed in early October with the Kissinger talks going well. The Nixon forces, however, were neither certain that the October 8 terms Kissinger had obtained in Paris would wash with right-wing voters, on the one hand, or that an announced settlement after October 15 would not appear to be overly political.

Nixon's doubts were partially solved by Hanoi's release of most of the terms agreed on and their further insistence on a formal signing by October 31, a week before the election. North Vietnam forced a Kissinger appearance before the press on October 26, at which the national security advisor made his famous "Peace Is At Hand" statement. But, by the time October 31 came and went, further doubts were appearing among voters about Nixon's Vietnam credibility. Henry Kissinger did not try for a final settlement in the last week of the campaign, but the president himself made a strong statement reassuring the voters that peace in Vietnam was close indeed. This made the difference, and his huge lead held up for 61% of the vote on election day.

Richard Nixon did play politics with Vietnam in those final sixteen days. His decision was not to consummate a final settlement which might endanger right-wing sentiment. But he used Kissinger's October 26 statement and his own election-eve talk to assuage most voters who were parched for word of peace. In fairness, Kissinger's press conference was professionally a necessity, given Hanoi's release of the terms. But Nixon read his own public opinion as requiring a tightrope walk—and it worked.

After Kennedy and Johnson had served out their time in the White House, and Nixon had finished his first term, there was ample evidence that the net effect of the twelve dramatic years from 1960 to 1972 had produced a divided, unhappy, and disenchanted American people. So a central question must be raised about all three of the last presidents: Did they really understand public opinion in their times? Put it another way: Were they such poor readers of the future that each in his own way allowed events in the short run to dictate their decisions, with the ultimate loser the very electorate Kennedy, Johnson, and Nixon all had so exhaustively pursued and finally won?

Kennedy essentially dealt with public opinion as an elitist, which befit his style and manner. Basically, he wanted to make decisions which were "best" for the country at home and abroad, trusting his sensitivity to political winds and his charismatic ability to communicate with the people to carry the day.

The key ingredients in the Kennedy perception were to surround himself with superior elitist brains who could come up with the "best" solutions and then to depend on the unwashed masses to rally behind his decisions. Of course, he did not disdain the very necessary politics of dealing with, manipulating, and even relishing the rank and file of the people.

When Kennedy was running for president, this writer asked him why he was pressing so hard for a bill to give aid to India. His reply was revealing: "I know there are few votes to be had from this effort. But there is an important layer of people in America who are thoughtful and decent. They are the essential leadership group across the country. To be a viable president later on, I need to show them I am willing to fight for sophisticated and even unpopular causes."

The Kennedy record finally was flawed in his real failure to inure himself to inside politics, specifically of the kind played in

Congress. In retrospect, Kennedy's elitism did him in as president, for precisely the reason Adlai Stevenson was undone in his bid for the White House: Both men communicated a disdain for the elected politicians who emerged from the people themselves. John Kennedy therefore ended an all too short tenure at 1600 Pennsylvania Avenue with the deep frustration of having been rejected by Congress on his legislative program.

Lyndon Johnson worshipped Franklin D. Roosevelt, his early political mentor. He honestly believed the old notion that "God must have loved the poor, because he made so many of them." In the Depression, helping the poor was good politics as well as good for one's soul, and was even doing God's bidding. Thus, the capstone of the Johnson philosophy was, "You never had it so good," meaning, of course, that the role of government was to be the provider of the good things the common folk could never achieve by themselves.

Translated into politics it meant promises unlimited. But in Johnson's terms, promises undelivered was the way to disaster. He believed a real leader had to deliver—and deliver he could, precisely where Kennedy had failed. "Delivery," to Lyndon Johnson, the product of Sam Rayburn in the Congress, meant passing legislation. So, by 1966, LBJ was on his way to historic heights, both in terms of social legislation passed and in popularity for his performance.

He had achieved his peak and had slipped downward by January 1968, when his old friend John Connally of Texas put it well in a private conversation with this writer: "Old Lyndon just can't do enough for people and the poorer they are the more he wants to do for them. I think he has smothered people so bad with 'you never had it so good' that he's got himself trapped into an impossible 'what have you done for me lately.'" Although close personally, Connally had differences a gulf wide with Johnson on social philosophy.

Johnson's troubles with Vietnam in many ways stemmed as much from his view of public opinion as from the soundness, or unsoundness, of his policies in that sad war. By clinging to faith in the less privileged masses and asking that he be trusted as a miracle-doer *inside* of politics, Johnson in fact disdained the thinking capacity of the people themselves, and their need for knowing the facts and deciding for themselves. In an odd way, Johnson displayed an old-shoe version of elitism, that "papa really knows best, and just wait until you see what I'm going to do for you!"

The ultimate reckoning on Vietnam never came during his time in the White House. Tragically, his time on earth ran out just on the eve of the final settlement announcement. In the end, Lyndon Johnson's faith that the people would follow him through "hell and high water" because he could always deliver on what he knew was best for them did him in politically. He underestimated the explosion of political literacy and, ironically, was the victim of the rapidly escalated educational system he felt so dedicated to. His fatal flaw was that, in pleading "to come reason together," he meant, "Let me take you on a faith ride. I'll make it good for you." Lyndon Johnson could persuade the ears off a deaf monkey in private; yet he always had an invisible shield that left him mute with the masses of the people. The reason? Essentially, in his perception of public opinion he did not really believe in mass decisions arrived at openly. He became a victim of the very doubts he experienced about Hubert Humphrey on June 6, 1968.

By the time he arrived at the White House, Richard Nixon had to have become a realist. He had lived at political death's door too long not to have stripped his view of public opinion down to an essential survival quotient: You operate off your natural political base as far as that will take you and then you improvise to make it the rest of the way. President Nixon's two successful runs for the White House find their basic keys in his partially yielding to public opinion (no matter what his own past record or statements of principle) and in his uncanny ability to exploit his adversaries' weaknesses in a no-holds-barred fashion.

The remarkable saga of 1968 and 1972 is not that they were two very different elections, resulting in widely differing margins of victory (less than 1 point in 1968 [5] and a 23-point spread in 1972 [6]), but rather how incredibly similar was the Nixon strategy in each case. In both elections, Nixon cultivated the increasingly conservative and Republican South's disenchantment with national Democratic politics and shored up normally GOP bases in the small-town Midwest and Rocky Mountain regions.

In both elections, he then let his major opponents destroy themselves in the big urban centers. In 1968, Hubert Humphrey undoubtedly was encumbered by his association with the unpopular Johnson Administration and the unpopular war it was fighting. But Humphrey also made some fatal mistakes of his own: (1) His failure to risk jumping the traces on Vietnam at the conclusion of the disastrous Democratic Convention, when he might have galvanized a suicidally divided party; (2) his failure to go after George Wallace until too late in October (he made his real gains when he finally began to polarize the electorate between himself and Wallace on race, an issue he avoided all through his dismal September run of 1968); (3) his seeming paralysis on the public stump in dealing with youthful protest hecklers (indeed, ultimately handled much better by his running mate, Senator Edmund Muskie, when he invited hecklers to share the mike with him on the platform).

In 1972, once again Nixon's opponent, another upper Northwest product, Senator George McGovern, provided him with at least half his final election margin. This time it was easier with George Wallace retired from the contest, for in both the South and in rural America, North and South, Richard Nixon had a political base from which to operate.

He then let McGovern destroy himself in the key industrial states, which George McGovern did in a way only rivaled in recent times perhaps by the political hara-kiri committed by Senator Barry Goldwater in 1964. In rapid succession, McGovern frightened both high- and middle-income voters with his $1,000-for-every-person welfare scheme; [7] he worried people employed in defense plants by demanding massive cuts in defense spending; he turned off many antiwar people by insisting America feel so guilty that it should accept defeat 50,000 American lives later in Vietnam; he then muted the young by seemingly showing in his handling of the Eagleton affair no compassion for those who have had mental troubles; and, finally, he soured new politics advocates by virtually promising every ethnic group a place in the cabinet, coming out for parochial school aid at a Chicago Catholic school and endorsing Louise Day Hicks *twice* in one day on a short visit to Boston (he did, however, carry Massachusetts on election day).

The secret weapon Richard Nixon employed in both 1968 and in 1972 was the enormous self-restraint he used in keeping himself visible only to his own base and positioning his opponents to allow him to back in when it came to the pivotal, populous states.

Limited visibility is a vital key to not only President Nixon's political successes, but to his perception of public opinion as well. One of his marks as a leader is to avoid bucking the mainstream of the popular tide on many key issues. Thus, he will perfunctorily carry out U.S. Supreme Court orders for busing to achieve racial balance, but will literally hold his nose while doing it to make it abundantly clear it is not *his* decision. And, indeed, a 1971 Harris Survey showed that while 33% blamed the U.S. Supreme Court and other federal courts and 24% blamed local school authorities for the busing actions, only 12% blamed Richard Nixon, the chief executive of the entire federal executive apparatus—the only enforcement arm the federal establishment has.

Similar examples could be cited on the Nixon approach to health care, social security, the Peace Corps, and other programs, where he has not particularly sought out credit, but has avoided confrontation which might violate the mainstream of public opinion.

Perhaps the ultimate tack in this studied avoidance of aborting the mainstream will is the approach to revenue sharing with the states and local governments. The key to Nixon policy on revenue sharing is that he satisfies two widely disparate constituencies in one fell swoop: He brings vast satisfaction to conservative ideologues who have been fighting big government and, at the same time, he is yielding to popular opinion which is so thoroughly disenchanted with the federal bureaucracy that it no longer wants to turn to government for an ultimate solution of nearly any major problem, no matter how moral it may be.

But if this were the sum and essence of Richard Nixon's perception of public opinion, he would quickly fall victim to his own inaction. Indeed, this was almost precisely the situation in July 1971 when the public expressed little personal confidence in him by close to a 2 to 1 margin. The other element in the Nixon perception of public opinion is, in fact, bold and daring —and thoroughly uninhibited. It is to assume that not only is there a prevailing public mood at a given moment on a given set of issues, but that changes are also in the wind. To catch a strong wind as it is beginning to gust upward will give any kite a real ride for the money. But one key precondition to catching hold of these winds of change is that you not be inhibited by your own past. If you are accustomed to riding south winds, you must be willing to turn 180 degrees to ride the north wind if need be. Another key precondition is that you be able to live with the change you have gone with over a sustained period of time.

The four major cases in his first term in the White House in which Richard Nixon launched his kite to changing winds were: (1) His de facto recognition of Communist China; (2) his courtship of the Soviet leadership and his rapprochement with Moscow; (3) his acceptance of compromise cease-fire terms to end U.S. military involvement in Vietnam; (4) his imposition of the wage-price freeze and his announcement that he had embraced Keynesian economic doctrine. A fifth major case may be his de-emphasis and redirection of federally dominated social spending programs. (This last, however, may be simply a massive variation of the Nixon principle of studied avoidance of frontal confrontation with the mainstream of thinking at any moment in time.)

In the case of China, public opinion had soured on the Cold War, particularly if Vietnam were to be the model such a Cold War would take in the future. It wanted to try accommodation rather than hostility, albeit cautiously so. With presidential blessings, this tendency of the American people was fanned into a strong east wind. At the same time, in the geopolitical real world in which Nixon and Kissinger live, exploitation of the Chinese-Russian rift dictated normalizing relations with both nations, but not simultaneously cutting defense spending here at home.

With the Soviet Union, public opinion did not need to take

such a drastic reversal. Rather, all the president needed was to give some substance to the latest public instinct that both countries had more to gain by competing in relative peace than by seeking ways to destroy each other. The public long had favored arms agreements, cultural exchanges, joint space ventures, and joint exploration of the oceans. But Nixon made these hopes become at least partial realities. And he could live with it, partly because it was good politics to be for peace, and partly because it fitted precisely his power-political view of supernation relations.

In the case of Vietnam, the overwhelming sentiment of the American people since 1967 had been to get out with at least a semblance of honor due a superpower. The Nixon policy of Vietnamization, of "winding down the war" bought time and slowly drained the bite of the hawkish conservative minority on Vietnam, a segment always vulnerable to forays from George Wallace. In the end, Vietnam hawks wanted out as much as Vietnam doves.

Yet the major problem still remained: How to get a government in Hanoi, dedicated to a 100-year struggle to take over the South, to agree to terms that would give the Thieu regime a chance for survival in the short run and also obtain release of American POWs? Though the full history of the Kissinger negotiations remains to be told, there nonetheless is ample evidence of the role of China and Russia in communicating to North Vietnam—through their own nonresponse to the mining of Haiphong Harbor and the earlier and later bombings of Hanoi—that they wanted a settlement.

The final settlement may be neither peace nor entirely honorable, strictly speaking, but few would quarrel with the rhetorical insistence by the president that it be termed "peace with honor." This tack was basically the formula suggested several years ago by the wise old Republican, Senator George Aiken of Vermont, when he said in effect that we should declare the war won and over and just come home.

Yet the final settlement also contained important concessions from the North Vietnamese, including a willingness to recognize free elections, to have an international supervisory force, to give de facto recognition to the Thieu regime, to respect the DMZ area, thereby implying that there are two Vietnams. However, it also contained some unpopular compromises by the U.S., not the least of which was to allow over 100,000 North Vietnamese troops to remain in South Vietnam and to give tacit recognition to the principle of coalition rule for the South with the Communists, although the initial coalition had no force or power.

In terms of public opinion, Richard Nixon on Vietnam could claim a major accomplishment. He caught the wind of final liquidation pretty far up in the sky, but change he did in his stated views on Vietnam. His best bet that he can live with the settlement is the strength of Thieu's army and the likelihood that neither Moscow nor Peking will risk a Communist government in Saigon that might be overly beholden to the other, thus probably precluding a Communist take-over, for purely internal Communist considerations, any time in the near future.

In the case of the wage-price freeze, Nixon violated all his previous statements about federally administered controls. But he sensed correctly, aided by careful scouting of poll results, that this is what the public wanted. Instead of moving meekly to some form of guidelines and jawboning as a halfway measure, the president went whole hog and again capitalized on the public's instinct for a more, rather than less, drastic attack on inflation. Since those last four months of 1972, of course, there has been a dissembling of federal controls over wages, prices, and rents; so the freeze itself was never something Nixon had to contemplate living with in the long run anyhow.

These examples pinpoint the essence of the Nixon perception of public opinion. Basically, public opinion is fixed, in that certain truths ought not to be violated, usually of a mother, God, and country variety. Moves designed to accommodate to the mainstream of thinking are always cloaked in the eternal verities. But moves to catch up new, major currents of change are trumpeted as examples of daring leadership, and history undoubtedly will mark them well as befitting such a definition.

In this respect, Richard Nixon on his international moves and Lyndon Johnson on his sweeping domestic legislation shared a common approach. In fact, both Johnson and Nixon shared another common perception of public opinion: People will judge actions and not really heed words. This tack finally undid Johnson when he mired in the quicksand of Vietnam. And it could undo Nixon the same way; as the Watergate scandal in 1973 has begun to do.

There is a more basic flaw in the Nixon approach to public opinion, however. Essentially, he does not appear to arrive at his approach to problems from his own inner convictions nor does he seem to "come down on the merits," in JFK's words. Rather, the Nixon approach is essentially exploitative. The set of popular will must be there for the counterreactive president to act. The gusts of new winds for change must be whipping upward before he will latch onto their swirl.

Perhaps, ironically, Richard Nixon fulfills the late Whitney Young's admonition to his fellow black leadership, "You have to run very fast to keep up with your following." [8] The pivotal question is not whether such a perception of public opinion works pragmatically, but rather what it does to the heart and soul of a people starved for inspiring demands upon it, seeking hope and national and world purpose, waiting for leadership which will take the promises Archibald MacLeish wrote about as far back as 1939, before World War II, before Korea, before the Kennedy and King assassinations, before the drug plague, before the full miseries of Vietnam and racial divisions were upon us. MacLeish's admonition that "America is promises . . . but only if we take them . . . now not later" [9] still holds. Yet none of our past three presidents has found it all: how to articulate the promises (JFK did), how to take them (LBJ and RMN did partially), and to provide the hope and the fulfillment together (none of the three have) in a central hope. Somehow, the people were ahead of the leaders and the shape of the times ahead of the people. As the mid-1970s approached, we were still adrift in a sea of confusion and division.

III

KARL MARX
UPSIDE DOWN

One of the great ironies of the late 1960s could be found in Detroit. There, America's largest car manufacturer had set up a research laboratory suggesting a whole new transit system, replete with underground pods, escalator belt highways, mass rail systems. "Imagine," exclaimed a young and enthusiastic professional at the lab, "we could end traffic jams in the future." That certainly boggled the mind. If successful, they just might make General Motors obsolete.

A bit of investigation back at GM headquarters, about ten to fifteen miles away, revealed little relationship between what the lab was doing and the major problems on GM management's minds. GM was thoroughly immersed in worrying about the onslaught of Ralph Nader, the new safety requirements laid down by the federal government, whether proposed emission standards could be practically met by new engines, and how much of a ruckus would be raised by investigations into shoddy servicing and repair work on American-made autos.

The fact is that while GM's management might be deeply concerned over a whole host of new federal regulations, they needn't have worried about a government take-over. For by the late sixties and early seventies, the number of Americans who would turn totally to governmental solutions for their problems had dropped to no more than 9% of the public. The threat of a federal take-over of nearly anything in private enterprise was highly remote. The further, more telling truth was that the threat of socialism was dead not only because government had grown so unpopular, but because there simply was no large, low-income mass in the country where radical or revolutionary ideas could germinate. The most status-quo-oriented sector of America could be found in those with incomes of $5,000 and under. The reason: 62% of all those in the lowest income bracket were 50 years of age and over. And it was still the case that the older people became, the less they could tolerate change, let alone advocate it.

Down the line, on the issues that overtook America in the 1960s and first years of the 1970s, the under $5,000 income group could be found consistently to be on the side of resisting change, while at the other end of the income scale, the $15,000 and over income, people were tuned in to change. The following table drawn from 1971–72–73 Harris Surveys illustrates this incredible fact graphically:

Contrast between the Under $5,000 and $15,000 and Over Income Groups on the Change Issues

	UNDER $5,000 %	$15,000 AND OVER %
Pro-Ralph Nader efforts	37	67
Willing to raise taxes to curb pollution	42	71
Pro-women's lib efforts	48	59
Against student demonstrations	54	38
Pro-U.S. Supreme Court school desegregation orders	48	69
Believe blacks asking for more than ready	56	41
Believe blacks have less native intelligence than whites	59	21
Favor legalized abortions	27	62
Ease criminal penalties for use of marijuana	30	43
Agreeable to coalition government in Saigon with Communists	32	57

	UNDER $5,000 %	$15,000 AND OVER %
Would turn in son or daughter possessing marijuana in room	57	27
Favor U.S. diplomatic recognition of China	42	68
Support newspapers on publishing Pentagon Papers	42	56

Ranging from support of the consumerist movement of Ralph Nader or willingness to raise taxes to pay for air and water pollution control to liberalized laws governing the use of marijuana or diplomatic recognition of China, the high- and low-income groups in America lived in quite separate worlds. By any of these and other standards involving the new issues which had their impact on America in the late 1960s and early 1970s, people of privilege tended to be far more amenable to change. By contrast, people with the least means appeared to be most resistant to change.

Of course, it might be argued that issues such as race, drugs, consumerism, pollution control, student demonstrations, women's rights, and abortion are not really "gut" issues, since their roots are not essentially economic. The following table puts this argument to the test—Is there any essential difference in point of view between the low- and high-income groups on a price-wage freeze, on "soak-the-rich" tax reform, on a federal jobs program for the unemployed, or on a federal compulsory, comprehensive health insurance plan? Results are drawn from an August 1972 Harris Survey:

Contrast between the Under $5,000 and $15,000 and Over Income Groups on Economic-Related "Gut" Issues

	UNDER $5,000 %	$15,000 AND OVER %
Favor tax reform with rich paying more	76	73
Favor federal program of productive jobs for unemployed	91	89
Favor return to price-wage freeze	53	53
Favor comprehensive, compulsory federal health insurance program	46	47

On key bread-and-butter issues there was essentially no real difference in attitudes between the high- and low-income groups. It was obvious that those better off were rather guilt-ridden about tax laws they could take advantage of, while at the same time they felt keenly that work ought to be provided by the federal government for the less fortunate.

The case of compulsory federal health insurance is fascinating. Pluralities of both the high- and low-income groups favored something akin to the Kennedy health bill by about the same margins. Yet, the two groups were not at all in the same position with respect to the impact of major illness on their financial condition:

> ——80% of people with incomes of $15,000 said they would be adequately covered financially in the event of a major illness
> ——No more than 46% of people with incomes under $5,000 felt secure enough financially to face a major health crisis.

Given these two widely different states of mind, it is incredible that a sizable majority of low-income people didn't rally to a compulsory federal health plan, and it is equally surprising that so many of the affluent supported such federal health insurance.

Yet, this was precisely the condition in America as it approached the last quarter of the twentieth century. Economic self-interest as the basis of public opinion was rapidly slipping away. The old New Deal assumption that the low-income masses could be depended on to support, and upper-income people to automatically oppose, any and all social measures which would put a floor under the status of the less fortunate just didn't hold water any longer. It would have been hard to believe in 1933 that by 1973 the upper 20% of the population incomewise would favor, by 73%, tax reform designed to soak the rich.

But if the affluent had grown to adopt more enlightened views, so had they grown rapidly in numbers. One set of income distribution figures from the Conference Board told an incredible story of the wholesale growth of affluence in America during the 1970s:

Income Changes in U.S.
from 1956 to 1980 ° [1]

	1956	1968	1980
	%	%	%
Under $10,000	82	60	39
$10,000–14,999	13	25	27
$15,000 and over	5	15	34

° Based on 1968 constant dollars, assuming average inflationary growth of 3.5% per year.

These staggering shifts in income redistribution tell a story of what has been happening to this country over a twenty-year period. Basically, America has been moving swiftly from a dominantly lower-middle-income to an upper-middle-income society. Privilege is becoming commonplace rather than the exception to the rule. While families earning $20,000 still can feel pinched when they aspire to live on a $50,000 scale, nonetheless the vast bulk of Americans (61% it is estimated) will have the means to live as well in 1980 as only a little over a sixth of the population lived only twenty-five years before. In one generation the traditional pyramid of income had almost been tipped upside down.

The implications for mobility, range of interest, and upward escalation of life style were beyond the imagination of the mass of Americans who had lived in Eisenhower's day. Significantly, despite the recession of 1969–71, the upward income surge continued to accelerate and the 1970 projections probably would underestimate the 61% with incomes of $10,000 and over or the 34% with incomes of $15,000 and over. Indeed, most projections underestimated the rate of change.

Yet, as incredible as the income redistribution going on might be, the changes in attitudes among the affluent are even more significant. It is worth pondering what America would have been like forty years after Roosevelt first came into office and the affluent had become the dominant majority, *if* attitudes had *not* changed. If privilege had remained as vested, stand-pat, and resistant to change in 1973 as it had been in 1933, the U.S. could easily have become the most plutocratic, stultified, and reactionary country in the history of the world.

But in the course of those forty years from 1933 to 1973, the issues of concern for the nation had vastly changed. The issue of race had moved front and center, and could not be solved by as simple a formula as "helping the poor will automatically eliminate the race problem." The racial question was deeply emotional, albeit with economic dimensions, but far more wrapped up in the psychological than economic hang-ups of middle-class white America.

One of the ironies of the racial issue was that, among whites, the more privileged, the more educated a person became, the more empathetic he became about seeing equality achieved by blacks and other minorities. Higher-income and better educated whites simply were infinitely more aware of discrimination against blacks; were far less prone to believe that blacks were "pushing for more than they are ready for"; were much less inclined to view blacks in stereotype terms; were more inclined to support black demands for new gains in jobs, schooling, and housing; and were far less frightened by black militants such as the Black Panthers. (Chapter XIII will amply document this fact.)

Even in parts of the economic sphere, the attitudes of the more affluent, the more privileged were where the thrust for change not only had begun but where it was the very heart of the engine to propel it forward. For example, take the case of consumerism. Traditionally in America, as perhaps in all places on earth, the less privileged have been fair game to be victimized by shoddy merchandise peddled at inflated prices. "Pay more and get less" has been a con game played by the sharp merchants on the poor from early mercantilist days. It is entirely probable that the less privileged still receive less for their money than other groups in America today. This is certainly demonstrably the case in food shopping studies in black neighborhoods.

But the impetus for support for the consumerist movement in America in the 1960s and in the 1970s came from the privileged rather than the underprivileged. The following table from late November 1972 illustrates the gulf between the low- and high-income groups on support of Ralph Nader's attacks on industry for failure to produce better quality performance:

Support for Nader in
His Attacks on American Industry [2]

	Nader Does:		
	MORE GOOD THAN HARM	MORE HARM THAN GOOD	NOT SURE
	%	%	%
Under $5,000 income	45	17	38
$15,000 and over	70	16	14

By any measure, the more affluent a person, the more likely he was to be a backer of Ralph Nader and a confirmed critic of the bottom line of quality in American life. "Improvement of quality of life" or "recognition of the repugnance of life" was a singular mark of a cause that had literally overtaken the rapidly growing privileged sector of America in the 1970s.

By contrast, the lower income group in the country, with the exception of the blacks and Chicanos, had by and large lost the impetus for pressing for change. Not only was it *not* any longer the case, as Lyndon Johnson grew up to believe, that "God must have loved the poor because he made so many of them," but there were not so many of them.

Indeed, by the 1970s, America did not have that proud a record on helping the poor. It was still the case that 6% of the families would admit in a Harris Survey that "someone close to me goes hungry for lack of food," and 12% [3] were still classified as in the poverty category—far too much, despite the decline from Roosevelt's "one-third of the nation ill-fed, ill-clothed, and ill-housed."

But any analysis of the 22% of the adult population with incomes under $5,000 would reveal that 2 out of every 3 were white and nearly that many were 50 years of age and over. Sadly, these were largely people who had experienced or grown up in the Depression days and had been the permanent victims of that miserable era. Some had achieved a better standard of living in their earlier adult years, but had plateaued out in advancement when they passed 40 years of age, and now were gradually receding into that blurred and tragically neglected growing mass of Americans called the "elderly."

They populated the fringe and dowdy areas of the downtown parts of the country's metropolises, holed up in fading shanties in all parts of the nation, struggled to make it to sunny Florida or Southern California to seek out a trailer camp or an old people's enclave. But for the most part, the whoop of protest, the thrust for change had left their bones. They had struggled for two-thirds of their lives, and, for better or for worse (most likely the latter), they had little appetite for rectifying their lot at this stage of their existence. Somehow, the art of rationalization grew stronger, the tendency to dwell on opportunities missed that might have been exploited grew weaker, the desire to cling to life as a realist took over.

Along with this rationalized sense of resigned accommodation, those growing old also felt a deep resentment of the new issues, the new ideas, the new manners, styles, and tastes that marked the late 1960s and early 1970s. Age wants more certainties rather than more uncertainties. Perhaps the ultimate certainty of death becomes pervasive. At any rate, the instincts of the old are mostly to cling to the status quo one grew up with rather than to push for a whole new ball game one is unlikely to see realized anyway.

Merely changing income distribution patterns, however, can hardly explain the phenomenon of why there was such a thrust for change among the affluent. The key must be found in the root cause for the growth of affluence itself.

In the course of the past thirty years, despite all of the criticisms leveled at our educational system (including Spiro Agnew's charge that too many were going to college who ought not to be there), the vast expansion of college exposure has probably been the single greatest stimulus for change in this country. The number in the population 18 and over with some college education (one or more years) has risen from 12% in 1960 to 34% in 1973, will pass the 40% mark by 1975, and will approximate the 50% mark by 1980.[4]

Whatever else results from some college education, there is a sure and inexorable relationship between higher education and higher earning capacity. The following classic table has not materially changed in many years:

Relationship between Income and Education [5]

	8TH GRADE OR LESS %	HIGH SCHOOL %	SOME COLLEGE %
Under $5,000	59	17	11
$5,000–9,999	29	41	26
$10,000–14,999	9	30	24
$15,000 and over	3	12	39

The essential fact, of course, is not so much that a higher income produces more extensive education (although certainly the sons and daughters of the privileged do generally receive some college exposure), but rather the other way around. When 93% of American parents said that one of their top ambitions was to send their children to college, they knew they had latched onto a real truth: A higher education in all probability will produce a higher income.

But many parents who experienced sending their children into the golden realm of a college education also had the rude shock of seeing those same children take on a whole new set of attitudes quite unlike those of their parents. Thus, the gap between the views of the college educated and those whose schooling never went beyond the eighth grade became the biggest gulf in America, even greater than those cited earlier between the under $5,000 and the $15,000 and over.

The essential truth was that, once a person was sprung loose from the traditional world of family background, ethnic environment, geographical neighborhoods, and exposed to the broader horizons of a college education, no matter how full of shortfalls, there was little likelihood of the college product returning to the mold from whence he came.

The college product had these earmarks which were distinctive: (1) An inquiring frame of mind to question many of the standard dicta one was raised to believe; (2) a sensitivity to realize there were others in society whose lot and interests were not identical to their own, but who should not suffer by dint of the lack of college exposure; (3) at least a tinge of guilt about having passed the threshold of potential privilege and, while inclined to reap the material rewards, nonetheless prone still to feel less than self-righteous about it.

These undoubtedly overgeneralized attitudes derived from a college education nonetheless were showing up in strong measure in the attitudes of the people classified as the "college educated" in public opinion polls. And, as the college educated inexorably moved up from 12% to 34% to 50% [6] of the population 18 years of age and over, just as inexorably America was going to change as a result. Bluntly put, the thrust for changing the country would accelerate and the areas of concern would focus far less on the economic issues which absorbed so much of American public opinion in the first two hundred years of our existence.

Ironically, much has been made of the lack of material aspirations among America's youth. Indeed, consistently it had been found among college students that most did not aspire to make higher incomes than their parents. This had been particularly the case with those who were the offspring of the college educated themselves. A few years ago, a Harris Survey found most college students' parents earning just over $15,000 a year; the students' own aspirations averaged out at just over $14,000 (undoubtedly an underestimation).

Such news had been greeted as meaning that college students had lost all ambition, that the sons and daughters of the privileged would end up with the menial, low-paying jobs, and that a new generation of blue collar children would pass these privileged scions standing still. There was much doomsaying in fashionable quarters along these lines.

But the odds were all against any such development—and for a simple reason: The most important door opener in America was still the basic requisite of having been to college. In fact, with the acceleration of education in the secondary years and the first two years of college, the chances were that two years of college would expose the average student to more and better math, science, literature, and language training than the average student graduating in the upper half of his class learned thirty years ago.

What was actually happening in the changing attitudes of the college-exposed was that prime, economic, bread-and-butter motivation was being overtaken by a greater concern for the broader quality of life. Slowly but surely, the economic trigger which for so long dominated our national political, social, and even economic life was being supplanted by a plethora of other concerns.

This trend, which might have emerged quite naturally from the internal process of college exposure, had been hurtled forward by still another coincidence that has a profound impact on American society: the fact that the American economy had gone from being essentially industrial-product dominated to being service-oriented.

A majority of people employed in the country now worked for service industries,[7] making America the first postindustrial society in history. One of the marks of such a society was that people were employed more as individuals with specific service functions to carry out, than as line workers on an assembly process. At the key executive level, more people were employed in professional than in line executive capacities. The one quality that divided most professionals from line executives in business organizations was that the professionals felt much more beholden to their outside discipline—whether it be systems engineering, teaching, scientific research, or other professional ties— than to the particular company or institution they worked for.

This difference between line executives and professionals in the emerging affluent society was a critical one. Back in the early 1960s, among the $15,000 and over group, line executives outnumbered professional people. A decade later, the professionals outnumbered the line executives and the gap is growing greater every year. By 1973, for every line executive there were almost two professionals in the $15,000 and over bracket.

The net result of the difference between the new professionals and the line executives could be found in their disparate attitudes in a number of key areas:

 ——On the subject of young people the two groups were far apart. By 63% to 37%, professionals said they were "not bothered by young people's styles, tastes, dress,

and language." But by 54% to 46%, a majority of business executives said they were "bothered by them." A
minority of 45% of the professional group felt today's
younger people were "more immoral than other
younger generations" in their use of drugs, but a majority, 62%, of line executives felt that things the
young did were more immoral. Close to half the professionals felt that student protests had stemmed
from "deeply felt injustices in the system," but almost
3 in 4 line executives wrote the protests off as the
work of "troublemakers."
——In the race area, 58% of the line executives were inclined to think blacks were "asking for more than
they are ready for," but no more than 37% of the
professionals agreed with them.
——On the final settlement in Vietnam, 61% of the professionals approved the U.S. agreeing to a continu-
ance of Communist rule in those parts of South Vietnam under their control until free elections could be
held. No more than 49% of the line business types
were in similar agreement.

These patterns, drawn from three key areas of attitudes toward youthful nonconformity, the press of blacks for equality,
and the compromise terms that ended U.S. involvement in Vietnam were only symptomatic of attitudinal differences on a
whole range of new issues. The very heart of the basic thrust for
change was the burgeoning professional group, now a majority
of those in the $15,000 and up group. These professionals were
the basic wellspring for change in America.

These professionals tended to be highly selective in their
tastes, preferring to cull their information from multiple sources
than from one monolithic source. They tended to resent cultural
media such as television entertainment shows which were predi-
cated on the least common denominator. They tended to fit
Daniel Bell's models of the new meritocracy.[8] Above all, they
tended to be most critical of American society the way it is now
constituted, although they were enough a part of the establish-

ment itself not to want to overthrow it for another system, but rather to want to overhaul it from top to bottom to make it meet the new challenges. They could almost take the economic question of making a living for granted, and not feel any real obligations to the status quo. These new professionals, who had as a group incomes higher than the line business executives, were the most dedicated to changing the system.

Implicit in this major finding of the affluent leading the charge for change was another key fact: The materialistic central pivot for making judgments and establishing the values in society was slipping out.

Issues such as Nader's consumerism and the thrust for an environmental clean-up were in many ways assaults on the economic system itself, although advocates of such programs would claim that they were trying to save the system in spite of itself. As pointed out earlier, the race question obviously was more than economics. The changing styles and manners of youth might be the product of an affluent society, but could not be laid to economic factors. Women might have a long string of grievances about discrimination with economic consequences, but, fundamentally, women now wanted psychological redress. The seemingly uncontrollable spate of violence across the land might stem in part from economic deprivation, but the claim that it resulted from excessive permissiveness certainly could not be laid to economic determinism. And the stark fear of American women on the streets could not be viewed as economic, but rather as deeply emotional.

Almost wherever one turned in America, the basic issues had become essentially noneconomic in nature. In almost all cases, they were the product of our own perceptions and consciousness as a people. And as a people we seemed wholly unprepared for the onslaught of the essentially noneconomic problems we were beset by.

With these new developments, much in America would be recast, altered beyond recognition. The last place they would be reckoned with would be in politics. The reason was not hard to find. The essential history of American politics was filled with coalitions of accommodation between groups and interests which found more reward in sticking together on election day than in canceling each other out.

The classic coalition in modern times was that put together by Franklin D. Roosevelt in the heart of the Depression. Roosevelt capitalized on the long-standing tradition of white Southerners to vote the Democratic column; brought to maturity the surge of Catholics to urban political power triggered by the unsuccessful candidacy of Alfred E. Smith in 1928; and then developed new bases among industrial unions, blacks, and the young. The fundamental glue of the Roosevelt New Deal coalition was its appeal to the less privileged, its promise to save the system by redistributing the wealth through social legislation.

Roosevelt had to use all of his charismatic qualities as a popular leader to win the 1940 and 1944 elections where issues of foreign policy and war took over from economic reform. The coalition was strained by defections among Catholics who displayed a latent isolationism in foreign affairs and a growing conservatism at home as they gained in affluence. Truman temporarily put a halt to the decline of the coalition by capitalizing on a Midwestern farm revolt. But the Eisenhower years were marked by what seemed to be a continued fading of Democratic ties with the Catholics, trade union rank and file, and white Southerners. In addition, the postwar years had created a whole new sector of American life: the rapidly growing suburbs, which were going Republican by 2 to 1 margins. The big city base of the Democratic party was weakening and no longer appeared dominant.[9]

Then came the Kennedy election of 1960. Mainly on the strength of the very real antipathy of white Protestants to have a Catholic in the White House, Catholic voters snapped back to the Democratic column, up from 55% to 72% in four years. The trade union vote came back in old-time numbers. Blacks came into the voting population in record numbers and went 4 to 1 for Kennedy. The white South did not come back, although adding Lyndon Johnson to the ticket proved pivotal in producing the Texas electorate's votes.

But under the aegis of a new, charismatic leader, the myth of the old New Deal Northern coalition was to carry on for another generation. By extending his appeal into the normally Republican suburbs, Kennedy seemed to present a convincing case that the essential New Deal base could have a new lease on life. When he succeeded to the White House, Johnson was convinced he could overcome his handicap as a Southerner by an even stronger appeal to the old segments in the coalition: appeals to the blacks with the promise of strong civic rights legislation, appeals to trade unions by extensions of social legislation, appeals to the poor through a poverty program.

The irony of the 1964 election was that the dominant fact of that year hardly involved Lyndon Johnson's populist fervor at all. The real story of 1964 was a powerful desire on the part of the electorate not to have three presidents in one year and, above all, not to have Senator Barry Goldwater, who worried voters with more than hints about rolling back social security and shooting from the hip with tactical nuclear weaponry. Nonetheless, on paper, all the old New Deal groups, plus sizable segments of the South, came back into the fold. Certainly by the end of 1964, it would have been hard to convince a Lyndon Johnson, elected with 61% [10] of the vote, that he was not the latter-day personification of the old Roosevelt coalition. Capitalizing on his legislative acumen, he pushed home a spate of social legislation that even dwarfed the record of his old mentor, FDR.

The war in Vietnam proved to be the final blow hastening the demise of the old New Deal coalition. The war appealed most of all in the white South, which had mostly been straying from the fold. But, with the rise of George Wallace and a third party, any potential Democratic gains from the war were largely aborted. Among the first to defect over the war were the young. They were followed by the blacks. The weakening trade union rank and file and the Catholics no longer could be held with JFK's charismatic personal appeal to both groups, by now faded, as Lyndon Johnson utterly failed to communicate a sense of credibility.

By 1968, Hubert Humphrey represented the last, best hope that the old coalition could make it. He had strong ties with labor though little appeal to the South. He tried to invoke the old clarion calls, but they fell on ears not tuned in. He brought the blacks back with a belated attack on Wallace, but he could not reach the Catholics and the essential big city coalition could assemble no more than 43% of the vote: A close effort to duplicate the Kennedy squeaker of 1960, but it was simply not enough.

By 1972, it was evident that no one was going to put together the old Roosevelt or Kennedy coalitions again, unless the surviving member of the Kennedy family, Senator Edward Kennedy, could invoke a nostalgic return to twelve years earlier. Even then, however, aided and abetted by a recession which worried Catholics and trade union members, the numbers in the old coalition were not enough to put together a majority any more.

The following table illustrates strikingly what had happened to the American electorate in just four years:

Changes in the Electorate
1968–1972

	1972 %	1968 %	CHANGE %
Shrinking in Numbers			
Under $5,000 income	21	25	−4
Catholic voters	24	25	−1
Small town voters	14	22	−8
Union members	18	23	−5
Democrats	44	51	−7
Increasing in Numbers			
College educated	36	29	+7
$15,000 and over income	20	12	+8
Independents	23	18	+5
Suburban residents	31	26	+5
Under 30 voters	23	18	+5
Blacks	10	8	+2

The mix of the electorate had overtaken the old New Deal coalition. The two parts of the old coalition still gaining in numbers, the young and the blacks, had soured over the war. The old coalition had few appeals in its porkchop approach to the college educated, the $15,000 and over group, or the growing political independents.

In a real sense, the New Deal coalition was counted out by

the growth of a new, educated, and affluent class. The numbers weren't there any more. But far more important was the fact that the issues had shifted. America was now entering a new era where the old divisions on economic issues would no longer bind. In many ways, George McGovern was a preposterous candidate in the end: Early on, he mistook the new, emerging groups to be almost wholly drawn from the young, and later on, he tried to resurrect the old New Deal coalition overlaid onto the new politics. Politics may be the art of compromise, but McGovern's inconsistent backing and filling in 1972 finally offended both the new and the old power centers of political life.

Politicians are widely thought to be highly adroit on putting together ingenious combinations to achieve remarkable victories. The truth is quite different. By the early 1970s, the anachronisms of the past literally abounded: A Daly in Chicago, the last vestige of the big city machine politics not much advanced over the models of the 1930s; a Jackson from the state of Washington who still wanted to parlay Cold War warriorship along with bread-and-butter New Deal appeals to the working man to the White House; a Meany of the AFL-CIO, who still saw his shrinking 18% constituency as the center of the political universe. Other lesser versions dotted the power points of both political parties.

In fact, the shapes and configurations of the new electorate, the new and emerging center of gravity of public opinion, were quite radically altered. The thrust for change—with the exception of the blacks and Chicanos—was now coming from the most privileged. It has been said that the American Revolution was essentially elitist in origin, and a case can be made for this proposition. Two hundred years later, the most privileged had in many ways become the most radical again, but not for revolution this time, rather for decisive change within the structure of the system. The old economic, class divisions had been blurred and were almost extinct.

Most illustrative of how thinking had lagged reality were the sadly out of joint efforts of young, militant activists, enamored of the Marxist ideas of Mao, who tried to combine their anti-Vietnam war fervor with drives to form coalitions with the suppos-

edly "unwashed working classes." The mix was like oil and
water. The time for an intellectual elite joining with "exploited
workers" had simply run out. That, too, was an anachronism
from the past.

In September 1971, this writer had a most difficult assign-
ment: to explain to the assembled staff of the Institute of the
U.S.A. in Moscow (the Russian equivalent of our State Department Kremlinologists) the basic set of American public opinion.
Many of the facts and conclusions in this chapter were laid out
for an alert band of Soviet students of the American scene,
headed by Georgi Arbatov, the chief Americanologist of the
government. For three hours, the assembled twenty-odd Russians patiently listened. Their questions were not unintelligent,
although most centered on highly topical matters such as the
climate in America for a SALT agreement and real suspicion
about improving U.S. relations with Peking.

Striking was the absence of questions about the emergence of
demands for change from the most privileged sectors in American society. The more this thesis was reiterated, the more the
Soviet hosts retreated from discussing it. The last straw came
when Arbatov, himself a Jew, asked the rhetorical question,
"And when are you going to put a stop to the JDL trying to
wreck U.S.-USSR rapprochement?" The meeting adjourned to a
gala luncheon, replete with four wines, champagne, and vodka,
where care was taken to smooth over any ruffled feathers from
the morning session.

Later that fall, a high-ranking Soviet diplomat in the U.S.
asked about the session with Arbatov's group. The strange lack
of response to the surge of the privileged for change in America
was raised. The diplomat smiled and said, "Well, speaking com-
pletely unofficially, you must understand that it is not pleasing
to Soviet scholars of the American system to know that what is
happening in America is Karl Marx upside down."

IV

VIETNAM
Out Damned Spot

The Vietnam War was the first test for an America where public opinion was no longer dominated by economic considerations. The experience tore the country apart. It exploded the lesson of World War II that if aggression is met early with democratic armed forces, long and draining larger wars could be avoided. It marked the end of such notions as the American Century.

We began the war as the most powerful nation on earth, indisputably ahead of all other nations in economic and military might. We ended the war as one of five major power centers on earth, perhaps still the most powerful, but with the Soviet Union, China, Western Europe, and Japan all viewed as superpower centers to be reckoned with.

For the past seven years, Vietnam has been two wars: one taking place in Southeast Asia and the other in the United States. The war in Asia was essentially military. The war in America was a war of public opinion—for our own hearts, minds, and souls.

It all started with the noblest of intentions back in those earliest days. In July 1963, a carpenter in Beckley, West Virginia, interviewed in the first Harris Survey on Vietnam spoke for much of the nation, "If we don't stand up for people oppressed by

Communism, we'll soon be oppressed ourselves." A farmer in the lush bluegrass country outside Lexington, Kentucky, added, "All Asia's at stake out there. I don't believe in looking down when you know you are right." By a 2 to 1 margin,[1] the people agreed that "if the Communist threat to South Vietnam grew worse," they would favor sending U.S. troops there "on a large scale."

Enough time had passed in the decade since the Korean War for some of the pain and anguish of that "no win" war to have eased. And the Vietnam War was still too new and the frustrations yet unencountered to make most people pause and to ponder.

Nonetheless, only two months later, by September 1963, some of the initial euphoria had begun to fade. Buddhist demonstrations in Saigon and Hue against the Diem regime in Saigon were put down brutally. On the home television screens, Americans witnessed self-immolations by seven Buddhist monks between June and October. U.S. troop commitments in Vietnam rose, in one year, from 4,000 to 15,000.

The tyrannical Diem regime had soured many Americans. A 27-year-old lawyer in New Hartford, Connecticut, put it for many when he said, "That Diem government there is bad and has lost the support of its people. Either they change or we pull out." President Kennedy's standing on Vietnam fell to 56% to 28% negative in our polls.[2] A majority asked, Why commit American lives to save a corrupt regime on the Asian mainland? This theme would play back with monotonous regularity over the next decade.

But on November 1, 1963, President Diem and his brother were assassinated in a coup by generals who took over the Saigon government. The wife of Ngo Dinh Nhu, Mme Nhu, denounced Kennedy and the assassination as U.S. interference. Yet a week after the Diem murders, Kennedy's rating on his handling of the Vietnam situation rose to 45% to 35% positive, by a 3 to 1 margin the public thought the generals should be recognized by the U.S., and by 68% to 5%, a big majority looked with disfavor on Mme Nhu's denunciations of this country.

Back in that fateful month of November 1963, a precedent

was set on Vietnam that would be repeated over and over again in the war of public opinion at home. A sudden and dramatic move by the president would rally public opinion behind him. In this case, Kennedy could depart on his final trip to Texas assured that the initial course he had struck in Vietnam had turned public opinion around, at least for the moment.

These November 1963 results never were published because another assassination of earth-shaking proportions was to take place on November 22 in Dallas. But the results of the poll were communicated to JFK just before that trip. His reaction was typically cryptic, "Well, I'm glad Mme Nhu isn't making more headway, but I wish I were more certain the generals were as right as I am sure Diem was wrong." When told of an additional finding that by 37% to 32%, a narrow plurality of the public would be willing to give up South Vietnam rather than get into a full-scale war there, Kennedy commented, "That's all well and good, easier said than done. This situation is going to get worse before it gets better."

How much "worse it would get before it got better" was a part of American history spared John F. Kennedy. However, he was only the first of three presidents who would find public support for the war sagging, faith in the Saigon regime fading, only to see it snap back with some development that again raised hopes among the American people. In the end, this war would destroy the credibility of Kennedy's successor, would materially contribute to the comeback of Richard Nixon, his arch political foe of 1960, and would dampen and cripple the American spirit for nearly a generation.

When Lyndon Johnson entered the White House, people were absorbed with the shocking loss of JFK, feeling guilty about the way blacks had been treated, and were worried about Castro and Cuba and tensions with Russia abroad. No more than 2% volunteered Vietnam as an issue of concern in late January 1964.

The new president could do little wrong. On a whole roster of issues he received high marks from the people, ranging from highs of 80% positive for "working for peace," 71% for "keeping the economy healthy," 65% for "moving the country ahead," to

53% for "handling Cuba." Such absolute majorities of public backing were all higher than Kennedy had achieved.

Almost unnoticed, however, was one specific area in which Johnson could achieve no better than a 45% to 40% positive rating early in 1964: his handling of the war in Vietnam. By April public opinion had again softened to 40% to 45% negative [3] where it stayed until August. To most, the war did not seem to be going better, even with the Diem regime disposed of, and the number of U.S. troops in South Vietnam had risen to 23,000.

Then, on August 2, the Gulf of Tonkin episode took place, in which two U.S. destroyers were reported to have been attacked by North Vietnamese motor torpedo boats. President Johnson ordered an immediate retaliatory air strike against North Vietnamese PT boat bases. On August 7, Johnson asked for and received the support he needed from Congress in the Gulf of Tonkin Resolution, empowering the president to "repel any armed attack against the forces of the United States and to prevent further aggression." Seven years later, with no end of the war yet in sight, Congress was to repeal that resolution and another occupant of the White House, Richard Nixon, would sign its repeal.

But the alleged attacks in the Gulf of Tonkin had an electrifying impact on public opinion. A high 88% of the public told the Harris Survey during that first week of August 1964 that they had followed the rapidly moving developments. The 58% who were critical of Johnson's approach to Vietnam before the incident dramatically turned around to 85% support for his policies. The plurality that had opposed carrying the war to North Vietnam overnight became a 2 to 1 majority in support of all-out involvement. [4]

In the presidential election against Barry Goldwater he was then waging, the issue of Vietnam had not been one of Johnson's strong points. But after the Gulf of Tonkin affair, the public closed ranks behind LBJ on Vietnam. Goldwater had been robbed of his charge that Johnson policies in the war were "no win." Johnson was winning the Vietnam issue both ways: He won over the militant pro-intervention people with his firm military response while, at the same time, people were still worried that Goldwater, his opponent, if elected, would plunge the country into a nuclear war.

Walter Jenkins, Johnson's closest aide during this period, called right after the post-Gulf of Tonkin poll had been published. He reported the president to be enormously pleased with the massive public backing given his action and especially with the passage of the congressional resolution.

This writer singled out a paragraph in the August 10 piece reporting the poll in the Washington *Post* which said, "The closing of ranks behind the President in this latest military crisis parallels national reaction during the Cuban missile crisis in 1962 and the landing of U.S. Marines in Lebanon in 1958 during the Eisenhower administration. In both instances, overwhelming majorities of the people registered immediate approval of presidential action. *It was equally true, however, that as each crisis receded, national unity diminished and criticism again appeared* " [5] (author's italics).

Walter Jenkins always noted any such comments carefully, especially if they were caveats. His comment on the phone that day was prophetic, "Well, I'm sure you are absolutely right, but you know the boss. He won't forget this big show of support for a long time to come." Not only did Lyndon Johnson use the Gulf of Tonkin Resolution as legal justification for all his actions in Vietnam, but he would recall the 85% support figure for years afterward. Mistakenly, he thought that kind of lightning would strike at his beckoning many a time in the years ahead.

In fact, as ten successive governments came and departed in Saigon, as rioting in South Vietnam accelerated, and military reverses mounted, the public once again retreated from its euphoric response following the Gulf of Tonkin episode. By election time, as Johnson swept to an unprecedented 61% of the vote against Goldwater, no more than 42% could give LBJ high marks on his Vietnam policy. By December, support had sunk below that to 38%. [6]

The Harris Survey findings of that December summed it up, "Only specific crises have galvanized the American people to full and united support of government action in Vietnam. Overall, there remains a sense of frustration and uneasiness."

In the face of these reverses, President Johnson escalated the war in February 1965 by ordering round-the-clock bombings of North Vietnam. Once again, the public rallied behind the president, with a massive 83% [7] who backed the new bombing policy. A retired man in Deerfield Beach, Florida, summed up the prevailing view, "I'm in favor of anything to prevent war, but as conditions are now, I see no alternative but to stay on and do what has to be done to end this thing." By 79% to 10%, a big majority felt that "if the U.S. withdraws from Vietnam, the Communists will take over Asia." The domino theory, so often articulated by the White House, had been sold to the American people.

Nonetheless, two other significant developments were shaping up in American public opinion. From November 1964 to February 1965, the number of Americans who simply wanted to pick up stakes and get out had risen from 20% to 35%. A big majority of 75% opted for a negotiated settlement. This meant that 3 out of 4 Americans as far back as early 1965 saw no chance for victory from the fighting. With over a third of the country against the war, in retrospect, it was apparent that this war would never achieve the national unity to sustain support over an extended period of time. The bombings of North Vietnam continued until May, when Johnson ordered a halt in the hope of eliciting a response from Hanoi to negotiate. None was forthcoming. Public support for the war again waned. In June the presidential response was to authorize the direct use of American troops to combat. Now the die was cast. By year's end, over 160,000 U.S. men were in South Vietnam.

Once again, the American public responded to the presidential call. Even though by 3 to 1, most people in the country had little faith in the Saigon government and even doubted we could mount a defense of South Vietnam to win a negotiated settlement, nonetheless 58% rallied behind the president that summer of 1965. In December Johnson's marks on handling the war reached 65%, a high point in public confidence he would never attain again on the Vietnam issue.

By January 1966, with LBJ's handling of the war still positive by 56% to 35%, the point of showdown in the war of public opinion was reached. The president by then had borrowed heavily into his election victory margin fourteen months earlier to obtain support for his mounting effort in Vietnam.

A substantial 73% had reported they found themselves often "deeply concerned" about the war and 61% had felt personally involved, even though most did not know anyone involved in the fighting itself. But, as a woman in Holyoke, Massachusetts, said, "Every night when I see our boys fighting in Vietnam on the television, I feel I know them all. They are the kids down the street I saw growing up."

On paper the people said they wanted to give the president what he needed: by 60% to 25% they favored sending up to 500,000 U.S. troops to Vietnam, but *only if that will shorten the war;* 59% favored another bombing pause, but a higher 61% also expressed the view that "bombings should be renewed if no negotiations are started during the bombing halt;" 62% favored the use of nausea gas, *only if that will shorten the war.*

At the same time, 73% of the public also favored a military cease-fire as the settlement they would opt for. The American people in early 1966 were saying they would be willing to try one more all-out effort to mount the military strength to win a cease-fire agreement. Two out of three were still willing to give Lyndon Johnson the benefit of the doubt; but, by late January, no more than 44% could give him high marks on his handling of the war. In effect, the public said to its commander in chief, Our patience is growing short, our pessimism about the war is rising, but if you can end it with one more show of strength, we will back you.

The Administration response came in June with bombings of the Hanoi and Haiphong areas, an effort Secretary Robert McNamara later was to admit was not effective. But right after these bombings, 85% said they supported them. Two in three Americans justified them in the hope that they would "shorten the war." Johnson's standing on handling the war went from 52% to 38% negative before the bombings to 46% to 42% positive.

That July 1966 ought to be marked well. For, when the bombings of Hanoi and Haiphong produced no visible change in the status of the war and no movement toward negotiations, never again would even a plurality of the public support the president's efforts on the war. In effect, the battle for public opinion had turned and Lyndon Johnson had lost the war at home. From October 1965 to October 1966, the number of Americans who gave the president high marks for his handling of the war slipped from 60% to 38%.[8] This rating would never rise above 44% in LBJ's remaining time in office; his final marks on Vietnam in December 1968 were 67% to 28% negative.

From July 1966 through the end of his term in office, it was downhill all the way for Johnson on the war issue. By 1967, he no longer cited public opinion poll results supporting him, for there simply were none to be found. The White House no longer called to inquire about the latest poll results. Visitors to the Oval Office came back and reported that the president had said, "It's a time we have to honker over and take it on the haid."

The singular mark of 1967 in the war in Vietnam was that it was a time of sharp escalation in the number of Americans sent there (up from 358,000 in November 1966 to 474,000 by December of 1967) and downright discouragement at home about the course of the fighting. In February of that year, by a narrow 44% to 42%, the public thought the actual military progress of the war was "better." But by August, the balance had been tipped to 63% who thought our side was "not doing better." In other words, there was ample evidence by now that the more U.S. troops were committed to the fray, the worse the public viewed the situation.

To make matters worse, the president's own credibility as a man "working for peace" had slipped from 61% in July 1966 to 41% [9] by July 1968. By the end of 1967, a majority of the people were prepared to level two withering personal criticisms of President Johnson: "He has not been honest with the people on sending troops to Vietnam" and "He has raised false hopes for the war too often." Gratuitously, a higher 79% said, "He has stood by his policies even though they made him unpopular."

Lyndon Johnson stated more than once that he had told Mrs. Johnson as early as October 1967 that he had no desire to run for another term in 1969. And well it might have been, for the

LBJ fortunes had sagged to new lows just about a year ahead of the 1968 elections. His rating on handling the Vietnam War was at an all-time low of 23% [10] positive, and in inspiring confidence personally he was given favorable marks by an identically low 23%. Obviously, he now was being judged exclusively on the war issue.

Worst of all news in the polls, when Johnson was pitted against potential Republican opponents for president in the October Harris Survey, he trailed Nelson Rockefeller 52% to 35%, George Romney 46% to 37%, Richard Nixon 48% to 41%, and Ronald Reagan 46% to 41%. Most shocking of all, however, was the additional news that LBJ was behind two young and relatively unknown Republicans: By 40% to 39% he was edged out by Mayor John Lindsay and by 41% to 40% he ran behind Senator Charles Percy. This was "taking it on the haid" with a vengeance.

The following January 1968, Johnson's close friend, Governor John Connally of Texas, came to New York to inquire of this writer further into these poll results and to explore the lay of the land in the upcoming presidential contest. The assumption throughout the three-hour session in Connally's suite at the Plaza Hotel was that the president would be running again. Another man who had been close to both Johnson and Connally in their early Texas days, C. R. Smith, chairman of American Airlines and later that year to become secretary of commerce, summed up the prevailing feeling earlier that month when he said privately, "The only way Lyndon will leave the White House is when they carry him out feet first."

Connally was puzzled at the evidence which clearly showed the president had lost the war of public opinion on Vietnam. He repeatedly said, "I can only judge from my own part of the country. But we feel in a war you stick by the president through thick and thin." He thought Johnson had run into deep trouble because he had told people too many times, "You never had it so good," a phrase LBJ had used many times in the campaign of 1964. Connally shrewdly observed that he thought the Roosevelt-Truman-Kennedy-Johnson old New Deal coalition was finished and probably could not be resurrected in 1968. Although, at LBJ's urging, he finally backed Hubert Humphrey in the election and helped him carry Texas, Connally felt that only Johnson could win nationally for the Democrats. But in the style of patriotic fervor that somehow sets Texans apart from their fellow countrymen, Connally simply could not understand that evening in January 1968 why LBJ could not win as a wartime commander in chief.

After a long hiatus of no communication, this writer received a call on January 31, 1968 to take dinner with President Johnson in his living quarters the following evening. The evening was memorable for three reasons: (1) That night was the second day of the Tet offensive the Communists had launched against the cities of South Vietnam; (2) throughout the over three hours spent with the president, he didn't mention the Tet offensive once, nor did he seem perturbed by it; and (3) rather than the Tet offensive, his attentions in Vietnam appeared to be totally centered on the small outpost just south of the DMZ, Khe Sanh, about which he said, "General Wheeler has sworn in blood that it will not fall," at least a half-dozen times. Khe Sanh held, but the Tet offensive was a disaster at home.

We arrived in the hallway-sitting room to hear the president practicing the speech he was to deliver in Georgetown the next day. After greeting us, he launched into a discourse on politics, the main thrust of which was that the new politics embodied by Senator Eugene McCarthy or Bobby Kennedy were not to be trusted. On the other hand, he extolled the virtues of Mayor Richard Daley of Chicago, as "the type of man in politics whose word is his bond and who can deliver for you when he tells you he will."

The evening divided into three parts. The first, before dinner, was essentially a monologue on how the established professional politicians in the Democratic party would control the convention in Chicago that August (leading this writer to mistakenly conclude that LBJ was planning to run and to bull his way through to nomination by cashing chips with the old pros of his party). At dinner, attended by three or four Johnson staff aides (Mrs. Johnson was out of town and Lynda Bird and Chuck Robb had eaten earlier in order to view a movie), the president dwelt on Vietnam, but mainly on Khe Sanh; the thrust of almost his entire conversation centered on the military conduct of the war. He also gave a blow-by-blow account on how he had stared down Kosygin during the six-day war in Israel, by daring use of the U.S. Sixth Fleet. After dinner, he took his guests on a tour of the living quarters, including some choice comments about the Lincoln Bedroom and the plaque Jackie Kennedy had put up in the bedroom Mrs. Johnson was using, indicating the "President and Mrs. Kennedy slept here." The evening ended in LBJ's own bedroom where he remarked about the stack of homework he had to go through before getting to sleep; then we all stopped to look at the president on each of three networks on the 11 o'clock evening news, on the three color TV sets that dominated his small bedroom.

As many before us learned, a dialogue with Lyndon Johnson in the White House, even on a relaxing evening, could be almost entirely a one-way conversation. Never did he ask about public opinion about the war, his chances for re-election, how the public might react to the Tet offensive, or a whole host of other subjects about which he might have inquired. The significance of the evening was what was never discussed. This writer has since pondered the evening and gone through extensive notes made just after the visit. The most significant conclusion is that President Johnson undoubtedly did not realize the impact the Tet offensive would have on American morale about the war. If the dispatches fed to him at dinner and throughout the evening bore disturbing tidings, LBJ never gave a hint of such. Other reports, however, indicated that technically the Tet offensive was viewed as a resounding military defeat of the Communists by our own military—which, technically speaking, was probably correct.

Post-Tet 1968 polling of the American people told a very different story, however. A big majority of 78% to 16% now thought the fighting was "not going better" for our troops. A substantial 43% expressed surprise at the strength of the Vietcong. A much higher 68% thought the use of suicide squads by the VC in the urban areas of South Vietnam gave a "real advantage to the Communists" in their seizing the initiative in the war. When asked if the fighting continued at this "stepped up rate," by only 43% to 42% did the public think "our side could win." Most shocking of all, by 61% to 23%, a majority thought the fact the VC had been able to enter the U.S. Embassy in Saigon was a sure sign "we weren't prepared for such a Communist attack."

In a way, public reaction to the Tet offensive in February 1968 sealed the verdict in the war of domestic opinion over Vietnam. Only 23% agreed with the military estimates that the Tet attacks were a victory for the U.S., 27% said it was a victory for the VC, and 33% a victory for neither side.

By his own admission, the following month Lyndon Johnson bowed out as a candidate for re-election in order to devote his remaining months in office to achieving the peace which had proven to be so elusive. He was never again to achieve better than a 2 to 1 negative response from his fellow countrymen in the polls assessing his efforts in Vietnam. He had become the war's most notable casualty.

President Johnson fell victim to Vietnam for as many complex reasons as could be found within the man himself. He worshipped Roosevelt not only for his social programs, but for rallying the nation to resist aggression in World War II. Roosevelt won a victory with unconditional surrender, but Johnson presided over a war of much longer duration in which victory was never in sight; and, in fact, at the time he bowed out, three-quarters of the country thought was going badly. Neither Lyndon Johnson nor the American people were prepared for a war in which there would be no victor. Roosevelt united the people in World War II. Johnson presided over an increasingly disunited and divided nation in the Vietnam War.

But perhaps the single most important clue to LBJ's undoing in Vietnam was his failure to see it as a two-front war. As on the second night of the Tet offensive, he seemed to assess it all in military terms. There is much which is heady about living hourly in the world of top secret communications that the public never will be privy to. But the temptation to therefore conclude that only those who know the presumed facts should be entitled to participate in the decisions can be fatal to leadership in a democracy. Implicit in this assumption is that the people are willing to give complete faith and confidence to their wartime leader, as Johnson himself liked to say, "To follow him to hell and back."

The American people followed Kennedy to hell on the Diem assassination and came back. They followed Johnson to hell through the Gulf of Tonkin episode and came back. They followed Johnson to hell on the first bombings of North Vietnam and came back. They followed him to hell in the bombings of Hanoi and Haiphong, but didn't come back. They followed him to the hell of the Tet offensive, but didn't come back. Nor would they ever come back to Johnson again on Vietnam. The war went sour because the more men we sent over to Vietnam the worse it seemed to go. The oft-repeated expressions of optimism by Robert McNamara, Henry Lodge, Hubert Humphrey, William Westmoreland, and even in the end, by the president himself became as hollow as Herbert Hoover's promise in the heart of the Depression of a "chicken in every pot."

The ultimate irony for President Johnson on Vietnam was that at the very moment in late 1967 that the bottom literally dropped out on his credibility with his beloved "people" over the war, 58% could also say they admired his "courage and fortitude" on the war. He had won the admiration of his countrymen with his unflagging willingness to "take it on the haid," but he simply had lost the power to lead them back from the hell of Vietnam. On Vietnam, Johnson went beyond the jaws of consent too often.

In the 1968 election, Richard Nixon was a beneficiary of the disenchantment with Lyndon Johnson's stewardship of the war. Despite his having been known as a hard-liner on the war during the campaigns, Nixon avoided any commitment to continue the Johnson course in Vietnam. He did hint that he had another plan to end U.S. involvement in the war and he did pledge to end that involvement during his first four years in the White House. But, basically, in 1968 Nixon allowed the Vietnam issue to spend its might against the incumbent sitting in the White House, Lyndon Johnson, and against his surrogate, Vice-President Hubert Humphrey.

Incredibly, as the "out" candidate in 1968, Nixon was helped by all of the disenchantment of the American people over the war, including the organized antiwar movement he was later to denounce from the White House, as well as the campaign stump. Looked on in retrospect, the antiwar protest movement succeeded perhaps beyond its wildest dreams both during the Johnson and Nixon years.

During the Johnson period, the highly personalized target of the demonstrations was not only the policies being pursued in Vietnam but the president himself personally. They reached a real low in the publication and later production on stage of the "MacBird" diatribe, a crude satire at best. But they were also directed against Johnson's handpicked successor, Hubert Humphrey.

Judged by the end result, Lyndon Johnson went out of office thoroughly discredited, with the war in Vietnam the prime reason behind the public wrath. Humphrey was defeated in 1968, albeit by a whisker. But the backlash over the war was undoubtedly the most severe handicap Humphrey labored under in 1968. After the wild and brutal show on the streets at the Chicago Democratic National Convention was ended, a substantial body of public opinion concluded that "if the Democrats can't run their own party any better than this, then how can they be expected to run the country if elected to the White House."

In the case of Richard Nixon, later on, the antiwar protests would have to wait four years, but, in the end, they would be successful in quite another way: The war would end and U.S. forces in Vietnam would finally come home. Nixon would survive and the protest movement would dissolve, but the war would end.

Of course, having made such an analysis, it must be added that rarely has American public opinion been so bitterly antagonistic and distressed by any force in recent times than in its fury over the antiwar movement. For example, in late 1967, when Johnson was hitting his all-time low in popularity on the war, by 68% to 22%, the people in the very same survey also thought the antiwar demonstrations were "acts of disloyalty against the boys fighting in Vietnam"; by 64% to 21%, that "most antiwar demonstrators are not serious, thoughtful critics of the war, but are peaceniks and hippies having a ball"; by 76% to 13%, that "antiwar demonstrations encourage the Communists to fight all the harder." An overwhelming 70% of the people felt the antiwar marches had "hurt the war effort."

At the same time, despite the almost despised status of the antiwar movement in the eyes of a majority of the public, by 61% to 30%, the people also respected that right to protest. By a substantial 60% to 25%, they agreed with the proposition that "the true test of our democracy is whether we allow people with unpopular views to express them without interference"; by 59% to 27%, that "antiwar sentiment is rising in the U.S. and people have a right to feel this way"; and by 58% to 34% that "demonstrations against the war are alright as long as they are peaceful."

The American people developed an enormous antipathy to the antiwar movement that continued throughout the Nixon years. For example, after his November 3, 1969 speech in which he pledged to withdraw all U.S. ground forces from Vietnam and he asked for the support of a "great silent majority," by 65% to 25%, the public agreed that "protesters against the war are giving aid and comfort to the Communists."

However, the same poll also revealed some interesting gains scored by the antiwar movement. Significantly, only two years later, by 55% to 33%, the public was prepared to deny the allegation that the protesters were "just a bunch of hippy, long-haired, irresponsible young people who ought to be cracked down on." And by 50% to 37%, the people agreed that "demonstrators have the right to say it is immoral for U.S. troops to be in Vietnam" and by 81% to 11% that "the protesters are raising real questions which ought to be discussed and answered."

Still later, in the summer of 1970, after the Cambodian incursion, when confrontations on the streets of New York, Pittsburgh, and other cities broke out between hard-hat construction workers and long-haired student antiwar protesters, similar ambivalence would manifest itself. A plurality of 40% of the public reported it sympathized with the hard-hats compared to no more than 24% who took the side of the students (a significant 23% said "neither"). But, when asked if they thought it right or wrong for the hard-hats to attack the antiwar young people physically, by 53% to 31% the public thought the hard-hats were "wrong."

It might be argued, of course, that the American people could have resolved their own determination on the Vietnam issue without the rancor, bitterness, and hate engendered by the antiwar protests and the counterprotests. Some might even claim that the antiwar movement kept alive support for the war just on the strength of the unpopularity of the people who took to the streets to voice their disagreements with Vietnam policy.

There is no way such contentions can be determined. There was an antiwar movement. It engulfed the sentiments of a majority of the young and over 35% of the adults. It changed a whole generation of college students. In the end, Johnson and Humphrey went out of office on a wave of antiwar feeling. And, also in the end, Richard Nixon did agree to a compromise settlement to bring back American troops and POWs, which he could later describe as "peace with honor" befitting the stance of a head of state of a modern superpower.

V

VIETNAM

The Nixon Light at the End of the Tunnel

Nixon took over the White House in January 1969 with 82% of the public convinced he really wanted to achieve peace in Vietnam. When he came to office, the American people did not expect any early settlement of the war; in fact, by 45% to 36%, they felt there never would be a settlement emerging from the Paris negotiations. Most people held the view that it was desirable to bring out U.S. troops even "if there never is a settlement."

Despite an announcement in June of a withdrawal of 25,000 U.S. troops, by July 1969, it appeared that the new president's honeymoon on Vietnam had ended. His rating on handling the war slipped to 52% to 38% negative after resting precariously at a 47% to 45% favorable standing the previous month. Two in three people took well to his idea of Vietnamization (a take-over of the fighting from the Americans by the South Vietnamese), but a plurality also thought it would never work.

The president's promise to pull out a hundred thousand more

U.S. troops in 1969 was doubted by more people than believed it. He was running into trouble on another account: By a narrow 44% to 43%, the public thought the draft was unfair, "because it made young men fight in a war they didn't believe in."

The negative vote of confidence on Vietnam continued for the president throughout the summer and fall, with 56% saying his proposals would end the war and 58% doubting the South Vietnamese army (ARVN) could fight nearly as well as American forces. In September, he was voted 57% to 35% negatively on the war. In October, hundreds of thousands of demonstrators took to the streets in "moratorium" demonstrations across the country.

Then on November 3, 1969, Nixon exercised his presidential prerogatives for the first time on the war. Essentially, he attempted to bring good news to the people to buoy sagging opinion at home. In principle, it appeared to be the same tack that JFK and LBJ had used before him: to say or do something dramatic that will raise hopes that a way can be found to bring the war closer to an end. However, there was one critical difference in the Nixon approach. As a careful reader of polls and public opinion, he gave top priority to the Vietnam War in the United States. He had been the beneficiary of Lyndon Johnson's losing war of public opinion and he did not mean to lose that advantage. To satisfy the war at home, his answer was to liquidate American involvement as fast as military conditions would allow.

Thus, the president announced an unspecified plan to withdraw all U.S. troops according to a secret timetable. The appeal worked. A substantial 82% said he seemed to "genuinely want to end the war as quickly as possible," thus re-establishing his good intentions. Two in three also thought he had demonstrated that he had and would continue to explore all means and avenues to a negotiated settlement, thus appearing not to cut off the route to peace through Paris. Finally, by 56% to 22%, a majority also felt Nixon was "right in saying he would never agree to a U.S. defeat in Vietnam," thus satisfying the hawks and right-wingers in his own party who might feel his troop withdrawal plan was a retreat and even a cop-out.

These three themes were to dominate Nixon strategy on Vietnam right through his entire first term in office: (1) keep accelerating the troop withdrawal under the rationale that Vietnamization was really working, (2) stress a willingness to negotiate, and (3) always insist American honor would not be violated.

His ratings on handling the war soared to 54% to 40% [1] positive and leveled out at 48% to 47% on the plus side as his first year in office ended. He sweetened the draft problem by announcing an ultimate end of the draft and the conversion to an all-volunteer army, both of which proposals met with close to 52% to 38% approval.

But by springtime, the progress on the war seemed to be lagging, reports surfaced of increased numbers of U.S. advisers being sent to Laos, and support for Nixon on the war sagged in April to 57% to 38% negative. On April 30, the president embarked on what was called an incursion by American and South Vietnamese troops into Cambodia, designed to destroy Communist sanctuaries along the border.

The reaction of the public at home to the Cambodian venture was robust and not all favorable. A majority of 56% felt the president was "justified" in his action, but most also thought U.S. troops committed to Cambodia would be bogged down there six months later, and a plurality thought Nixon had triggered another Vietnam War. The campuses erupted into violent protests, culminating in the fatal shooting of three students at Kent State University by National Guardsmen.

Even though U.S. troops came back from Cambodia by the end of June, Richard Nixon would bear two scars from the episode with American public opinion. By 49% to 39%,[2] the people now doubted his credibility on the war, and his rating on handling the war went into a permanently negative set. It would not be until December 1972 that a majority would again give him favorable marks on the war.

In the fall of 1970, both President Nixon and Vice-President Agnew would learn that trying to win an off-year election by making whipping boys of American student protesters simply would not wash. The White House missed a golden opportunity to pick up seats and even control of the U.S. Senate in the No-

vember elections by not stressing the president's desire to liquidate American involvement in Vietnam. The GOP that fall had
to settle for a stand-off—and for Richard Nixon who went all
out in attacking youthful protests and in appealing to the "silent
majority," that election was tantamount to defeat, as indeed his
own people would later admit privately.

About three weeks before that 1970 election, this writer had a
call in New York from White House aides who came around
with their own statistics designed to show that Harris Survey results had a consistent anti-Nixon tilt. After a rather pointless
two hours of argument, this writer offered some unsolicited advice to the effect that Spiro Agnew had already lost his effec-
tiveness on the anti-youthful protester issue and that if the president followed the same tack it would prove disastrous. The
reason: Unlike rats, human beings do not eat their young.

Two weeks after the election, Charles Colson, then the presidential special counsel, who had been one of the visitors, called
from Washington to say, "Although we won't admit it publicly,
we bombed out in the election, and you were absolutely right."
In ensuing discussions, a truce of sorts was reached between us.
It was natural for Nixon people to worry about Harris Surveys,
since in 1960, Harris polls had been used by John F. Kennedy to
help defeat Richard Nixon. In 1962, Governor Edmund "Pat"
Brown also used Harris polls to defeat Nixon for governor of
California. However, in 1963, the Harris firm had abandoned all
political polling for private clients and the Harris Survey was
launched in the Washington *Post* and *Newsweek*, under the
sponsorship of Philip Graham.

The essence of the truce was that the White House would receive the twice weekly Harris Survey as a courtesy each Friday
prior to publication when the subscribing newspapers received
it. A similar courtesy arrangement had been in existence in the
Kennedy and Johnson eras. In addition, this writer agreed to answer any queries the White House might have about the poll results published, a practice the two previous Administrations had
followed. Finally, in return, the White House agreed not to send
emissaries out on missions to "get Harris," as Herb Klein had
done after the 1968 election, when at an editors' meeting in San
Diego he observed that "Harris ought to be put out of business."

This truce has been kept by both parties since the spring of 1971. In fact, it is not an overstatement to make the judgment that in the 1971–72 period, Richard Nixon probably was a better reader of public opinion than either of his predecessors in the White House.

The year of 1971 in many ways shaped up for Richard Nixon as a repeat of Lyndon Johnson's disastrous year of 1967. Despite public approval of a renewal of bombings of North Vietnam's panhandle in January, 61% favored a total withdrawal of U.S. troops by the end of the year. Support for a coalition government in Saigon as the price for peace grew to a point in May where a 42% to 39% [3] plurality favored it for the first time. That same month, for the first time, a majority of 58% felt it was "morally wrong for the U.S. to be fighting in Vietnam."

A literal race was on between successive Nixon announcements of further troop withdrawals and a growing public appetite for faster and faster removal of troops from Vietnam. The president's credibility on the war was still negative, as were his ratings on handling the war. By 2 to 1, the public did not think the ARVN "could hack it" as Nixon stoutly maintained, and a record 71% thought the U.S. becoming involved in Vietnam in the first place was a "mistake."

The number who thought the troop withdrawal was "too slow" went up from a low of 26% in late 1969, to 34% in 1970, to 45% in May 1971, to a majority 53% [4] in November of that year. Majorities opposed the U.S. leaving 50,000 noncombat troops on the ground in South Vietnam, using U.S. bomber and helicopter support to back up South Vietnamese fighting forces, or giving $1 billion in military aid to Saigon after we had left the country.

By late August 1971, it was obvious that the withdrawal of some 300,000 U.S. troops from Vietnam would not be enough. Nixon credibility on the war had reached a 57% to 31% negative mark and close to 7 in 10 expected no end of U.S. involvement in the war by election time. Most telling of all, with the 1972 election approaching, was the 46% to 20% charge that "Nixon has not kept his 1968 promise to end our part in the war before the end of his first term."

The situation in early 1972 was no better. To be sure, the dramatic Nixon visits to Peking and Moscow had sent the president's ratings on "working for peace" soaring to new heights, as his Phase I and Phase II economic control programs had aborted disaster on the domestic side. But Vietnam appeared by all measures to be the Achilles heel of any Nixon re-election bid. Vietnamization didn't wash, according to 60%, who thought the South Vietnamese could not stand militarily on their own. In May, by 51% to 31%, a majority said they would settle for a standstill cease-fire with the Communists controlling that part of South Vietnam they occupied. An even 60% were willing to get rid of President Thieu as the price of such a standstill cease-fire. A massive 76% wanted *all* U.S. troops home by the end of the year. The only sticky point in an otherwise "let's cut and run" prevailing attitude was the 75% to 13% majority who said they wanted to stay in the war "until our POWs are released."

Then President Nixon made a bold strike. In early May, he ordered the mining of North Vietnamese harbors. The public rallied to his new move by 59% to 25%, although a majority also feared this move might draw the Russians and Chinese into the war. When there was no response from Moscow or Peking, Richard Nixon reasoned he would squeeze out one or two more escalations of the war—if they worked and if they promised to shorten the odious war.

When Nixon continued bombings north of the twentieth parallel into the fall, the public once again backed him by 55% to 32%. This backing shrunk to a narrow 46% to 44% as election day approached. And there were distinct signs toward the end of the campaign that the Vietnam quicksand could entrap another incumbent.

The basic problem of George McGovern, however, in exploiting Vietnam was McGovern himself. Early on, by 51% to 34%, a majority credited the South Dakota senator with "having been right about Vietnam long before most other men in public life." But after a whole spate of fiascos in August on the war issue, ranging from the Ramsey Clark visit to Hanoi, the dispatch of Pierre Salinger to Paris to talk with the North Vietnamese, Sargent Shriver's claims that Nixon could have obtained peace early in 1969, and McGovern's statement that Thieu would flee

Saigon if he won the election, all of which met with a negative response from the electorate, McGovern had blown the war issue. By 47% to 32% the public simply did not think McGovern's terms for ending the war were honorable. A decisive 49% to 33% believed Richard Nixon rather than George McGovern could better and more quickly end U.S. involvement in the war.

The Nixon years on Vietnam turned out to be ironic. After buying time on the Vietnam issue for two years by accelerating U.S. troup withdrawals and cutting U.S. casualties, Richard Nixon gambled on escalation through mining of harbors and bombing cities in North Vietnam and the gambles worked. The greatest irony of all, however, was the "gift" of the Vietnam issue from George McGovern, who bought the president more time by convincing the electorate that, no matter what reservations about Nixon's credibility people might have, they could trust McGovern even less.

By election day, although his ratings on handling the war were still negative, Richard Nixon was sitting with a 40% to 29% plurality who believed he would achieve right and honorable terms in the October 8 Paris agreement surfaced by Hanoi and that he "could not have attained such terms back in 1969." The year of 1972 ended with Nixon's standing on the war at 51% to 46% positive, for the first time since before the Cambodian incursion in the late spring of 1970.

Perhaps the greatest presidential gamble of all took place in the final days of 1972, when Nixon ordered heavy bombings of Hanoi and other North Vietnamese population centers. This time, the public opposed the bombings by 51% to 37% and his rating on the war slipped overnight to 56% to 39% negative. Had this escalation gamble not worked, it would have been a sour morning indeed when Richard Nixon was sworn into his second term in office on January 20, 1973.

But the gamble did work, the peace terms were agreed to and signed, the POWs and remaining troops came home, and the sad and tragic Vietnam chapter seemed closed for a war-weary and frustrated American people.

The open wound may have been finally closed in January 1973, but the scar tissue is likely to remain on the American conscience for a long time to come. What, then, is this scar tissue made up of?

First, for the American people, the romantic mask has been ripped off wars, for a long time to come. Thanks to the nightly TV news shows, for close to a decade, the blood and guts and sounds of jungle warfare spilled out into American living rooms. This was no war movie with fictitious characters who died heroic deaths or emerged as conquering heroes. Modern television did not spare the viewer's sensitivities.

When surveys asked what troubled people most about the war, easily the dominant reply at any point from 1965 onward was, "All the killing." Above all, this was a personal war, conducted on faraway soil, air, and waters, but with heavy loss of American men. The personalization of the men who fought was more graphic than any other war. This fact alone will be a memory that will sear all who were witnesses for many years to come. For those who lived in this time, any war will likely never be the same. American soil has not been invaded in well over a century, but the sensitivities of a majority of our people were deeply invaded by the Vietnam experience.

Vietnam also aroused the people's consciousness of guilt about the country's morality. As much as 65% of the public believed the U.S. role there was "immoral." This is a far cry from the old, romantic notions that God fought on "our side," which has pumped zealous purpose into many nationalistic wars.

Yet the morality issue is fraught with delicate and painful dilemmas. Woe betide the politician who preaches to us that we should suffer so much from guilt and blood on our hands that we deserve to lose. George McGovern did not say this, but came perilously close to communicating it—and it cost him dearly.

Most troubling about the moral issue is that it collides with our normal pragmatism, so ingrained in the American character. Two illustrations will demonstrate this terrible trauma that remains deep in the Vietnam scar tissue. Both involve questions difficult for any American traveling abroad to answer with any credibility.

One deals with the My Lai massacre, the episode in which an American platoon cold-bloodedly shot down old men and women and small children. In April 1971, when the My Lai case was front page news, 58% of the public labeled American involvement in Vietnam as "morally wrong." Yet the same cross-section of people also felt, by 65% to 24%, that the guilty verdict rendered by an army court-martial of Lieutenant William Calley was also a "mistake."

The main reason people felt Calley should not have been convicted for his part in My Lai was that he was being made a "scapegoat," a view held by 77% of the people. Why? Well, 81% said they were sure "there were many other incidents like My Lai involving U.S. troops that have been hidden"; 77% also believed "the soldiers at My Lai were just following orders from their higher-ups"; and 56% felt that "by finding Lieutenant Calley guilty, all soldiers who kill anyone but enemy soldiers should also be found guilty." By a massive 88% to 6%, most Americans agreed that "it is unfair to find just Lieutenant Calley guilty and not put higher-ups on trial who gave Calley his orders."

The key rationalization obviously was that Calley was taking the rap for higher-ups who were responsible for the My Lai massacre. Therefore, justice was being meted out to the wrong man—the small man instead of the big man.

But what of the claim that exonerating Calley would have put an official stamp of this nation's approval on the shooting of innocent children and old people? When the question was put to the same cross-section, by 53% to 33%, a majority said it *disagreed* with this line of reasoning. Yet the logical consistency of the answers does not drive away the haunting concern that what was done at My Lai could be justified. To the contrary, by 53% to 35%, a majority felt the killings were wrong. Wrong and immoral, perhaps, but not so wrong that the platoon's lieutenant who fired the machine gun and ordered another to fire should be prosecuted for it.

Another tough question to answer abroad is the justification of President Nixon's orders of heavy bombings during the holiday season of late 1972. The public opposed those bombings by 51% to 37%. Yet a closer examination of people's reasoning is revealing. By a thumping 67% to 17%, the public rejected out of hand the claims that hospitals and residential areas were hit in those raids. Less than 50% (46%) felt "it was inhuman and immoral for the U.S. to have bombed Hanoi's civilian centers the way we did."

Rather a big 71% of the public agreed with the proposition that "what we did in bombing Hanoi was no worse than what the Communists have done in the Vietnam War." And a plurality agreed that "the only language Hanoi will listen to is force, such as our bombing their cities."

What, then, was the reason for the opposition to the bombings? It was concern over human life, but mainly American lives. By 55% to 30%, a majority agreed that "we lost many American lives and B-52s unnecessarily in the bombing raids." Is this a double standard on human life or merely another case of "war is hell and it's too bad if civilians are hit?"

Perhaps the deepest scar tissue of all is the divisions that might well linger on from the long and agonizing experience. Older and younger members of families were torn apart on this war, with older people generally defending the "resist aggression with force" argument and the young generally seeing their generation sent to needless and useless slaughter. The division between blacks, dominantly opposed to the war, and many whites was exacerbated. The division grew between North and South, with the latter infuriated by the tolerance of the former of compromise, draft evasion, flag burning, and other acts viewed as treasonous and unpatriotic. The divisions went on and on, including small towns versus big cities, the affluent with sons who went to college versus the less affluent whose sons went to Vietnam. Perhaps the most basic split was between husbands and wives, with the women opposed to the taking of human life much more than men. Basically, Vietnam created new divisions that the country had not experienced before. There was little in anyone's training or upbringing to cope with the shock of the impact of the war.

In foreign affairs, the tendency to withdraw from any commitments in the future to other allies will be great. Some 61% [5] of the public came to hold the view that "we achieved little by going to war and in the future we should let other countries defend themselves." Does this portend a new kind of isolationism, as Dean Rusk so often feared; or does it simply mean that, in the future, the U.S. will realize that initially small commitments can lead to long, bloody, and costly conflicts that can tear the country apart?

Polling on Vietnam for ten years had to set some kind of record for sustained, continuous data on measuring changing public moods and attitudes on a single subject. Yet this long vigil of watching a nation tie itself up in knots of frustration paled before the realization that every result published would be immediately analyzed not simply by a president or his staff in the White House, but also by comparable power centers in Moscow, Peking, and Hanoi.

In December 1967, the Russians sent a new man to the staff of the UN in New York, a former chief political officer who had served in their Embassy in New Delhi during the Nehru years. Among his regular chores was to monitor the attitudes of Americans, particularly the Harris and Gallup polls. Dr. K., as this writer and his staff came to know him, would regularly inquire about the meaning of our survey results, especially if they dealt with foreign policy and relations with the Soviet Union or China.

Dr. K. turned out to be much more than a Russian expert on American public opinion. This writer will never know his real role in the Soviet apparatus, except that he was high-ranking and, by his own terminology, "unofficial." He was highly literate, knew good paintings and music, and was not at all the prototype of the blustering, rigid, party-line adherent that so often populates Soviet bureaucracy (most other bureaucracies, too, for that matter).

Dr. K. is important to this story of Vietnam because, in the month of October 1968, he returned from his annual leave home and announced that it was "a great time for great games." For their own reasons, the Russians that fall had decided that it was to their benefit to help work out a settlement of the Vietnam problem. Earlier that year, Dr. K. had tried out a line of communication through this writer that had worked.

After he declined to run again, President Johnson wanted to

set up another summit meeting with Premier Aleksei Kosygin. In May a Russian intellectual who often wrote important policy pieces in *Pravda,* wrote a full-dress analysis of U.S.-Soviet relations. The press of this country did not pick up some of its subtler meaning.

Dr. K. paid this writer a visit, armed with a copy of the original *Pravda* article and an English translation. He made his point directly, pointing out that the article contained an important bid by the Russians to open up a new era of better relations with the U.S. This writer was sufficiently impressed with the message, particularly after consulting with old White House security hands, to ask to see the president directly on the subject. During the subsequent meeting with President Johnson, in which he paid close attention to the message, he also hauled out with enormous pride originals of his secret correspondence with Khrushchev and Kosygin and reviewed a number of them with obvious relish.

Toward the end of June, a message came from the president to the effect that he wanted this writer to ask Dr. K. to find out why Kosygin had been so slow in replying to his last communiqué concerning a summit meeting. Now the connection had been made both ways, for apparently within a few days, a reply from Kosygin was received. The summit was never held because of the Russian invasion of Czechoslovakia.

When he returned in October, Dr. K. came prepared with some disarming information. He explained that the Russians had felt it necessary to go into Czechoslovakia because they were having the same rumblings of insurrection in the Ukraine in the provinces along the Czech border, and had had to partially mobilize 300,000 troops in that region.

Then, in a lengthy, six-hour session he got down to business on Vietnam. He quickly sketched in a plan for "a suspension of all offensive military activity" by all parties in Vietnam. This was to be a military settlement of Vietnam and the political settlement would have to be worked out internally by the Vietnamese themselves. When I probed him to find out if Hanoi would agree to this, he gave me elaborate explanations of how the Soviets had been successful with Hanoi by following a skillful policy of parallelism to North Vietnamese policy. But that this policy in turn now presented the Soviets and ourselves with unprecedented opportunities to achieve a Vietnam cease-fire.

This writer immediately called McGeorge Bundy, an old acquaintance from Kennedy days, and asked his advice. Bundy suggested it be taken very seriously, that it sounded to him like the John Scali episode during the Cuban missile crisis in 1962 when the Russians used a newsman as a conduit to transmit messages for a settlement. Jimmy Jones, a close aide of the president, now a congressman from Oklahoma, was called by phone and the basic message transmitted, including the bit about the Ukraine.

Three days went by and there was no response from the White House. Then Walt Rostow called back to say the president was grateful for the message, but there was no need to pursue it further. He did ask for more details about the Ukrainian matter and admitted that was an intriguing piece of new intelligence, which obviously had been let drop to add credence to the Vietnam signal.

This writer did not let the matter drop there. Bundy had another suggestion: That George Ball, by then out of government, but a former undersecretary of state, ought to be approached and that he might take the message to Dean Rusk, who might take it to the president. Ball was impressed and did talk to Rusk, who in turn called personally to ask me a series of probing questions.

Rusk took the message to the president and then a series of intensive meetings with Dr. K. and Ambassador B., attached to the UN and the "official" source of the offer, took place in the garden at the United Nations, at Charley O's restaurant in Manhattan, at this writer's house in Riverdale, and other such unlikely places for the Vietnam War to end.

The terms suggested were simple and basically revolved around the key phrase "a suspension of all offensive military operations" by all parties, but also including a halt of all bombings of North Vietnam. Ambassador B. went through essentially all the points originally put forth by Dr. K. All this was duly relayed to Secretary Rusk. A few days later a cryptic message came from Jimmy Jones: "Can you see if you can get agreement to guarantee the inviolability of the DMZ [the demilitarized zone separating North and South Vietnam]?" The question was put to Dr. K. who said it would take another nineteen hours due to time differences in Moscow and Hanoi. But within twenty-four hours, in a meeting in the UN gardens, an affirmative answer came back.

All this was accomplished between October 6 and 19. Then there was nothing but silence, except a single message that parallel channels had been confirmed in Paris by Ambassador Averell Harriman and that discussions would proceed directly with Ambassador Anatoly Dobrynin and the White House.

Finally, in the early evening of October 31, this writer's home phone rang and it was the president himself on the line, speaking obviously from a conference setup, for he sounded as though he were at the bottom of a well. He said, "Lou, we are doing our damnedest to get this agreement to end this war. But we are running into real trouble with that fellow in Saigon, who is being put up to resisting by people here in Washington, such as Mme. Chennault. We have ways of knowing what cables go in and out of this city. Anyway, we are going to end the bombings in return for getting down to business in the Paris talks. Not quite as much as you got from them, but still a stride ahead. The country owes you a debt and you'll read about your contribution in my memoirs."

Six months later, at a chance meeting with Averell Harriman in Washington's National Airport, this writer swapped stories of that wild October period. He basically confirmed a similar signal from the Russians in Paris, but attributed the breakdown of a cease-fire agreement to not only General Thieu's refusal to go along, but also to Walt Rostow's and the Joint Chiefs' unwillingness to give up "search and destroy missions."

Still later, in January 1971, Rostow appeared on a TV show on public opinion that this writer was associated with on ABC. Afterward he took me aside and said, "You know, that war is really won. It is just a matter of a short time before it will be officially recognized as a victory for our side. All we need is a few more months. It would have been a mistake to force it prematurely back in 1968."

If the strange episode initiated by Dr. K. in 1968 did not come to fruition, then another equally unexpected development in 1972 did allow the Harris Survey to play a part in finally arriving at a settlement of Vietnam. Dr. Henry Kissinger informed me of the episode late in October 1972.

The Harris Survey of October 9, 1972, showed Nixon holding a 27-point lead over McGovern. Throughout the campaign, Frank Mankiewicz, McGovern's spokesman, had insisted that, by October 10, the race would narrow, McGovern would take the lead, and go on to win. Apparently, the Russians, Chinese, and North Vietnamese were keenly aware of this prospect and had a rather avid interest in what our poll would show in the first week of October.

On Friday, October 5, the October 9 poll showing Nixon ahead by 27 points arrived at the White House, as it did in the offices of over 250 newspapers across the country. Kissinger carefully put a copy of it in his brief case to take to Paris for his scheduled secret meeting with the North Vietnamese in Paris on Monday, October 8.

That same day brought a call from Dr. K. at the UN who wanted this writer to meet him and another Russian, Mr. K., a high-ranking Soviet diplomat, that afternoon. They queried me about the election, trying to get me to make a flat-footed prediction that Nixon had it all wrapped up. I balked, saying that with a month to go anyone would be a fool to say it was all over. Two hours later, the best the Russians could learn was that the next Harris Survey would show Nixon "not losing much," meaning, of course, that he was 25 points or better in the lead.

On October 8 in Paris, Dr. Kissinger reported that for the first hour, the North Vietnamese came in with the same intractable position they had held for months. Finally, he took out his copy of our October 9 Harris Survey and showed it to the North Vietnamese. They asked a number of questions about it, adjourned the meeting for an hour or more, returned, and presented a whole new set of terms which essentially became the final settlement.

As Henry Kissinger put it, "When they finally realized President Nixon would indeed be around another four years, they changed their tune and fast. Your poll carried a lot of weight." He agreed that the Russians, in their usual "parallelism" with Hanoi, undoubtedly confirmed to the North Vietnamese the authenticity of the October 9 Harris Survey.

By early February 1973, as our final Vietnam survey was being prepared, I suddenly realized that the long vigil was coming to an end, and a strange chapter for polls and a sad, frustrating experience for one particular public opinion analyst was being closed out.

VI

WOMEN
The Struggle To Be
"More Equal"

Back in another time, before the 1950s, it was not uncommon for the poll taker to ring a doorbell and have the woman of the house say that she could not honestly tell whom she was voting for, because her husband had not yet given her the word. The general rule then was for each man's vote to count twice—one for himself and another for his wife. The vote of any woman meant as much as that of any man; but, in fact, in the Orwellian concept, the man's vote was "more equal." [1]

By the 1970s, under the impetus of women's liberation stirrings, women were making a determined bid to be viewed in a different light. Rather than being sex objects, alternately put on a pedestal and then taken for granted, many women wanted instead to be respected as whole people—important in their own right. Populationwise, women were now close to 52% [2] of the population in America. This was no longer a case of a minority seeking sufferance from a more powerful majority. Instead, women's lib advocates would argue, it was a case of a majority asserting its right to full qualitative and quantitative status in the emerging social, political, and economic scene.

Unfortunately, it was not quite as simple as that. Many of the most direct targets of women's lib did not arouse the sleeping giant of female protest. For example, 55% of all women reported they were "hardly annoyed" by "pictures of nude women in *Playboy* and other magazines"; an even higher 65% were not troubled by "a man talking about you as a 'girl' and not as a 'woman' "; and 67% did not become upset by "jokes about women drivers, mothers-in-law, or dumb blondes."

In fact, as the 1972 Virginia Slims Women's Opinion Poll, conducted by the Harris firm, pointed out, by 49% to 39% [3] most women viewed women's lib groups in a negative light. Converts to the cause could be found among single women, black women, those under 30, and women who lived in the big cities. But solid majorities of women who were married, over 30, who lived in small towns and rural America recoiled with aversion at the thought of women's lib speaking for them.

The dominant imagery of women's lib tended more often than not among women themselves to run to words and phrases such as "radical," "revolutionary," "aggressive women," "silly and faddish," "women trying to get into things they don't belong in," "frustrated," "insecure," "hysterical," and "masculine type women." Only a minority could conjure up such dreams as "freedom for women," "better jobs and better pay," "equal pay with men," and "liberation from housework."

Yet, the idea somehow was proving to be more potent than the movement. In 1971, by 42% to 40%, most women in America held a negative view of efforts to strengthen women's status in society. But only a year later, the corner seemed to have been turned and by a clear 48% to 36% a crucial balance of women had changed their minds and gave high marks to the idea of women's lib, even though they still could not bring themselves to enlist in the cause itself.

Women themselves clearly spelled out this distinction between their convictions and their assessment of the organized women's lib movement:

————The charge that "leaders of women's organizations
are trying to turn women into men and that won't
work" met with agreement among women by 51% to
43% in 1972. Even more serious was the criticism
that "women who picket or participate in protests are
setting a bad example for children and such behavior
is undignified and unwomanly." The trigger words
which would evoke a special caveat to women's lib
professionals were "bad example for children," "undignified," and "unwomanly." Raising children properly and maintaining a special and unique female
dignity were indispensable preconditions which any
protest movement must reassure women will be respected above all else.

————But the idea of protest had some real appeal. The
rallying cry that "it's about time women protested
the real injustices they have faced for years" met
with 48% to 43% approval among women nationwide.
The proposition, "if women don't speak up for themselves and confront men with their real problems,
nothing will be done about those problems" was
agreed to by a substantial 71% to 23% majority.

————Thus, the perfectly logical conclusion: "Women are
right to be unhappy with their role in American society but wrong in the way they are protesting,"
which met with 51% to 34% agreement.

It was evident that the success of any movement seeking to
redress injustices to women in the last quarter of the century
would depend on a keen understanding of what women perceive
to be the heart of their frustrations.

In the 1960s and early 1970s, much had been said and written
about women's "second class citizenship" in the jobs they were
offered and held. Yet the evidence was massive that it would be
some time before equality of career opportunity became the engine powering the women's protest movement. It was a fact that
most women did not feel they were discriminated against in get-

ting white collar or clerical jobs, in obtaining work in the arts, in landing manual labor jobs, in getting skilled labor employment, or in obtaining top positions in the professions. Nor did most women give credence to such common claims as "often a woman will do the real work and a man will take the credit" or "a woman usually gets the dirty, boring chores to do" or "when a promotion opens up, a man from outside the department will be brought in to fill it, instead of it going to a deserving woman."

Most telling of all was that women who held down jobs by and large did not feel they had an "unequal chance" in the responsibility given them, in the salaries paid them, nor in their chances for promotion. By a convincing 59% to 25%,[4] a majority of working women felt they were "viewed on the job as equals to men."

In fact, the one exception to a perception of rather equal treatment was the discrimination women felt against them in "obtaining executive positions in business." Women as a whole felt discriminated against here by 50% to 32%. Working women said they were blocked from rising to top executive posts by 46% to 33%. Though it must have come as a bitter pill to some women's lib activists who saw a world dominated by "male, chauvinistic pigs," the truth was that a much higher 59% to 32% majority of men felt working women did not have an equal chance to attain the utmost rungs of executive position. And men also were inclined to see discrimination against women in promotions and pay, while most women did not.

There were reasons, of course, why women did not feel the pangs of discrimination more. No more than 35%[5] of all women 18 years of age and over are employed in paying jobs. The vast majority of 71% of all women felt "taking care of a home and raising children is more rewarding for a woman than having a job" and that "a woman's household chores are as important as a man's job at work." When asked the most enjoyable part of being a woman in America today, the top three volunteered reasons given by women themselves: "being a mother, raising a family" (cited by 53%), "being a homemaker" (23%), and "being a wife" (22%).

Most of the roughly 1 in 4 women who were employed simply were not in it for the long pull. Many worked for 3 to 5 years and went off to the greener pastures of marriage and babies and household chores. Later on, when their kids became teen-agers, many women went back to work, but in many cases they were to take part-time employment or jobs which they didn't view as full-blown careers.

But another reason was that women themselves had not been exposed for long to the notion that they might be exploited on the job. After all, sex discrimination in employment had only recently become unlawful. In a landmark case, in early 1973, the Equal Economic Opportunity Commission (EEOC) forced a settlement of $38 million in back pay from AT&T for discrimination against women and minorities in the Bell System.[6] The Nixon Administration had served warning that in its second four years discrimination against women in employment would receive a high priority.

Many employed women may be pleasantly surprised in the next few years to learn that the male-dominated work society was indeed yielding to the pressures to provide them with a better break on the job. And it then is entirely predictable that the cause of becoming "more equal" in work could become far more a front-burner issue among women themselves. One of the hallmarks of progress in America has been an awakening of public awareness and clamor *after* the U.S. Supreme Court or the Congress has taken initiative in the civil rights area, instead of an aggrieved segment of society pressing fruitlessly for years before finally being rewarded with friendly legislation or court decisions. The Brown case on school discrimination against blacks was resolved in 1954, a good nine years before the civil rights movement bloomed into a major and massive force in the country. Nonetheless, much would have to happen to turn a rather passive female population into a marching army out to square the issue of equality on the job for women. Any movement organized around better job opportunities could well flounder for lack of support.

What, then, in the early 1970s did women feel were their "real problems" which 71% of them said if they "don't speak up for themselves and confront men on them," nothing would be done? A real clue to what bugged women as the mid-1970s approached could be found in these results: (1) A massive 82% of all women felt annoyed that men told women "to be quiet because they aren't supposed to know anything about some serious subject"; (2) by 49% to 39%, most women believed "most men find it necessary for their egos to keep women down"; and (3) by 50% to 41%, most women felt that "most men think only their opinions about the world are important."

The basic fact is that women felt strongly about many issues of the day, but believed they were the victims of a male putdown when it came to their point of view being taken seriously. With the close to 3 in 10 women who had had some college education, with America rapidly moving into an era in which noneconomic issues were coming to dominate our lives, women had just about reached the point where they were not only entitled to their own opinions but that their views on the world were every bit as sound and as important as men's. Of course, implicit in this feeling was a growing awareness that the attitudes of men and women were indeed different.

Just where women part company with men was one of the important keys to understanding where America is headed in the next ten to twenty years. All the evidence pointed to the fact that where women felt most intensely about a subject was almost unerringly where they held different views from men.

The Vietnam War profoundly disturbed the women of America. War ceased being a man's business the moment the blood and guts of rice paddy fighting spilled into the living rooms of America on a nightly basis. Two out of three women reported that seeing the war on television made them feel "more against the war," compared to less than a majority of men who felt the same way. Thus, when a young draftee was shown dying on television, 67% of all women said they felt "upset" about it, (only 49% of men felt the same). The reasons for feeling upset made up the litany of women's curses against all wars: "all wars are senseless," "a terrible waste of human life," "too young to die," and "violence is detestable." A substantial 61% of all women said they simply "do not believe in war as a way to settle anything."

Consistently, during the Vietnamization period, when Richard Nixon was in a race with public opinion to withdraw U.S. troops before the bottom dropped out of the support for his war policies, women were 10 points higher in saying the pace of withdrawal was "too slow." The women of America led the mounting chorus to demand ultimate liquidation of U.S. involvement in Vietnam.

When President Nixon escalated the bombing of North Vietnam in August 1972, 64% of the men, but only 46% of the women [7] supported that military move. When it appeared that the bombings had had some effect in bringing Hanoi to agreement in early October, two-thirds of the men of the country agreed that bombing was effective. But fewer than half the women would agree.

In October 1969, when antiwar demonstrators had their moratorium marches, men stood 50% to 35% opposed to the protesters. Women went on record 43% to 40% in support of the demonstrations. When the My Lai case of Lieutenant Calley surfaced, a plurality of men in the country felt that "shooting of civilians in Vietnam by U.S. soldiers" could be justified. However, a plurality of women disagreed and could see no justification at all. On the antiwar Hatfield-McGovern bill in the U.S. Senate, men were opposed to the legislation but women supported it.

By nearly every measure, women were more opposed to Vietnam than men. Fundamentally, women viewed war as a last recourse, as a point of no return. They hated war more than men, mainly because they felt more keenly and more sensitively about the loss of human life than men. In a way, this was ironic, for war always and invariably takes the lives of many more young men than women. Women in the end cared more about young men's lives than the young men themselves. Perhaps it was the maternal instinct. Perhaps it was because women felt things more than they intellectualized them. Perhaps it was because women had a more profound appreciation of the value of human life.

In any case, the measurable fact was that women were more distressed over war than men and that, in the case of Vietnam, their will came to prevail, albeit after extended pain and anguish. On the controversial issue of amnesty for Vietnam draft evaders, 58% of men were opposed to amnesty, compared to no more than 48% of all women.

As important as these differences might be, in retrospect, the Vietnam era will also be marked well as the time when the women of America not only parted company with men on a massive scale on a noneconomic issue, but it also marked a critical point where women would no longer sit by in silent acquiescence to dominant male policies on matters of war and peace. This essentially humanistic, pacifist sentiment on the part of women could be a new source of searching, questioning, demanding more forthright answers in the formulation of future foreign and defense policy. For example, in 1972 women were more than 10 points more opposed than men to increasing spending on defense research and development. Even more notable, women were far less inclined to favor the U.S. making defense commitments to some of our most traditional allies. If Western Europe were invaded by the Communists in 1973, 55% of the men believed we should go to war to defend our oldest allies. But no more than 40% of all women agreed. If Australia were similarly invaded, men supported going to war by 48% to 35%, but women opposed such a commitment by 41% to 33%.

War and peace were not the only areas of concern in which women part company with men in significant numbers. On passage of strict gun control legislation, men stood 62% to 36% in favor, while women came in with a much more lopsided 78% to 18% [8] backing. Once more, women came out more decisively against violence than men were prone to do. One key and long-standing split between the sexes apparent in the early 1970s was over the subject of capital punishment. Women were opposed to the death penalty for any crime, even when the life of another has been taken, by 46% to 39%. Men favored the death sentence by a substantial 56% to 37%. This raised serious problems about the legitimacy of trials by jury which guaranteed universally that a person accused of murder be tried by a jury of his peers. If nearly half the women of the country would become "scrupled jurors," eliminated by their own self-profession that they could not sentence the accused to death, then the question must be raised in turn: Can a person being tried for murder be tried by a jury of his peers?

Of course, the U.S. Supreme Court had in effect put a moratorium on the death sentence, by calling it "cruel punishment," so such questions might well be moot for the moment. But, if, as some observers believe, the high court was sensitive to public opinion at any given point in time, then it must be concluded that it was the body of female rather than male opinion that was being adhered to in the trend to outlaw capital punishment. With President Nixon advocating a return to capital punishment, women can be expected to provide much of the popular will in support of the U.S. Supreme Court's position.

There was further evidence that women were different in their views about the poor and minorities from those of men. For example, when President Nixon proposed elimination of the Office of Economic Opportunity, the agency running the antipoverty program, women opposed abolishing OEO by 48% to 34%, while men split down the middle on the subject 44% to 44%.

On the matter of race, women tended to show a greater sympathy toward progress for blacks than was the case among men. On the principle of school desegregation, women stood 50% to 34% in favor of integration in public education, compared to a much narrower 46% to 42% favorable view among men. A substantial 66% of women felt that discrimination against blacks was "widespread," as compared with 55% of men. On the controversial subject of open housing, now the law of the land, although hardly a reality in terms of integrated housing, women stood 52% to 34% in favor of open housing while men showed a narrow 47% to 43% margin on the support side. When asked if "blacks were asking for more than they were ready," 55% of all men felt this was the case, while 53% of all women felt it was not.

Perhaps no figure of the white establishment is more associated with the long series of desegregation decisions than former Chief Justice of the U.S. Supreme Court, Earl Warren. When he finally ended his long tenure and resigned in 1969, the public gave him mixed marks on his record. Men were 45% to 43% negative about Warren, but women were 52% to 34% positive about him. For the women of the country, Earl Warren had a special place, and they shared this view quite apart from the prevailing attitudes among men.

These differences held to a pattern, centering on two crucial elements: the higher priority women place on human life and their equally strong aversion to violence. In the 1970s these deeply felt instincts of women were having a rather profound impact on the quality of life of these times. The Vietnam War brought them out on the single issue that absorbed America for the longest period of frustration in this century. In the process, women crossed that invisible barrier between harboring their thoughts to themselves and a new-found willingness to express their views in the outside world—not as Democrats or Republicans, not as suburban or small-town residents, not as older or younger people, but first and foremost as women.

How far these stirrings of women as an organized group would go in the years ahead was difficult to estimate, let alone measure with precision. But some of the instinctive feelings of women, if pursued to their logical extensions, could pose serious challenges to the time-honored ways of a man's world. At the moment, women were not terribly upset at not being admitted to all men's clubs nor to bars exclusively reserved for the male sex. Those avant-garde women trying to break down such barriers even had a taint of exhibitionism in the eyes of most women.

A far more potentially significant idea widely held by women was that, by 60% to 29%, a sizable majority simply denied the proposition that "winning through competition is one of the greatest experiences in life." A majority of men disagreed. They regularly enjoyed their competitive victories at work, at play, either as participants or as exuberant rooters for their favorite football, baseball, basketball, or hockey team. Women saw far less need for there to be winners and losers in life. This was an instinctive view, undoubtedly turning back to the central sensitivity of humanity they felt, although it was undoubtedly also a reflection of being taught it was "unwomanly" to win, at least not too often.

Up to 1973, a majority of women had not taken up the challenge of many of the basic assumptions which underlie institutions in the American establishment. But if they turned their fire that way, some sacred notions were bound to perish or at least be changed rather drastically.

One conclusion was certain about the phenomenon of the women's movement in the 1970s: A new coalition of women activists was being forged that was likely to hold and to continue into the next decade. This coalition was immediately apparent from the following table showing the division among key groups of women on the efforts to strengthen or to change women's status in society:

Efforts to Strengthen and Change Women's Status in Society

	FAVOR %	OPPOSE %	NOT SURE %
Women Nationwide	48	36	16
Single	67	20	13
Married	46	38	16
Divorced, separated	57	29	14
Widowed	40	40	20
Black	62	22	16
White	45	39	16
18 to 29	56	30	14
30 to 39	49	36	15
40 to 49	42	41	17
50 and over	41	40	19
Eighth grade	42	34	24
High school	43	40	17
College	57	32	11
Cities	52	31	17
Suburbs	51	35	14
Towns	44	38	18
Rural	40	43	17

Leading in consciousness of the new women's surge for self-identity were single and divorced women, black women, those under 30, the college educated, and women who lived in the large metropolitan centers of the country. Taken together, by the early 1970s, they had convinced enough of the rest of women that there was real merit in the cause of women's rights to carry the day.

There was significance in the make-up of this coalition. First, it was essentially young, which means those women who felt most strongly were more likely to be around a long time into the future. Second, they were well educated for the most part, so they were likely to be highly articulate about what they wanted. Third, they were located in the large metropolitan areas of the country, so they were likely to have an inordinate impact on the major media of communications.

Both interesting and poignant were black women who, before the Virginia Slims Women's Opinion Polls of 1971 and 1972, were widely believed not to be turned on by organized efforts to change women's status in society. Consistently, however, on samples large enough to be significant, black women have placed themselves in the vanguard of the movement. Black men, by contrast, showed no more than 47% sympathetic to the women's efforts—a gap of 15 points between black men and black women on support for the principle of women's lib.

Before there was hard data on the subject, the theory was that blacks had so many troubles as blacks, the cause of womanhood in addition was a burden simply too much to bear. In addition, black men had suffered so much emasculation from slavery onward that black women were willing to submerge their own woes in deference to their men. The theory turned out to be patent nonsense in the light of the facts which have now been assembled. Black women were tired of being extolled for their heroic efforts to hold together broken families, of working their fingers to the bone on jobs away from home and then assuming large measures of responsibility for family discipline when they came home at night. A black woman in New York's Harlem put it for many of her black sisters when she said, "You know, a woman is a human being, too. We bear the children and we bring them up. We work to feed them. We want our men and we want them to want us. But all we ask is that they respect us for what we are—human beings. We don't want it easy. But we want it nice, because living, not dying is what it's all about. And we mean to get it as women as much as we do as blacks."

One key to breaking the vicious circle of welfare which so often and inevitably trapped black ghetto mothers was the expansion of child day-care centers, where working mothers can leave their children. The child day-care center had been the subject of much controversy in the budget battles which raged across federal, state, and local lines in recent years.

Women favored more child day-care centers by a sizable 64% to 26%. Men wanted them, too, but by a much lesser 49% to 36%. Leading the drive in advocating the centers was the new coalition of women's activists: women in the big cities (72%), single women (73%), women under 30 (74%), divorced and separated women (82%), and black women (86%).

When women with children under twelve years of age were asked if they would look for work if there were a reliable child day-care center near where they lived, 24% nationwide said they would seek employment. But, among the welfare affected groups, a much higher number expressed a desire to work: Among those with incomes under $5,000 a year, 43% said they would look for employment and, among black mothers, an even higher 46% voiced the same desire.

The child day-care center issue was one which was essentially a women's issue. It was the kind of cause which the emerging women's movement was likely to press for in the months and years ahead. It fit the ingredients that made women different in the 1970s. It was a cause women felt more keenly about than men and one in which men would follow rather than lead. It affected the lot of women in their desire to achieve dignity for themselves and their children. It bridged the work world but also had a large pay-out in the happiness of the home, so central to American women's existence. Finally, child day-care centers would benefit the poor and the minorities—and that was a subject that interested women, whose main concern, after all, was humanity and the nurturing of human life.

In the 1970s, the women's movement was directed largely against the male-dominated establishment. As with other forces striking out for change, the women's movement groups were skeptical of early surveys of women's attitudes. Our own first study, conducted in 1971 and paid for by Virginia Slims, for example, was coolly received by leaders such as Betty Freidan and Gloria Steinem. The second study in 1972 simply could not be ignored. It documented many of the changes (most favorable to their cause) which have just been reported in this chapter.

Gloria Steinem's magazine, *Ms.*, finally did a full spread on the second Virginia Slims Poll. The study itself had been conducted by one of the able, young Harris analysts, Carolyn Setlow, a woman. In reporting the survey's findings, Ms. Steinem throughout called it the Harris-Setlow Poll of Women's Opinion —a testimony, indeed, that equal rights had come to the polling profession.

VII

WHERE HAS ALL THE QUALITY GONE?

In 1962 this writer was in the last year of his "former life," a period dating from 1956 during which he conducted surveys for an estimated 240 candidates running for public office, ranging from the president of the United States and the prime minister of Canada to state legislators in a number of states. One of the most dedicated members of the U.S. Senate and an old client, Democratic Senator Philip Hart of Michigan had invited me to lunch in the Senate Dining Room to try out a whole new idea: to begin an investigation into food packaging in supermarkets.

The thought was a shocking one, for perhaps more than any other American institution, the supermarket stood out around the world as a symbol of this country's wide lead in our standard of living and our superior methods of bringing the good things of life to the masses of the people. Just before our meeting, the Justice Department had taken the nation's biggest food chain, A&P, into court on antitrust charges. A&P had responded by taking out full-page ads in newspapers arguing that the net result of the antitrust suit would result in a crippling of the great benefits consumers received from modern supermarketing.

We had done some polling on the subject, and by a 3 to 2 margin, the consumers were backing A&P. The lunch with Senator Hart and the group he had assembled began by my telling him he certainly had a lot of courage taking on as formidable a sacred cow as the nation's supermarkets. Hart's aides were undeterred. They had done their homework. They had case after case of peaches which looked like standard size but in fact contained much less than a full measure, and package after package which looked bigger but contained less.

As the luncheon meeting came to an end, this writer reiterated his previously reported facts and recommended against Senator Hart's undertaking the investigation. Senator Hart answered for the group, "You are dead wrong. Things are changing, and consumers will respond to the truth. This country needs a truth-in-packaging law. The time of consumer advocacy has come. This movement will grow." Indeed, I could not have been more wrong, Senator Hart was right and the man who later picked up the consumerism thread was Ralph Nader, who had an idea.

By the early 1970s, the time of consumer advocacy and Ralph Nader had come to America. In a period when the men running department stores could evoke no more than 28% of the public who would put high confidence in them and when business leaders generally could attain no higher than a 27% top confidence rating, Nader triggered 60% who viewed his efforts favorably. Even 63% [1] of all the business executives in the country gave Nader high marks, the $15,000 and over group backed his criticisms of industry with 70%, and the college educated with 72%. Nader had caught fire and, most of all, in the heart of affluent America.

This appeal of Nader and his consumerist activities must surely rank as one of the real concerns of the 1970s, a period marked by a greater growth of affluence than the country had ever known before. A sure-fire formula for accelerating sales in the 1960s had been to cultivate the growing suburban and affluent market, the end of the spectrum which bought a disproportionate share of the goods and services. For example, in 1968, the 39% of the population with incomes of $10,000 and over a year represented an estimated 52% of the total dollar purchases made in the country. As the number of families with incomes over $10,000 a year was projected to rise to 61% by 1980, the outlook for a surging market for higher quality, higher priced products and services could not have been brighter. The American consumer economy should have been poised on a truly golden era of consumption. Buttressing this optimism, in 1966, American business was credited with bringing better quality products by 75% of the American people.

But something went terribly wrong with the reputation for quality of American products and services in only a few short years. Consumers became increasingly reticent and selective. They asked more questions about quality and they found quality wanting. After a quarter-century buying splurge previously unknown in the history of the world, a new kind of doubt appeared to be replacing traditional faith in American know-how. Instead of that know-how being capable of solving nearly any problem the country faced, it was beginning to be viewed as the creator of products that could contaminate, poison, or kill you.

By the 1970s, massive numbers of people came to see substantial danger in the use of many of the staples of the American material way of life, as the following table indicates:

Perceived Danger in Use of Products [2]

	BELIEVED DANGEROUS %
Pesticides and bug spray for home use (poisoning)	85
Children's toys (poisoning, sharp edges, flammable)	83
Automobiles (manufacturing defects)	77
Room heaters (fire, asphyxiation)	76
Power lawn mowers (inadequate safeguards)	72
Auto tires (blowouts)	69
Artificial additives in foods (poisoning)	65
Fabrics as children's clothes and curtains (flammable)	64

Perceived Danger in Use of Products (Continued)

	BELIEVED DANGEROUS %
Detergents (allergic reactions)	64
Power tools (inadequate safeguards)	62
Appliances (electrical shock, fire)	56
Hair sprays or coloring (poisoning)	54
Canned goods (poisoning)	48
TV sets (radiation, fire)	48

While by no means a complete roster of all the major consumer goods people were buying, the list nonetheless encompassed enough of the mainstream to prove the point: There was a risk to the material wonders now available in the marketplace, one that could be dangerous to health and life and limb. The traditional warning to the buyer, "caveat emptor," now had a bite with a vengeance.

But worries about cutting oneself, catching fire, one's safety in jeopardy, being shocked, radiated, or poisoned were not the only new dimensions which seemed to be souring the American material dream. Once the consumer bought a particular product, substantial minorities reported having trouble making the product work the way it had been promised in the blaring advertising copy and in the soothing, syrup words of the salesman.

The world of repairs for major products in the 1970s could be traumatic. Four in ten new car owners reported trouble with their autos requiring repairs and 61% said the bill they paid was "too high." One in three new television set owners had similar repair troubles and 58% said they paid an exorbitant bill to have their TV set fixed. Over one in four stereo set owners reported troubles and 47% thought they were "taken" in the bill from the repairman. The pattern for refrigerators, air conditioners, vacuum cleaners, new stoves, toasters, and new auto tires was not much different.

Many of the products people bought might be viewed as dangerous in the first instance, but after struggling through repairs and inordinate charges for them, by the early 1970s a veritable army of exasperated consumers had mushroomed across the country. The combination of quality concerns before owning a product along with frustrations in dealing with service personnel after you bought it was altogether too much. Not only was confidence in product quality deeply shaken, but in an unheralded change, America had converted to a dominantly service economy, where more dollars now were going for service than for products as such. When asked if they were receiving generally satisfactory service from each of 21 different major suppliers of services, a majority of the public who used each service came up negative on 11 of the 21.

Literally hundreds of thousands of doors were being slammed in the faces of door-to-door salesmen with less than satisfactory experiences being reported by 91% who were called on by a door-to-door appliance salesman; 89% who had an encounter with a door-to-door book salesman, and 68% who were visited by a door-to-door cosmetics salesman. Used car salesmen, the butt of many a traditional joke, were no laughing matter to 74% who gave them votes of no confidence. Credit loan company personnel were believed not to be helpful by 67%, garage and auto mechanics came up a negative 66%, home improvement and repair contractors had let 64% of their customers down.

Real estate brokers have never won popularity contests, but in this period 62% of those who had bought or sold homes from them were critical. Radio and TV repairmen came up short in the estimate of 58%, followed by new car dealers who weighed in with a negative 56%. Personnel of mail order companies were rated as unsatisfactory by 55%.

Ten other major service areas of the economy had the distinction of having disenchanted only minorities of their customers: radio and TV dealers, 42%; furniture dealers, 40%; appliance dealers, 40%; supermarket operators, 31%; clothing store personnel, 30%; record dealers, 29%; department stores, 29%; pharmacies, 26%; and shoe repairmen, at the head of the list, who only made 20% of their customers mad at them.

In fairness, the average for all 21 service industries on customer disenchantment came out to 49% generally satisfied and 51% not. But what it meant for the average consumer in the early 1970s was that the odds were just about even that he would have a satisfactory service experience. Every other time you might call on a store or some repairman, the chances were that you would receive service that did not upset you. But, then, every other time the chances were that you would come out of the store either grumbling or resigned to your fate.

It is little wonder that when asked directly about it, 2 out of every 3 people in the country favored the establishment of a "complaint bureau" in every community in the country, where the beleaguered customer could find some redress.

In a way, two cases, one in the product area and one in the service area, point up the type of problem besetting American consumers these days. One of the fastest growing forms of packaging in the past decade has been aerosol containers. Many traditional products have been repackaged and now come to the consumer in the form of aerosol cans. They obviously have the advantages of being self-contained, the product can be dispersed in neat and controlled doses, and can even be shot or sprayed out of the container if that's the way the consumer wants it.

But is this the way, indeed, in which most Americans view the aerosol can? When we surveyed a cross-section of homes on the subject in 1972, it began auspiciously: 81% of the public was convinced aerosol containers were less likely to spill and 53% credited them with being more leakproof. But from then on it was downhill all the way for the aerosol can: 51% worried that children could get at their contents more easily, 60% that their contents might catch fire, 74% that their contents might be inhaled by mistake, and 82% that they might explode. When asked if this new form of packaging were more safe or more dangerous than alternative forms of packaging, 56% of the public opted for "more dangerous," only 4% for "safer," and 28% saw little difference. The advent of the aerosol can, called the aerosol bomb in the early days, certainly has been received as a mixed blessing for American life.

The financial service which has penetrated nearly every segment of American life is insurance, owned in some form now by 92% of all households. In 1972 we tested public reaction to insurance agents and representatives. Generally, 66% of the public felt that agents were "helpful and friendly" and 53% thought they made a genuine effort "to arrange insurance plans to fit people's individual needs."

But after that it was rough going for service people in the insurance business. On the pivotal issue of "being honest with their clients," a requisite in any personalized relationship, the results showed a 45% to 45% standoff. "Providing a good service for the premiums people pay" met with a negative 49% to 42% response. "Giving enough factual information about insurance policies" came up with 54% to 38% on the minus side. By 46% to 36%, most people said insurance men "did not avoid using gimmicks." On "not trying to sell people more insurance than they need," the public was 57% to 32% negative. Finally, on "keeping their prices down," insurance agents were scored a thumping 71% to 21% negative. Obviously, the art of selling insurance was not doing much better in enhancing public confidence than aerosol containers.

In the case of financial services, by the 1970s a real crisis of confidence had arisen, for a highly specific reason. People had become skeptical of representatives of financial institutions coming to them in the guise of wanting to sit down and work out a financial plan and then, in the end, invariably telling them that the particular financial product the agent was peddling was just what they needed to give them security and a sound "estate plan." What has been reported for insurance agents could have been documented even more readily for mutual fund or securities representatives. The ultimate irony was that at precisely the time when an increasingly affluent public had the money and the appetite to make their money earn for them, financial institutions were falling back on the tried and true methods that had worked ten and twenty years ago.

The net conclusion of the public in both the product and in the service areas was that no more than 18% could say that quality had improved in the past ten years. Scarcely more, 24%, believed there was substantially no change over the decade. But a majority of 56% [3] had no doubt that product and service quality had grown worse. Perhaps most telling of all was the fact that 60% of all business executives felt that quality had deteriorated. If the men generating the goods and services admitted such a decline, then things had reached a sad state, indeed.

Nearly 3 in every 4 Americans had reached the point in the early 1970s where they felt something was seriously wrong with quality control in the country. Yet when asked if they thought some kind of federal regulation of quality of products and services was the answer, the public balked at the thought. No more than 25% could say they thought a system of federally regulated quality control would be "very effective." The reason: Public skepticism about government doing anything well had reached all-time lows. The heavy hand of federal bureaucracy could hardly be viewed as an exciting corrective for business which had seemingly forgotten what quality meant.

By 70% to 24% [4] the public felt industry itself had to devote more attention to "repair and service." But if not by governmental fiat, how? The answer was to be found neither in government nor in industry. Instead, people turned to a new vehicle: consumer advocacy. By decisive margins of 2 and 3 to 1, the public was willing to opt for a form of self-organization to do the job. A sizable 66% said they saw a "real need" for consumers to join together on the issue, with no more than 22% feeling they could obtain adequate protection from government or industry. Although it was unlikely to happen, 32% of the public, 1 in every 3 persons 18 years of age or over, expressed a desire to take an "active part" in such a consumer movement. This meant the consumer activist movement could become as large as all the professional, social, or political groups in the country combined, for their members totaled no more than 35% of the adult population.

If Ralph Nader and groups of consumer advocates had not emerged in this period, the public surely would have invented other Naders to speak for them. By the early 1970s, there was every indication that the consumerism appetite of the American people had only begun to be whetted. Now 75% of consumers favored a universal system of printing "final dates" on all perishable packaged food products, such as milk, cheese, and other dairy products. Real merit was seen by 3 in every 4 in "unit pricing," a practice under which the supermarket shopper would know precisely how much he was paying for the amount of merchandise received—regardless of how the product was packaged. The spreading idea of "no fault insurance," which held out the promise of compensation for people involved in auto accidents without extended litigation, was favored by almost a 3 to 1 margin nationally. Among the affluent $15,000 and over group, support for no fault insurance rose to nearly 4 to 1.

There seemed to be no end to the changes in marketing practices and the shape and delivery of services the American people were willing to support by lopsided majorities. The consumer had become far more articulate, selective, and, most of all, unafraid to speak out and advocate change.

While all kinds of changes were meeting with high public approval, the chief vehicle and voice of the establishment in the consumer field, paid advertising, appeared to be in the deepest trouble. On any list of institutions tested for respect by the people, advertising almost invariably finished at the bottom, with no more than 14% who could express high confidence in the men running the profession. No more than 12% of the consumers could bring themselves to describe most claims in advertisements as "generally accurate." More than 7 times as many people, 86%, said they thought such claims were "exaggerated."

For years, advertising spokesmen had dismissed such criticisms as nonsense, with pat answers as "it is fashionable to complain about advertising, but then go out and buy only advertised products" or "people just don't want to admit they are influenced by advertising, even though they know they are." Yet by the early 1970s, the more reflective leaders in advertising were deeply troubled and privately admitted they had wildly underestimated the consumerist revolt. Committees were formed to work out studies to measure the depth and impact of the decline of public confidence in advertising. In New York City, the heart of the profession, bills were introduced in the City Council requiring proof for all efficacy claims in the advertising of products. The Federal Trade Commission came up with a series of crackdowns on false ad claims more sweeping than ever before in its history. Even the sacred cows of aspirin products, one of the great success stories in the advertising trade, were under cease and desist orders on their claims—from Bayer to Bufferin to Anacin to Excedrin.[5]

Clearly things had changed drastically from the days when "the man in the gray flannel suit," the prototype of the smooth Madison Avenue advertising executive, was viewed as sitting in the cockpit of the most powerful communications apparatus in the world. Now the advertising profession found itself in a highly defensive stance, if not, indeed, in the eye of the hurricane of consumerism.

Yet the lack of credibility for advertising was but part of the more general problem of the decline in reputation for quality which beset the business establishment. The 75% to 19% high marks for product and service quality recorded in 1966 dipped to a bare 47% to 46% in 1971, and by late 1972 had gone to a rather sour 52% to 42% negative [6] standing with the public.

Three basic trends all coalesced to give the consumer advocate movement a position of unusual power and prestige. First and foremost, the credibility of American know-how had come under a cloud, not so much concerning our national ability to produce new products and services, but more because, for all of our skill and know-how, actual deterioration of quality now seemed evident at every hand. Second, because the establishment itself had lost much of its credibility, its efforts to throw up a believable defense were seriously hampered. Third, people did not see government, at any level, as the primary source of protection for the consumer.

Inexorably, then, in the spirit of the original colonists two centuries before, the public became prepared to take matters into its own hands. Men such as Nader, who seemed willing to become consumer advocates, seeking to reform the system from a position staked out in the private sector, literally were hailed as folk heroes.

Solid majorities of the public expressed the view that "Nader's efforts can go a long way toward improving the quality and standards for goods and services" (64%), "Nader is right when he says the average consumer should have a voice in top corporate decisions" (52%), "There never would have been strict federal safety regulations for cars if Nader had not crusaded for auto safety" (65%), and "It's good to have critics like Nader to keep industry on its toes" (80%). Even when Nader had the audacity to compile an assessment of every incumbent congressman's record in 1972, a majority of 56% agreed with the statement that "Nader performed a public service" in taking on Congress.

By the same token, some of the criticisms regularly directed toward Nader and other consumer advocates by professional defenders of the system meet with pitifully little public support. For example, the claim that "Nader is a troublemaker who is against the free-enterprise system" was soundly rejected by 68% to 11% by the public.

Over the past five years, one of the few places where Nader has been received with a full and open welcome is on the college campuses. Although he has avoided becoming an activist in popular campus causes, such as the war and black militancy, Nader has openly associated himself with the younger end of the generation spectrum. Yet the aversions of the public for activist students have not been transferred to Nader. By a thumping 61% to 14%, a majority of the public denied the charge that "Nader's efforts are just part of the way-out and unfair protests of young people against the establishment."

On only one count did any vulnerability in public opinion emerge for the Nader cause: By 46% to 30%, a plurality of the people agreed that "Nader gives a one-sided picture of what American industry does, leaving out many good things industry does." The public was beginning to believe Nader did not present a full and balanced analysis of American business operations. However, this was perhaps less a Nader weakness than an opportunity for industry to present its case. This result suggested that the public would welcome a dialogue between industry and Nader. Yet, so far, almost the only answer given to Nader by business had been a denial of his charges, a wholly defensive effort on which business has essentially lost the battle. Mainly due to its own inability to articulate and report its positive efforts, the good works of business remain virtually unknown.

As incredible as Nader's rise and sustained support from the

American people might be, an even more amazing fact was that virtually no mainstream candidate for president has picked up the Nader cause as his own. In 1972 Senator McGovern peripherally endorsed the aims of Nader, but consumerism certainly was not one of his major thrusts. Senator Muskie had taken the leadership in managing the Clean Air and Clean Water bills through Congress, but never embraced the Nader cause, reportedly because he did not want to unnecessarily "antagonize large segments of the business community."

Part of the reason for the studied avoidance by politicians of Nader's cause could be traced to the steadfast refusal of Nader himself to embrace political candidacies or parties. In fact, if anything, Nader has handled himself in a way almost to deliberately cut himself off from mainstream candidates. In early 1972, when the Muskie candidacy seemed to be promising and when Nader might have established some real ties with the Maine senator, Nader chose instead to criticize Muskie's efforts on environmental legislation as being "inadequate" and "falling short of what ought to be done."

But the fact remains that the consumerist movement survived 1972 handsomely, while the Democrats went on to disastrous defeat and disarray. The chances are that the full political impact of the consumer cause will be realized only when its most visible leaders emerge as political forces in their own right. It will be interesting, for example, to follow the budding political career of former Miss America-turned-consumerist, Bess Meyerson, in New York politics. In 1973, when New Yorkers rated Mayor Lindsay 72% negative on the job he had done, Bess Meyerson was rated 71% positive as consumer affairs commissioner.

If the establishment has consistently underestimated rising consumer disenchantment with the quality of products and services, then much the same can be said for the closely allied cause of cleaning up America's physical environment. Henry Grunwald, the managing editor of *Time*, told this writer in 1970 that the issue of air and water pollution control was "essentially a faddist, style issue that soon would pass." His reasoning was a common line that ran through most of the business community and the media establishment.

The heart of the discontent about pollution is that it challenges the engine of technology which is so central to the complex economy and society that America had become by the 1970s. The young who feel so strongly about air and water pollution at the same time find the automobile an indispensable part of their lives. The affluent and educated who are so agitated by the despoiling of the environment nonetheless live in a maze of electronic and other gadgets which are the direct output of the same industrial system which also produces pollution. And, to top it all, according to this pragmatic put-down, is the deep aversion nearly everyone has for paying the higher taxes necessary to clean up the environment.

All of the foregoing makes perfectly good sense until placed against the reality of the state of mind of the people themselves. Shortly after Grunwald denegrated the potential of the environmental issue, the Harris firm conducted a test of public opinion on the domestic issues of concern in the country. At the top of the list of "most important" priorities at home emerged air and water pollution control, singled out by 72% of the public. When asked if they actually believed pollution could be cleaned up, by an even higher 76% to 19%, people said "it can be done." At a time when federal spending was highly unpopular, 72% of the people opted for increasing federal funds to improve environmental quality.

This concern over air and water pollution took hold in earnest as the country entered the decade of the 1970s. In 1967 public opinion was by no means committed to clean up the physical environment. On a key question of paying $15 more taxes per person to finance air and water pollution control, the division nationwide was 46% to 44% in opposition. The lines were drawn by region, by where people lived, their incomes, and their age. People on the East and West coasts were alarmed by pollution but in the Midwest and South they were not. Suburban residents were upset, but big city and rural residents were not. The higher income people were aroused about air and water contamination, but low income people were not. The young were willing to pay higher taxes to curb pollution, but those over 50 were not. A majority of 51% of all the public could say pollution did not affect them personally.

But only four years later, as the 1970s arrived, the set of public opinion had changed drastically. Now by 59% to 34%,[7] a majority was willing to endure higher taxes of $15 per person to curb air and water pollution. Underscoring this dramatic turnabout was that sentiment to pay more taxes for environmental control was going up at precisely the same moment that willingness to pay higher taxes for other new federal programs was going down. A 2 to 1 majority of the American people felt they were receiving poor value for their tax dollars. The desire to pay more taxes to clean up pollution was so deeply felt, however, that it was capable of overcoming the tide of the tax revolt.

The biggest shift over the four-year period had been the rising concern of big city dwellers over the quality of the air they breathed and the worries of rural people about the deterioration of their streams and rivers and lakes. The case of blacks in the big cities was most interesting. In the 1960s, no more than 1 in 3 blacks expressed concern about air pollution. In explaining this lack of concern, urbanologists had a pat answer: Blacks had so much wrong with their inside environment—holes in the ceilings, broken toilets, rat-infested flats—they could scarcely be expected to pay much attention to the air outside on the streets. Thus, liberals and other elitists tried to square their own worries about ecology with blacks' lack of concern. Yet in the 1970s, there is ample evidence that blacks have awakened to the alarm over a deteriorating big city environment. In fact, more blacks than whites expressed the view that air pollution was growing worse. In the cities, opposition to paying higher taxes to curb pollution switched from 51% to 38% opposed in 1967 to 56% to 34% [8] support by 1971—mainly due to a major shift in the concerns of blacks over the state of air pollution. Air that makes a person choke is color blind, and by now blacks and whites stand side by side in being appalled by it.

That same year, top Nixon Administration people also expressed skepticism that the pollution issue was real. In St. Paul in late 1970, Bert Cross, who then ran the Minnesota Mining and Manufacturing Company, told this writer about his experiences on a Nixon pollution advisory board. "Everybody gives lip service to the decline of quality of the air and water, until they come face to face with the twin realities involved. First, they don't know how expensive it will be to do the clean-up job and how it will add to the cost of the products they buy. And then, they haven't begun to face the curtailment of jobs that will take place if the government really got tough about pollution. Just wait till they have to choose jobs or pollution, and you'll see how fast they'll get off this pollution kick they are on." A year later, President Nixon himself was to express similar skepticism on the issue of jobs versus pollution in a private conversation the writer had with him in the White House. However, Nixon was far less categorical than Cross had been a year earlier.

Partly as a result of these highly placed doubts about just how much the people were playing for keeps, we undertook a series of tests of public attitudes pitting jobs head to head against pollution controls. The results nationwide were revealing: When confronted with a choice between cutting unemployment in their community in half or cutting air and water pollution in half, by 51% to 37%, the public opted for cutting pollution. Other measures bore similar tidings from the rank and file of the people to the skeptical leadership.

But perhaps as telling a test as any was the case of the state of Washington, and most particularly the greater Seattle area. Seattle had been beset with as much economic disaster as any city in the country when the dominant employer in the area, the Boeing Company, came upon hard times, with the cutbacks in the SST and other new plane programs. Unemployment in Seattle soared over the 14% mark and western Washington resembled the dark Depression days of the 1930s. Because aerospace is an industry employing relatively highly paid professionals and paraprofessionals, the affluent were reduced to near poverty almost overnight, making Seattle an acid test for the environmental issue. When a Harris Survey was conducted there,[9] the results were striking. Twice as many people selected "reducing air and water pollution" as the most serious problem facing the state than picked "increasing employment." In fact, in Seattle, more people (51%) opted for controlling pollution than did for "attracting new industry" (22%) and "increasing employment" (23%) combined. A high 83% said that air pollution was a "serious problem" and 82% said the same about water pollution.

When the people of Seattle were asked to name the leading cause of air and water pollution, 76% put the finger on industry in the case of air contamination and 54% on industry for polluting the waters; in both cases industry was the top culprit. When asked to rate the job done by the federal and state governments to curb pollution, Seattle residents came up 3 to 1 negative. Local government did better, receiving only a 3 to 2 negative assessment. But local industry came out on the short end of a nearly 4 to 1 negative rating on the pollution issue.

Finally, the issue of attracting new industry to the area was raised. In Seattle 90% of the public affirmed the need for new industry, an obvious response to a deep-felt problem of employment. Yet when asked if they would favor a new plant coming to Seattle which would cause a "large increase in pollution" no more than 28% of Seattle residents supported it. Then, when asked if they would tolerate a new plant that caused "a slight increase in pollution," the total who would acquiesce rose to 47%, still not a majority. Only when given the choice of a new plant that would cause "no increase in pollution" did 89% offer their support. Leading the opposition to new industry at the price of increased pollution were professional people, those with a college education, and those in the highest income brackets.

Whether it was hard-hit Seattle or other areas of the country that had ridden out the recession with less trauma, it was patently apparent that the environmental issue was going to be around for a long time to come and that the people were playing for keeps about cleaning up pollution. Nor was the bite of the issue limited to air and water pollution. The environmentalists were broadening their attacks to encompass visual pollution—eyesores that dotted the American landscape. The sight of soft drink, beer and other bottles and cans strewn along the side of roadways and in recreation areas offended 85% of the people. Objections were raised by 38% to visual pollution from billboards, 40% to auto junkyards, 60% to utility poles and overhead wires, and 83% to litter generally.

Fully 80% of the people were willing to blame "the public" for this kind of littering. Although there would always be a tendency to say that "others" were worse than themselves, the fact remained that America in the 1970s was suffering from a bad conscience over the way its great natural resources had been plundered and despoiled.

But, most of all, the people were prepared to take the action needed to rectify the mistakes of the past—and their terms were going to be tough. They were not going to give a mandate to industry to spend money on pollution control and simply "pass along the increased costs to the consumer by charging higher prices," a proposition that might be ratified in many board rooms, but which met with 71% to 22% rejection by the public itself. Their toughness was evidenced by the 73% to 17% majority who favor "fines for companies who are warned and continue to pollute" and by the 64% to 24% majority [10] who support "a ban on any product manufactured through a process that pollutes the environment."

The steel fist of the public in the 1970s on an air and water pollution clean-up did have a velvet glove over it, however. The proposition of "direct government aid to manufacturers to assist in a clean-up and in pollution control" was favored by 59% to 33% and "tax benefits and write-offs to manufacturers to encourage and assist them in pollution control" was supported by 59% to 29%. The majority willing to pay higher taxes to do the job was also willing to spend that money on a system of incentives and assistance to make possible and to speed up an environmental clean-up.

The phenomenon of the air and water pollution issue was an important signal for America coming into the latter quarter of the twentieth century. It was a fair warning to the establishment and particularly those vested with responsibility for technological progress that the American people would no longer give a blank check to any and all "advances" put forth in the name of science and industrial know-how. The day when nearly any technological breakthrough meant it was automatically good appears to have come to a close.

A case in point is that of the supersonic transport, the SST. Consistently, a majority of public opinion had opposed the U.S. building an SST, despite the fact that the plane could transport people across the continent or to Europe in half the time, despite the acknowledged loss of leadership for the American aerospace capability in not building the plane, and despite the number of jobs that would be gained by going ahead with the SST. Outweighing all of these considerable benefits was the simple, believed fact that the SST would pollute the stratosphere. Until this central environmental objection to the SST was answered or corrected, there would be no American SST. A majority of the public stood behind the decision of the U.S. Senate to kill it.

By the same token, neither had the American people turned their backs on the legitimate benefits wrought by science for mankind. Over 8 in 10 people believed this country "never could have achieved its high standard of living without scientific progress," "without a strong scientific effort, the U.S. would become a second-rate power," and "modern life is better off due to the wonders that scientific progress has brought." Those avant-gardists who saw a return of America to a Rousseauian cultism that rejects any and all technologically derived progress were doomed to a long wait.

Basically, people had been alerted to a new state of consciousness in which they wanted to selectively decide for themselves whether an act in the name of "scientific progress" is indeed progress at all. For example, by 54% to 36%, people worried that "science has put so many artificial additives into good products that many foods are now unsafe to eat."

The central criticism, however, was summed up in the substantial 62% to 27% majority who agreed with the statement, "scientists have thought too much about what will work and not enough about how their discoveries will affect the lives of people." This failure of the technologists to see the human implications of their creations struck close to the heart of the revolt.

The surge of consumerism and environmental concern was

also a classic example of the thrust for change which is now running strong in affluent, educated, and young America. The issue of restoring quality to American life had been largely initiated by the more rather than the less privileged sectors of this country. Yet, the growing minority at the top end of society had enlisted majorities of middle Americans, as witnessed by the fact that 65% of the union members and 55% of all small-town residents gave favorable marks to Ralph Nader.

This pattern of change initiated from the top seemed likely to accelerate rather than diminish for the rest of the decade of the seventies. Not only were the numbers at the top expected to grow rapidly, but the quest for better quality in life was an idea that could be and was shared by nearly all people, whatever their status.

Congress had passed reasonably tough Clean Air and Clean Water acts. President Nixon signed them both and had attracted an able team to work on environmental matters. Yet when Congress appropriated more funds for pollution control than the president felt his budget could take, he announced he would impound the funds and even vetoed the appropriation bill. Congress promptly overrode the veto. The public backed Congress by almost 2 to 1 in this dispute, although it meant more federal spending. Consistently, the president had come up with negative ratings from the public on his handling of air and water pollution, in spite of allocating increasing amounts of federal funds for environmental controls.

Yet, one might ask, how could President Nixon remain relatively popular in the face of this criticism on an issue of such deep concern to the people? The answer was that, as in so many areas, the politicians were almost the last to get the word in these strange times. Much of the establishment still privately voiced the skepticism of *Time's* editor Grunwald. In the elections of 1972, environmental bond issues were on the ballot from one end of the country to the other. Almost without exception, they passed in the same vote that re-elected President Nixon with 61%.

The answer was that the full political impact of the quality of life issue had yet to be felt. That it is there can be testified to by ex-Senator Gordon Allott of Colorado, whom most political observers and politicians thought was safe in his re-election bid in 1972. But Colorado was rocked by the environmental issue in that election with a referendum on the Winter Olympics of 1976. The voters turned down the Olympics on ecological grounds and Senator Allott woke up the morning after a defeated office-holder. He had failed to take the environmental issue seriously. A relative unknown beat him technically, but an analysis of the vote revealed it was an issue that caused his political demise, an issue sparked by affluent and educated Coloradans—the issue of environmental control.

It was as good a bet as any that in 1976 and in 1980, the quality of life issue would be as pivotal in determining the make-up of state houses, the Congress, and the White House as any other question facing the country. It was a time bomb ticking under a rather cynical establishment. When most of the men currently in power were climbing to the top, the conservation issue was something to give lip service to, but it had little bite. As recently as 1963, only a decade ago, Kennedy had found out in a cross-country speaking trip that conservation bored his audiences.

As a University of Connecticut sophomore put it in an interview we conducted with her shortly after Earth Day, 1972, when it seemed the earlier enthusiasm for an environmental clean-up was fading, "Don't they understand that we have only begun in our drive to save the physical world we live in. We will expect more and more faster and faster. We just won't go away."

VIII

THE POOR
"The Living Sick"

Willie Jefferson, a black sharecropper in Columbia, Mississippi, thought about the lot of people as he has known them, shook his head, and concluded, "Well, I suppose people didn't used to be as sick as much as they are today. They just died when they got sick and didn't live sick."

"Living sick" was the common lot of the 25.6 million Americans [1] who still, by the latter third of the twentieth century, would qualify as the poverty segment of this most affluent society. In one sense, the country had come a long way since the 1930s when Franklin D. Roosevelt said America would no longer tolerate "a third of the nation ill-housed, ill-clothed, and ill-fed." By the time of Lyndon Johnson's Great Society in the middle of the 1960s, the number who could be officially classified as the poor had shrunk to 18%. And by the early 1970s, the number had diminished again to 12%, although the latest counts began to show an odd shift upward after a long drift down.

Poverty was every bit as much an American dilemma as the race question. As a people, we were full of bad conscience about the fact that 1 in 8 people were poor. At the same time, in a land of enormous affluence, where most families throw away enough food daily to feed 6 families in Bangladesh, over 8 in 10 went along with the shibboleth that "most people on welfare are lazy and should be made to go to work." There might have been much left to be desired in the way the work ethic was lived up to by most Americans in their own lives these days, but there was virtual unanimity in commanding those on welfare to leave the dole and go to work. By 88% to 6%, an overwhelming majority favored the vastly oversimplified but highly popular idea of "making people on welfare go to work." [2]

At the very same time, a majority also favored increasing federal aid to the poor by 58% to 30%. An even higher 89% in 1972 supported the proposition that the federal government provide jobs for the unemployed. By 70% to 23%, a sizable majority also agreed that "low income people will never have adequate housing unless the federal government pays some of the cost of building the housing they live in."

Bred into the American ethic was the twin notion that we should feel guilty about receiving the handout, but also that it was dead wrong for people to be living in the squalor and misery of poverty. The New Deal, of course, was created to help the less fortunate and to redistribute the wealth, with programs ranging from relief and temporary jobs to a patchwork system of social insurance.

The second Nixon term apparently was going to be marked by a sharp and divisive debate over whether or not the long-hailed social legislation of the New Deal and the Great Society could be selectively pared and winnowed (in the name of dropping what didn't work). Opponents to the Nixon social budget chopping charged that any substantial cutbacks in spending for social welfare would mean the country was callously willing to condemn the poor to a permanently hopeless state of poverty. The debate was classic because each opposing side represented a deep strain in the American ethic. Ironically, by the 1970s neither side was likely to win this struggle, for the simple reason that the people themselves were ambivalent and were not prepared to abandon their conscience, on the one hand, or their disdain for those who would not or could not work, on the other.

The big difference between the 1970s and the 1930s, however, could be found in the fact that in FDR's time the welfare state idea could rally enough votes of self-interested disadvantaged people to win election after election. Roosevelt could appeal to people's pocketbooks by promising them that the New Deal would raise them out of their underprivileged misery. The beneficiaries of income redistribution in the thirties vastly outnumbered the affluent who would have to pay for social reform. By 1972, when George McGovern put forth his later retracted program to give $1,000 to each person as part of an income redistribution plan, more than half the people were earning over $10,-000 a year and the poor were a small minority. The political potential of putting together an underprivileged majority had evaporated, the victim of growing affluence.

What remained was a dilemma of conscience. Nearly 90% felt it was "a disgrace in plentiful America for people here to still go hungry," and three-quarters believed it "morally wrong not to care for the poor, the disadvantaged, and the elderly who cannot provide a decent standard of living for themselves." Somehow, the pangs of bad conscience, perhaps the memory of parents or grandparents who had suffered the pangs of poverty, would not go away. And, while the idea of those born to poverty rising Horatio Alger-like to fame and fortune still had some real appeal, the growing sophistication of an educated people told them there would likely be a bitter residue left who would always be poor. And that was wrong.

Regardless of the more esoteric moral dilemma that might have been besetting the rising affluent, the lot of those still mired in poverty remained dismal by any standards. They could take small solace in the knowledge that people with incomes of $15,000 had some feeling of guilt over their misery. Much has been reported and written over the past forty years about the psychological degradation of being unemployed, of living in slums, of the haunting experience of being hungry.

But perhaps no more pervading sense of being poor could be seen than in the perceived state of health of those living in poverty. For 2 out of 3 people in the population, when they were "feeling fine," it meant nothing is the matter with them. But for nearly 2 out of 3 of the urban or rural poor, "feeling fine" meant literally, "not as sick as usual."

More than any other group in society, the poor placed a higher priority on trying to achieve health. For example, 66% of the poor gave health a higher priority than having a good job, compared with 51% of the American people as a whole. As critical as "earning enough money to make ends meet" might have been to the poor, 61% of the poor still rated good health above it.

An unemployed 27-year-old black in the heart of Brooklyn's Bedford-Stuyvesant area put it for many when he said, "When you have no learning, you don't know where to begin to learn. If you can't learn, then you can't learn nothing. And after a while, you want to give it all up. But if you are feeling down and sick all the time, you can't even get started to learn or earn." Good health, in the eyes of the poor, was the lifeline to everything else.

Most Americans were aware of the fact that each succeeding generation was taller, weighed more, was in presumably better physical shape than the previous. When asked to compare the health of their own family with times gone by, three-quarters of affluent Americans answered unhesitatingly that their health was better. They cited a long list of advances in drugs, doctor's care, research breakthroughs, and, significantly, better diets and abundant food.

But when inner-city blacks and Appalachian poor whites were surveyed by our organization, the story was diametrically the reverse. By 51% to 29%, black ghetto dwellers felt their health had deteriorated, was worse than their parents' or grandparents'. Rural poverty whites felt the same sense of discouragement over their health, by an even more sizable 63% to 16%.

A 47-year-old poor white in western North Carolina whose family had received government rations explained, "My mother lived to be 106 years old. People didn't live out of tin cans then. They had good pure water to drink then. It wasn't doped up like the water is now." To the North in Lebanon, Virginia, a 71-year-old retired white said, "At least in the old days you could eat fresh food. Now it's too expensive to buy." In El Paso, Texas, a 24-year-old Chicano housewife pointed out, "The only kind of food you can afford to buy makes it easy to gain weight and hard to control weight. It's awful unhealthy food we got to eat, mainly fats and leftovers."

The complaints of the poor centered on the food they ate. One in six believed the key to deteriorated health was lack of proper food and diet. Ironically, with the poor, the subject of food was a distasteful subject—by a 16 to 1 margin. Of the poor interviewed, 2% reported they simply did not "have enough food to go around," although a much higher 3 in 10 said they knew "someone who did not get enough to eat." But far and away the most frequent problem with food among the poor was the quality of the food available. Many complained that the food was filling but not nutritious, was loaded with fats, might be weight-adding but was not health-giving. There appeared to be fairly widespread distrust of Department of Agriculture programs for food distribution, but the food they could afford to buy with their own money was widely believed to be inferior. As the poor, they were reduced to purchasing the cheapest fare available—and their distinct impression was that it was not healthy food.

But another reason cited by the poor for a worsening of health today was that proper medical care was more difficult to come by. A black woman on welfare with six children and no husband on Chicago's Southside put it this way, "The doctors charge more money and there's no money to pay for the doctor. If you have no money, you can't buy medicine either. To get it free, you have to go through red tape, and after everything it just isn't worth the bother. So people can't get the right care, so then people are sicker and sicker."

The prevailing mood of the poor was an acute awareness of being "living sick." Outside of Hazard, Kentucky, an unemployed poor white man quoted a biblical saying that cropped up in many different parts of the country, "The Bible says we will get weaker and wiser. My children aren't as healthy as I was. Only thing is if we're supposed to be getting wiser, then we ought to have enough sense not to get sicker."

Illness and disease are unwelcome visitors to any home. But

with the poor, they were constantly present, a pervading and seemingly permanent condition. As one put it, "I always get a visitation from the miseries."

The continuing survey of the National Center for Health Statistics largely confirmed these instinctive feelings of the poor. The official numbers were a grim litany: "four times as many heart conditions as those in the highest income group; six times as much mental and nervous trouble; six times as much arthritis and rheumatism; six times as many cases of high blood pressure; over three times as many orthopedic . . . and almost eight times as many visual impairments." [3] When our own survey asked poor and nonpoor alike if they had "someone in the family seriously ill," only 7% of the affluent reported such illness. Among the Spanish-speaking, it was 24%, among inner-city blacks an equal 24%, and among Appalachian whites it was a higher 31%.

If the poor suffered a much higher incidence of serious illness than the rest of the country, they also tended to feel bedeviled more by a whole host of minor afflictions, as the following table indicates:

Minor Afflictions Suffered from Recently [4]

	AFFLUENT	POOR
	%	%
Bad colds	39	49
Nervous tension	34	49
Headaches	32	42
Sore throat	30	35
Indigestion	21	28
Exhaustion	16	23
Constipation	15	25
Shortness of breath	10	24
Bad cough	10	18
Insomnia	9	15
Sores that don't heal	1	6

These results, of course, did not mean the poor actually suffered more from these ailments. But more of them felt they did than was the case among the affluent. Similar patterns emerged when the Harris Survey tested feelings about a whole roster of psychosomatic feelings: The poor felt more "worried and nervous," more "lonely and depressed," less "able to sleep," more often "too exhausted to get up," more often "no appetite," more "emotionally disturbed," more often "can't cope with pressures," more often "faint and weak," and more often "overly tense." As a black in the Watts area of Los Angeles said, "When you're living sick all the time, you're living sick all over from your head to your toes."

Most public thinking about health among the poor and nonpoor alike centered on "what to do if serious illness strikes." Much of the health system itself was geared to how to meet such crises, leaving much of the area of preventive medicine to chance. Both the poor and nonpoor had the same high expectations of what they hoped would happen in a medical crisis. Their first thoughts were for obtaining "the best medical care," followed by "finding a good doctor." Next on the priority list if "serious illness strikes" was a deep wish for a specific magical agent who had clearly seized the health imagination of the public: the "specialist." Over half the public, 56%, gave a high priority to obtaining the services of a specialist in case of serious illness. An even higher 69% of the poor singled out a desire for a specialist.

Of course, the expected health experience of the poor differed sharply from that of the rest of the American people. While 42% of the general public would worry over the "price the specialist would charge," a much higher 67% of the poor held such apprehensions. While a minority of 39% of the public at large were concerned that their health insurance would prove to be inadequate, a higher 54% of the poor worried about lack of coverage.[5] A majority of the poor, 54%, said they simply did not know where they might turn for help in a health emergency.

Between 1963 and 1973, medical facilities, particularly hospitals, in the United States improved considerably, to the point where there was solid evidence that the country had probably overbuilt its hospital capacity. However, a majority of 62% of the poor still complained about the inadequacy of facilities, compared with only 32% of the rest of the public.

The poverty groups registered a lengthy list of grievances. A North Carolina sharecropper put his worry about the shortage of rural doctors this way, "A lot of the time you can't get a doctor. If you get your throat cut on Saturday or Sunday, you might as well sew it up yourself. They're too busy and the hospital is too far away to get to." In Jeff, Kentucky, a 67-year-old Appalachian white summed up the situation, "Many more doctors are needed. There are not nearly enough doctors here. You have to go to Hazard to get the nearest doctor. Then you sit there for over a day before you can see him. None will make a house call anymore."

The woe called the "waiting sick" was cited by others. A woman in Bedford-Stuyvesant in Brooklyn put it this way, "The doctors won't come to the house when someone is sick, the hospitals and the clinics make you wait all day before they take care of you. You can die before you get any attention." In San Antonio, Texas, a Chicano reported, "I went to the county hospital and the girl next to me had to wait so long, she had her baby in the hall." In El Centro, California, a part-time farm worker said, "People have to make an appointment when they are sick two weeks ahead. Old folks wait longer then anyone else and they are on Medicare. You can never get in on the weekends." A housewife in Siler, Kentucky added, "Our clinic is always filled up. It's so hard to get to see the doctor. Sometimes you will sit all day and then be turned away and have to go back."

The haunting reservation of the poor was that in an emergency, "you might pass away before they get to your turn in line," as one black observed. The specialist was God among the poor, who rated him higher than any other point of medical contact. More than the rest of society, however, the poor were more critical of private doctors. They did not question the doctor's competence, although a majority believed that "lots of doctors prescribe medication when it is not necessary" and 40% felt "a lot of operations are unnecessary; doctors do it just for the fee." The heart of their complaint about doctors was that "they are primarily interested in making money" (a view held by 53% of the poor) and "most doctors don't want you to bother them" (believed by 74%).

A black mother on welfare in Detroit said, "The doctors charge more money and medicine costs so much. To get it free is a real hassle. When there is no money, there is no doctor's care or medicine. When you can't get the right care, people have got to be sicker." A 68-year-old poor white in Bakersville, North Carolina, said, "I have lost faith in all doctors. All they want to give you is a big bill. My wife could get well if she had proper care. I'm so old now, there is no use. So I'm scared—all the time."

All of the foregoing strongly suggested that even if one went along with the recently published conclusion of Harry Schwartz of the New York *Times* that the crisis in health delivery has been vastly overdrawn, there could be little doubt the poor suffer real neglect in the health area.

What had been reported about the "living sick" could be repeated about the condition of their urban and rural slum housing, their lack of preparation or access to fruitful employment, their broken homes, the hopelessness of growing up in a house of despair. The felt condition of health or the lack of it among the poor was merely symptomatic of nearly all parts of the life of those in poverty that might be examined.

In the course of surveying house to house in nearly all of the fifty states, the memories of interviewing the poor were easily the most poignant and moving. One such instance occurred in Leylands, West Virginia, a poverty-stricken coal mining town, during the 1960 presidential primary, when we were polling for Kennedy in that make-or-break primary. The writer and columnist Joseph Alsop were foraging public opinion by foot. Leylands was a small town, typically on the incline of a "holler," as West Virginians call them. On the other incline of the hollow, or valley, were the remains of the by then abandoned coal mine. There were the telltale marks of how the unemployed scraped out a pitiful living in the strip mines here and there in the hollow.

About halfway up the incline, I conducted an interview in the home of 43-year-old Edgar Webster, an unemployed miner. As is common in the homes of the poor, the visitor was welcomed into the kitchen, and Webster, his wife, and five children, from 4 to 14, crowded around the kitchen table. The room was neat and had a scrubbed look, although the linoleum on the floor had frays on the edges and four or five holes in the middle of it.

Coal miner Webster told his story, "Times are hard around here. The mine's been down two years and the unemployment insurance has run out. I get a little work doing gardener chores in a place down the road, maybe one day every two weeks. I do a little strip mining one or two days a week. So maybe we have $14 or $15 a week to live on. We get the dry rations and the powdered milk from the government and that helps to feed all these kids." At the mention of the powdered milk, Webster's 6-year-old daughter grimaced and made a sound that came out, "Icky." Mrs. Webster hushed the girl and told her to mind her manners.

Webster went on to relate how his oldest son and daughter, 17 and 16, had left Leylands to make their way in Washington, D.C., where they had found employment. When asked why he didn't leave Leylands and move somewhere else where he might find better prospects for work, his answer was typical, "Look, first of all, I'm a coal miner and I can earn $7,000 or $8,000 a year. That's enough to raise this whole family on. Maybe pretty soon the mine will open up again. We keep waiting for that, but the weeks get to be months, and now the months get to be years. So it's hard times."

At this point, Mrs. Webster took over. Her voice grew almost shrill with the optimism she was voicing, "Yes, but we are lucky. Our hard times look like they are over now. Edgar went over to the clinic in Beckley last month for an examination of his lungs. And our lucky day came just yesterday. Edgar has the black lung, and that means we can get the payments from the government. That'll tide us all through. We're just luckier now than most, isn't that right, children?" The Webster children looked at each other a bit embarrassed and then smiled politely back at their mother. Edgar Webster closed the interview by observing philosophically, "Misery feeds on misery. So I guess we'll make out."

The Depression of the 1930s had probably never left Leylands nor the Websters by the time the 1960s had arrived. But for most of the rest of the country, the steady march of affluence had taken over. Yet, some of the Depression-born insecurities lingered on. For example, in interviewing in 1958 in Indianapolis, a poll taker could run into home after home of laid-off Delco workers who were fearful of losing their television sets because they couldn't meet the time payments. For them, the specter of losing their black and white TV sets seemed nearly as calamitous as not being able to feed the family's children was back in the 1930s. Thirteen years later, in 1971, much the same phenomenon could be observed among families where unemployment or a cutback in the work week had taken place; but by then losing a *color* TV set for failure of time payments was the focus of apprehension.

By no stretch of the imagination could the middle-income worries about job insecurity or the squeeze of the high cost of living be compared with the gnawing, degrading miseries of the poverty groups. But during the 1970–72 period, 2 out of every 3 people were convinced that prices were rising out of control, that unemployment in their own community was rising at a faster pace, and that the country was in a recession. One of the marks of the period, different from other economic downturns, was that white collar and even executive jobs were placed in jeopardy. And the twin pressures of high prices and high unemployment, a phenomenon that upset many set economic theories, left some deep scar tissue on affluent America.

This recent experience with economic insecurity was significant, for it provided an important bridge between the relative security of an affluent society and the abject misery of poverty. Many aerospace engineers in Seattle would go through the rest of their lives, no matter how high their future incomes, constantly reminded when seeing someone who was unemployed or when observing ghettoes in a city or slum living in the open countryside, "There but for the grace of God, go I."

So it was not simply a matter of an increasingly dominant affluent society feeling pangs of conscience about the poor and disadvantaged who live on the other side of the tracks. It was not just a question of the fortunate rich or well off taking pity on the less fortunate. There was rather a sense that there was something deeply wrong when over twenty-five million Americans find themselves living in substandard, even subhuman, conditions. The sight of it was a condemnation of a system that worked to widen rather than to narrow the gap between the rich and the poor.

It was therefore no happenstance that from 1966 to 1972 the number of Americans who believed the old shibboleth that "the rich get richer and the poor get poorer" jumped from 48% to 68%.[6] Or that a substantial 43% of the public by now was prepared to say "those who have power are out to take advantage of me," or that 74% believe "the tax laws are designed to help the rich rather than the average person."

Taken together on a carefully worked out scale of alienation or sense of powerlessness, the number of disenchanted people in the country rose significantly from 34% to 46% from 1966 to 1972.[7] Among those with incomes under $5,000, the alienation reached 63%, or nearly 2 out of every 3 of the poor. Among the $15,000 and over group alienation ran under 30%. The poor in America were those who felt most powerless, while the affluent, albeit for change, did not.

These wide differences in alienation between those at the top and at the bottom of American society were psychological reflections that mirror the findings of the U.S. Census that the actual income gap between the poverty and affluent groups increased rather than decreased between 1960 and 1970. The inescapable point was that the felt differences were real. And such facts became more unbearable as an affluent society becomes more worried about the overall quality of life in the country.

In effect, over twenty-five million people [8] living in abject misery amid the greatest abundance and plenty in the history of the world was no more and no less than a blight in America. For these people, no matter how they arrived there, their continued existence in a state of poverty contaminated, degenerated, and polluted the rest of American life. It certainly can be argued that any claims that the quality of life was improving in the next five or ten years would contain a ring of hollow mockery until ways could be found to substantially reduce and ultimately eliminate poverty.

The chances were, then, that the problem of the poor in America would come back to haunt the new and rising affluent society. The chances were good, too, that the emerging shape of programs would change drastically. No one seemed to have come up with a welfare system that was either viable economically or politically, let alone both. Straight income maintenance may have had its human advantages, but it did not come to grips with how to root out the causes of welfare families, who in some cases were now entering their fourth and fifth generations. Neither President Nixon's exhortations to "get them to work" nor the liberals' traditional flat payments accompanied by a social worker's solace appeared to work. Neither the easy panacea of giving the states the money and responsibility to solve the problem, nor the traditional Great Society approach of a massive centralized war on poverty had worked. Neither the temporary outbursts that, in effect, said, "cut them off the dole," nor the counterarguments that said, "how can we be so heartless about the poor," produced solutions that worked. Most of all, leadership, whether "hard line" or "compassionate," which did not come up with answers would not last long in the new and emerging articulate, educated society that America was becoming in the 1970s.

Meanwhile, the poor, always living in a very real world, continued to live in the rot and denial that is poverty. Human pollution was the state they were living in, no matter how revulsive it sounded. This writer remembers vividly tramping around the Southside of Chicago on July 4, 1966, with Washington *Post* editor Ben Bradlee who was then head of *Newsweek*'s Washington bureau. An elderly black man was standing next to a mound of rubble that had a most unappetizing mixture of broken down walls from crumbling houses, human refuse, and garbage. He pointed to the mound and said, "Things are so bad around here for me, man, sometimes I can't tell which is the dung heap—me or that mound there."

IX

ORGANIZED LABOR

New Defender of the Status Quo?

Throughout most of its history in the United States, the drive to organize workers into unions was marked by violence and bloodshed. Old union men still remembered the bloody confrontation between the United Auto Workers and Harry Bennett's goons at Ford on the bridge leading into the Baton Rouge Plant in Detroit in the 1930s. In Aliquippa in Western Pennsylvania, old steelworkers recalled the bitter struggles to win recognition for the United Steelworkers in the same period. And in the 1970s, the efforts of such as César Chavez to organize farm workers had not been without violence.

The primary aim and objective of mainstream trade unionism in the U.S. had almost always been to win the right of workers to belong to a union, so that they improved their pay, their working conditions, their security, and allowed workers to have a bigger slice of the pie through the collective bargaining process. Unionism was resisted because the rise of trade unions meant that the absolute power of employers over conditions of work of the employed would be broken. Unions versus management in our system had always been a classic power struggle.

Yet by the 1970s, organized labor was no longer viewed as radical or even a threat to the establishment. Instead, big labor, personified by AFL-CIO President George Meany, had become part of the establishment itself. Two of the five people called by Richard Nixon's White House staff when bombings were halted in Vietnam in January 1973, just prior to the final Paris negotiations, were Meany and Frank Fitzsimmons, chief of the Teamsters Union. Both had given Nixon powerful support on the war. Both were courted assiduously by Nixon in his bid for re-election. Fitzsimmons had made an outright endorsement of the president. Meany, after a break with Nixon the year before over the wage-price control program, had blocked any AFL-CIO endorsement of Democrat George McGovern and made no secret of his personal preference for Nixon.

After the election, the Phase II wage and price control program was scrapped, reportedly as the result of an agreement between Meany and the new secretary of the treasury George Schultz, an old Meany friend with whom the labor leader played golf. (Old Andrew Mellon, Hoover's secretary of the treasury, would have rolled over in his grave at the thought of his Republican successor at the treasury fifty years later cavorting socially with a labor leader.) President Nixon talked of a "new majority" in American politics. This majority included Southerners, the newly affluent, the modern establishment, and a measure of organized labor. Pictures of Nixon's meetings with hard-hat union leaders in 1970 adorned the walls of several White House aides in 1972. Indeed, a hard-hat himself, New York building trades leader Peter Brennan was now the secretary of labor.

By the 1970s, organized labor was a far cry from the surging organizers of the 1930s. Radicalism, both at home and abroad, was every bit as much a target of George Meany as it had ever been of the rugged individualists who had been the captains of industry.

It was not always this way for trade unions, however. For many years, of course, dating from the labor upheaval of the 1930s, trade unions had emerged as the spokesmen for the underdog. Workers were underpaid, exploited in foul working conditions. Under the impetus of the New Deal, organizing workers into unions appeared to many an act as noble as putting a minimum floor under wages, social security for the aged, or programs designed to help the unemployed or the indigent. Unions were the force that could organize the disadvantaged, the poor, the exploited. They would be a powerful counterbalance to big industry which had been largely in control of the economy and Republican government during the 1920s and had brought about the Great Depression through mismanagement. Above all, business stood for the status quo. Its bogeyman was big government, which in turn raised the specter of socialism. Unions were viewed by much of the business establishment as part of the socialistic conspiracy to destroy private ownership, initiative, and free enterprise. The classic struggle of the 1930s was between growing unions and entrenched business.

By the thirties the country's employment was dominated by the vast mass production complexes, symbolized by the automotive industry. The drive to unionize the auto plants and the steel mills, aided and abetted by a friendly Roosevelt Administration and a lopsided Depression-born liberal Democratic Congress, produced a spate of hours and wages legislation, designed primarily to tip the balance of government to labor's side. The Wagner Act was hailed as the Magna Carta of labor in the U.S.

Because the mass employment industries cutting across state lines were the natural target of unionization in the 1930s, federal legislation had a strong impact on accelerating membership drives. Because the wage patterns in these mass producing industries tended to be flattened out, with relatively small differences between the highest and lowest grades of work, industrial unionism became a major force. These developments were to give rise to a new type of labor leader.

The new union chiefs were to be far different from the prototype of Samuel Gompers, the founder of the American Federation of Labor, half a century before. Gompers's whole philosophy was that organized labor should be concerned almost exclusively with the immediate wages, hours, and working conditions of working people. Craft unionism, under which workers were organized according to skills, was the order of the day in the late 1800s and early 1900s. The notion of labor identifying with larger social and political movements was essentially foreign to the Gompers philosophy. In Europe, the trade union movements had a much different history, openly identifying organization of members with a working-class social and political movement which in turn formed labor parties that as often as not were socialist or social democratic.

In Europe, many trade unions advocated nationalization of industry. In the U.S., the union movement shied away from such radical political and economic programs, merely wanting to represent workers' interests in bargaining for better wages, hours, and working conditions with privately held, controlled, and operated business.

But in the 1930s and 1940s, a new breed of labor leader emerged out of the mass production industries, best exemplified by Philip Murray of the United Steelworkers and Walter Reuther of the United Auto Workers. Encouraged by FDR's New Deal philosophy, both Murray and Reuther were dedicated not only to improving conditions for their own union members, not only to legislation which would improve the lot of workers throughout industry, but to much broader social reform in society as a whole. The idea of commitment to changing the entire society, to schemes for income redistribution, to broad measures in the health and welfare areas, even to establishing links to trade unions abroad was the sharp break of industrial from craft unions. One of Reuther's pet programs for many years called for limiting incomes to any one individual to $25,000 a year.

Under the leadership of John L. Lewis, head of the United Mine Workers, most industrial unions split off from the AFL in 1937 and formed the Committee for Industrial Organizations (CIO). The AFL's strength under President William Green's stewardship was derived from the craft unions, epitomized best

by the building trades, the construction unions, more conservative politically, philosophically still the blood descendants of
Gompers.

For many years, however, both wings of labor developed separate political arms that nonetheless tended to come out for the
same candidates. By and large, with rare exceptions, candidates
who were pledged to support pro-union legislation (the AFL
criterion) were also pledged to work for extension of New Deal
reform under Roosevelt, Fair Deal reform under Truman, and
the generally liberal Democratic platforms of the 1950s and
1960s.

A perennial debate within the union movement itself was
whether the social reform commitments of CIO leaders were in-
digenous to their movement or were mainly ideas grafted onto
trade unions born out of loyalty to essentially Democratic party
liberal political leadership. As long as the trade union movement grew rapidly in membership and also continued to espouse
liberal social causes, the distinction was a moot one. To most
liberals and to most union members, labor unions in America
were "progressive forces" working to help the lot of downtrod-
den workers everywhere.

But, by 1955, most mass-producing industries had become organized and the combined AFL-CIO membership leveled out at
a high of sixteen million U.S. members, where it has remained
since. Two key developments were taking place, however, that
would change the role of unions by the 1970s as a force for
change in American society. Both had to do with the make-up of
the work force. More rapidly than most trade unionists were
aware, America was shifting from an industrial production to service industry country. This meant that white collar workers were
rapidly overtaking blue collar workers in the population. The
second development taking place was within mass industries
themselves. Specialization was accelerating with more sophisticated automation. This, in turn, led to a widening of the spread
on wage rates, which gave rise to a growing demand for craft
unionism within industrial unions. Both in the steel and auto
unions, craft movements emerged in the late 1950s and early
1960s. The more highly skilled workers saw their economic in-

terest as different from the rest. They demanded separate bargaining, separate councils, and most of all, felt more of an affinity for the craft than for the industrial type of unionism.

The last straw for industrial unionism came during the Eisenhower Administration in the 1950s, when the political climate changed and social reform was no longer the dominant drive of the federal establishment. Once they had lost their political allies in the White House, trade union leaders became less and less ideological. More and more of their attention was turned to fending off legislation that would restrict union rights won in the 1930s. Although they still worked hard politically for the Democrats, and found themselves largely backing liberal candidates, without a social reform leader in the White House, faced with a failure to recruit new members among the growing white collar groups, and beset with internal division between their own skilled and semiskilled worker members, the trade union movement in 1957 reunited under the banner of the AFL-CIO.

With the death of Phillip Murray and the increasing isolation of Walter Reuther, the top leadership of organized labor slowly but surely moved from a position of advocating social change to one of holding the line. And, despite mighty efforts at registration of voters in the 1960 and 1964 campaigns, both of which helped the Kennedy and Johnson causes in those years, it was rare to find innovative social ferment emanating from the trade union movement.

By the 1960s, George Meany, out of the craft building trades in New York, had taken full command of the AFL-CIO. Meany had two abiding interests: to protect the economic status of his own membership, and, as a kind of strange carry-over from the world-wide interests of American trade unionists in the 1940s, an abiding, tough, and fierce commitment to fighting communism abroad.

During the late 1950s this writer gained much of his experience in political polling on surveys financed by the AFL-CIO Committee on Political Education (COPE), headed then by the late James McDevitt. In fact, in the 1958 Democratic sweep, the Harris firm looked invincible by registering twenty-one winners for the U.S. Senate and governors out of the twenty-three races we polled that fall.

COPE National Director McDevitt and his assistant, Al Barkan, who succeeded him, used to complain in those days that it was difficult to get George Meany interested in their work to elect men to office who would be pro-labor. McDevitt once said, "Meany is more interested in what the communists are doing in Tanganyika than who is going to carry Timbuctoo." The attention of labor politically took on overtones of being more worried about right-to-work laws and less with progressive social legislation, albeit labor worked long and hard for almost all of the Johnson Great Society program in the mid-1960s.

But this writer remembers well a day in 1963, the year the Harris firm abandoned polling for candidates to report public opinion for the newspapers and television. I was prevailed on to make one last appearance before an AFL-CIO state directors meeting in Washington, D.C.[1] The civil rights movement was stirring in early 1963 with sit-ins, freedom rides, and other signs of nonviolent protest. The AFL-CIO had not been prominently associated with the movement of Martin Luther King, except for Reuther and the die-hards from the industrial unions. Meany preceded me on the program and I was struck by his complete failure to take cognizance of the civil rights question. A number of craft unions still had Jim Crow locals (separate white and black unions). I took note of the absence of Meany's recognition of the times, especially the surging civil rights protest movement, and suggested there was a serious question of just how "progressive" the AFL-CIO could claim to be if it ducked the minorities question or just gave lip service to it. Meany had lingered on in the room as I began to talk. As I finished the part on minorities, he snorted through a cloud of cigar smoke, put the cane he was using hard on the floor, and stomped out of the room.

The trade union movement had stopped growing in absolute numbers all during this period, as it failed to organize substantial numbers of the growing white collar workers and failed to penetrate the growing ranks of blacks in many industries. From a high in 1964 of 28% of the electorate, it went down to 24% in 1968 and finally to 18% of all voters by 1972.[2]

By the 1970s, George Meany was presiding over an increasingly status-quo-oriented trade union movement. His base was no longer the poor, benighted, disadvantaged underdogs, as an examination of the profile of union members would show. The median income of the rank and file was $12,350, much higher than the $8,440 annual pay for nonunionized people in comparable jobs. Fully 46% lived outside cities, mainly in the suburbs. Although 78% of all blacks were in jobs eligible for union membership, only 35% of these blacks were in fact in unions. A much higher 59% of comparable whites belonged to unions. Over 6 in 10 union members were drawn from the ranks of skilled labor and semiprofessional people. Only 10% of union members held white collar jobs, although 18% of the entire population was non-blue collar. The education of 8 in 10 never went beyond high school.

Clearly, by 1973, the trade union movement was more white than the nation's work force, drawn heavily from the upper middle income among working people, and had largely a skilled labor constituency. The poor and the disadvantaged were by and large untouched by the movement. The profile strongly suggested a base of craft workers, not far off the mark set by Samuel Gompers almost one hundred years earlier. But there was one vast difference: By now the rank and file of labor was relatively affluent, with 1 in 4 earning $15,000 and over. The trade union movement had become thoroughly middle class. And in 1972, union members voted 56% to 44% for Nixon over McGovern.

Given these facts, some had already jumped to the conclusion that the rank and file of labor had gone conservative. The prevailing image of the union members in the minds of many was best summed up as hard-hat. Construction workers wore hard-hats on the job and even some presidents of the United States had donned hard-hats when entertaining their union leaders.

Perhaps the one event which triggered the stereotype of the hard-hat union member in the 1970s arose from the events following the Cambodian incursion in May 1970. Students took to the streets all over the country to protest what they viewed as an escalation of the war. In New York, Pittsburgh, St. Louis, and other cities, construction workers organized counter-demonstrations supporting the president.

In New York in late May 1970 the ugliest confrontation of all took place. For days before, throughout the Wall Street area, impromtu bands of workers and assorted hangers-on trooped through the streets, carrying handmade signs saying "Back the President on Vietnam" in response to the students. The center of one procession was a bedraggled simulation of the famous trio in the "Spirit of '76" painting, one with a drum and one bearing the American flag. No fife was to be seen in the crowd, however.

On the day of the confrontation, a planned pro-Vietnam demonstration organized by the building trades unions began near Wall Street whence construction workers erecting the new massive World Trade Center marched to City Hall in support of the war. Along the fringes of the march, antiwar student protesters heckled the workers with catcalls and obscenities. When passing Pace College en route, word passed that some students were burning an American flag. This was the trigger. The ranks of hard-hats broke and students, or anyone resembling a student, were set upon with pipes, wrenches, and fists and pummeled until they fled or fell.

The hard-hats continued to City Hall triumphant in all ways that day. They had put the hippie, long-haired peaceniks to rout once and for all. Within a few weeks, their leaders would be honored at a White House visit. And so a myth was born—at least in the minds of those who saw labor turning to the right.

In July, the Harris Survey went to a cross-section of the public across the nation to find out reaction to the hard-hat confrontation with the students. By 40% to 24%, a plurality said they had more sympathy with the hard-hats than the students. But a significant 23% said they sympathized with neither side.[3] Thus, it could be concluded that the balance of public opinion turned away in disgust from both sides. Union members reported sympathizing with the hard-hats by 37% to 24% with an additional

26% who said they were turned off by both parties to the confrontation.

But easily the most significant result emerged when people were asked if they felt the use of violence by the hard-hats was justified. By 53% to 31%, a majority of Americans felt it was not. The only people who applauded the hard-hat action were those who preferred Governor George Wallace of Alabama for president, by a 56% to 35% margin. Rural residents, far away from the canyons of Manhattan, also tended more than others to feel violence against the students was justified. Union members condemned the hard-hat action by 53% to 30%. Their chief reason: "Might does not make right," as a steelworker in McKeesport, Pennsylvania, put it for many.

A careful and fair analysis of just what union members think was then undertaken over the next two years by the Harris firm. In an era of instant communications, followed by snap judgments by establishment leaders, indeed there had been a tendency to read the temper, mood, and views of the rank and file of labor, as the stereotype TV character in "All in the Family," Archie Bunker, a bigoted, hot-headed, hard-hat who would like to return to Herbert Hoover days.

As with the rest of the public, union members shared some views that would fit the stereotype. It was true that union members opposed busing to achieve racial balance by 78% to 16%, but so did the rest of the public by 76% to 18%. The facts did show that union members opposed legalizing marijuana by 79% to 18%, but so did the country as a whole by 80% to 14%. Trade unionists supported stiffer penalties for drug pushers by 71% to 23%, but so did the rest of the public by 73% to 20%. Union members wanted to "make people on welfare go to work" by 90% to 6%, but so did most other people by 89% to 6%.

So a first conclusion about the views of union members was that they shared almost identical convictions about people on welfare, racial busing, the war, and drugs as most of the rest of the population. Give or take a few points, union members by the 1970s held views just about the same as the mainstream of American public opinion. The most one could conclude from the fact that 55% of union members, compared with 49% of the public, were "bothered by the styles, tastes, manners, and language" of young people or that by 45% to 41% they would "turn in to the authorities any child of theirs they caught smoking marijuana" (slightly higher than the 43% to 43% standoff among the public generally) was that union members were a bit more annoyed by nonconformity among the young and a bit more uptight about young people using marijuana. But in no way could any analysis of these, or literally hundreds of other questions like them not reported here conclude that union people had sharply more conservative reactions than most of their neighbors.

Nor were trade union members much different from the rest of the country on some issues that might affect their own union membership. When the public favored a wage-price freeze by 52% to 34%, union members backed the freeze by an almost identical 52% to 37%, thereby giving the lie to those who claimed union labor would never stand for tight controls of wages. Much as their neighbors felt their pockets were being picked by inflation and that escalation of wages would mean another round of price hikes, over 8 in 10 union members said they would opt for "lower wage increases if prices can be controlled" over "taking their chances on higher wages with fewer controls." On the issue of *cutting* defense spending, a position *supported* by 58% to 30% of the public, an even higher 60% to 29% majority of union members took the same position. The assumptions of Senator Henry Jackson and many union leaders that workers were wedded to continued high levels of defense spending out of patriotism and the jobs they gained from defense industry proved to be patent nonsense in terms of the facts themselves.

On a whole roster of other issues the similarity rather than differences between labor's views and the rest of the public was also evident. For example, by 90% to 7%, an overwhelming majority of the public favored a federal program to give jobs to the unemployed, a point of view shared by 89% to 7% by the rank and file of unions. The 83% to 9% division among the entire country in favor of spending more federal funds for pollution control was close to the 85% to 9% lopsided margin among union members. On federal aid to education, 76% of the public and 80% of union members expressed a desire for more federal spending. When, in late December 1972, the public turned by 57% to 37% against President Nixon on renewed bombings of Hanoi, trade unionists also opposed the bombings by 52% to 37%. When, in early 1973, the public backed recognition of Cuba by the U.S. by 51% to 33%, union members wanted to open diplomatic relations with Castro by 50% to 36%. And when the public massively favored closer relations with the Russians and Chinese by 77% to 13%, unionists favored better relations with the Communist superpowers by 77% to 12%.

There were significant areas where trade union members differed from the rest of the public and these were important to examine. Union people were more sensitive to negative economic news than most. For example, in late 1972, at a time when the public thought the recession was over by 43% to 41%, union members believed by 48% to 39% that the recession was still here. While 61% of the American people felt President Nixon and the Republicans were "too close to big business," a higher 72% of organized labor felt the same. Although the average union member was relatively more affluent than others in the same job categories, the psychological pinch of economic insecurity had left deeper scar tissue on the union worker.

Another important area where union members differed from the rest of the public was the question of helping the poor. While most Americans in 1972 wanted to increase aid to the poor by 58% to 30%, union members favored help to those in poverty by a higher 63% to 27%. Compared with the 48% to 30% plurality the same year who supported a federal, compulsory, comprehensive health insurance plan, a more decisive 51% to 25% majority of union members favored health insurance such as Senator Kennedy has proposed. While the public split only 45% to 44% in agreement with the proposition that "if public housing projects are not subsidized by the federal government, the poor, disadvantaged, and elderly will be condemned to a life of misery," a 51% to 38% majority of union members felt this way.

Perhaps no area had received more attention than the antiblack sentiment believed to run rampant among trade union members—again, part of the hard-hat syndrome. The 18% of the union vote cast for Governor George Wallace in 1968 was cited as proof of it. This feeling again was widely reported in the state of Michigan in 1972, where Governor Wallace won the Democratic primary, largely by exploiting the school busing issue. Yet the evidence simply did not bear out the claim. In the country as a whole, in late 1972, most of the public held the view that "blacks have tried to move too fast, before they are ready" by 47% to 44%. Among trade union members, this charge was denied by 47% to 44%. Among the public generally, the proposition that public schools should be desegregated met with 51% to 40% approval. Among the union rank and file nationwide, desegregation of schools was approved by a much more decisive 55% to 35% margin. More union members felt that blacks were discriminated against in obtaining a quality education in schools, in obtaining decent housing, in getting manual labor jobs, in getting into labor unions, and in the way they were treated as human beings than the rest of the public as a whole. This was not to say that many white trade unionists did not feel strongly on the race question. But, put in perspective, union members were measurably less upset by black demands and by integration than the public as a whole. The protests of the Machinists Union about the misrepresentation of the trade union point of view on the television series "All in the Family" appeared to be well founded. Archie Bunker in life proved to be more fiction than fact.

Even in areas such as crime and youth, some interesting differences between union members and the rest of society could be found. The idea of "preventive arrest," an approach surfaced in the first Nixon Administration by then Attorney General John Mitchell, under which people with known criminal records or suspected of engaging in criminal activities could be picked up by the police before they commit a crime, was opposed by the public as a whole by 47% to 38%. But a more decisive 50% to 37% of union members were against the use of "preventive arrest." Ralph Nader might have been a hero to young people, but he also had wide backing among union members, with 70% giving him high marks on his consumer advocacy, compared with 65% of the public at large. In an interesting test in 1973 where people were asked to choose between "more safeguards to individual privacy—or a stricter crackdown on permissiveness," the public as a whole opted for safeguarding privacy by 56% to 34%. Trade union members also chose protection of individual privacy but by a higher 60% to 32%. In the foreign policy area, when Peking was up for admission to the UN in early 1971, the public generally favored seating the People's Republic by 48% to 27%, but union members supported the UN's action by a higher 53% to 24%.

Out of this welter of evidence, it began to be clear that trade union members were far from the hard-hat stereotype that existed in the minds of so much of the media, among establishment politicians, and even in the perception of many union leaders themselves. To be sure, men such as Lane Kirkland, the national secretary-treasurer of the AFL-CIO and Meany's number two man, pointed out that organized labor still supported a spate of social legislation in Congress, including the Kennedy Health Bill, although early backing was more evident from Reuther and Leonard Woodcock's United Auto Workers. In 1972, the contests for the House and U.S. Senate, labor's political arm, COPE, backed many more Democrats than Republicans. And Al Barkan, head of COPE, was one of the leaders of the group who deposed Ms. Jean Westwood, McGovern's hand-picked chairwoman of the Democratic National Committee, thus indicating labor still has deep Democratic ties. But the major thrust of the Barkan line within the Democratic party was that most of labor now opposed change in society and demanded a centrist stance by the Democrats in the future. Implicit in his reasoning was that the hard-hat syndrome, as it erupted in mid-1970 on the streets of New York, was the prevailing mood of the rank and file.

Al Barkan, of course, was by now George Meany's chief surrogate in the political area. In 1972, after many years hiatus from the heat of political battle, Meany staked out a headquarters at the Democratic Convention in Miami Beach, which by pure chance happened to be next door to this writer's suite at the

Americana Hotel. Meany maneuvered long and hard with his lieutenants to stop the McGovern nomination. He correctly forecast the McGovern defeat, but for the wrong reasons. George McGovern lost in 1972 among labor and nonlabor segments of the electorate, not because he stood for change and not because he espoused the causes of the young, but because he first stood for an extreme redistribution of income at home and in effect demanded that the American people feel so guilty about Vietnam they should welcome a North Vietnamese victory. Having overkilled in one direction, McGovern then became a trimmer, as one Chicago Democratic leader put it, "trying to be more regular than Mayor Daley himself." As part of the total electorate, the rank and file of labor was turned off by the McGovern show and voted him down on election day.

Ironically, in a little-reported story out of the 1972 campaign, McGovern in August showed he could misread the mood of American labor as badly as George Meany. He went to a meeting of two hundred Illinois labor leaders in Springfield. On the way to the meeting, the head of the Illinois AFL-CIO told McGovern that Meany would not allow him to back the senator, having declared a moratorium on all AFL-CIO local bodies making endorsements for the presidency. McGovern then asked if his opposition to wage controls might not loosen up the labor leaders. He was told that such an approach might work. McGovern then startled his labor audience by announcing that "ninety days after I'm in office, I will remove all price and wage controls." At the time he said it, a majority of the membership of the AFL-CIO favored even tighter controls than the federal program in effect called for.

After the Democratic Convention, the Harris firm polled the public on its reaction to George Meany and his politics. Although 46% of the public had no real knowledge about the labor leader's politics, the remaining 54% divided 36% to 18% in disagreement with Meany. Among the rank and file of labor, union members also disagreed with Meany by a slightly closer 33% to 22% margin. When asked if Meany's opposition to McGovern made them feel more or less like backing the Democratic nominee, 10% of the public said "more like backing him,"

8% said "less like backing him," and a big 73% said "it makes no difference at all." Among union members the results showed 10% who felt "more like" supporting McGovern, 11% who felt "less" that way, and 71% [4] who said President Meany's position made "no difference at all."

In the end, however, George Meany had some real chips to cash with President Nixon. Union labor did go for the president by an estimated 56% to 44%, a real turn-around from the 14-point edge labor had given Hubert Humphrey, the Democratic nominee of four years earlier. On the surface, Meany could claim that his opposition to McGovern was decisive in the change in labor's voting preference. But the Harris Survey had shown McGovern 53% to 35% ahead of Nixon in May with the union vote.

The only thing wrong with such ex cathedra reasoning was that in May McGovern was only behind nationwide by a 48% to 41% margin and on November 4 he lost by 61% to 37%. While labor shifted more than voters as a whole, the fact was that the rank and file of unions were more or less reacting to the McGovern debacle as most other Americans in the summer and fall of 1972. The facts showed that George Meany had little to do with it, though his tacit backing was happily received in the White House and by President Nixon personally.

In fairness to Meany, it must be pointed out that, for many years, those running labor's role in politics have known that union endorsement of candidates by itself was not a critical influence even among union members. While 21% of union members felt a union backing of a candidate made them feel more like voting for him, 7% had a negative reaction, and 72% said it made no difference one way or the other. Nonetheless, the rank and file did not object to such endorsements, saying by better than 3 to 1, such backing generally did more good than harm. Two in every three union members felt that it was right and proper for their union to work around election time to get out the vote.

Indeed, it was precisely on registration that COPE and other union political arms had been effective. In 1960, labor's registration efforts must be credited as one of the key elements in Kennedy's victory. In 1968, although Humphrey lost by a whisker, again labor worked effectively to bring out its vote and in dissuading dissident rank and filers from voting for George Wallace. In 1972, however, it was doubtful that all of labor's horses and king's men could have saved the shambles of the McGovern candidacy even if George Meany had not blocked an endorsement.

In a sense, the role of labor leaders with their own rank and file in the broader political area is a case of advise and consent of the governed. Better than ten years ago, the Harris Survey found that while over 8 in 10 union members believed their union should be active in pressing for legislation that affected the life of the union (Taft-Hartley, Landrum-Griffin, etc.) and also that affects the work life of the members (factory safety, workman's compensation, unemployment insurance), a majority of 3 to 2 also opposed their union becoming deeply embroiled in broader issues affecting society, ranging from war and peace to race and environment at home.

This put a severe limit on the actual mandate union leaders had to operate in the larger area that affected their members as citizens. Yet, in fact, these restraints had never been exercised. To the contrary, both the AFL and its individual international unions annually passed platforms and policy resolutions which covered the entire gamut of national and world problems.

In a way, this missed connection between the rank and file views and the positions taken by the leaders was precisely where labor leadership ran into trouble. Among the public, the number who had a "great deal" of confidence in the men running the nation's unions had declined from a meager 22% to 14% in the period from 1966 to 1972. Among union members, confidence fell from 34% to 23%, higher than the general public, but low by any standard.

When probed in depth, the public came up with the conclusion that labor leaders were more likely to be "manipulators" than "dedicated" leaders, to represent "special interests" rather than to be "public spirited," more likely to be "unethical" than to be "imaginative and creative." However, they were believed to be "hard workers." Basically, it was a profile of tough but industrious men, uninspired but clever in a manipulative way. The rank and file gave its own leadership better marks on dedication and hard work, but integrity and public spirit did not emerge large in the union member's view of the men who speak for him.

The irony was that members of unions have shown many times that they would throw out their leaders when they fail to deliver on the crucial business of collective bargaining. They could even overturn corrupt leadership, as the remarkable victory of the insurgent group in the United Mine Workers in 1972 proved. But, beyond this limited sphere, the union leader had a relatively free hand to exert his influence on the power structure. James Hoffa, the former head of the Teamsters Union, had obviously remained popular with his own members, despite having served a prison sentence. The reason was apparent nearly every time a Teamster's local president who supported Hoffa spoke out: "Jimmy delivered at the bargaining table." The rank and file undoubtedly agree.

But in the affairs of a nation, the limited scope of the mandate allowed union leaders to roam far and wide on a whole host of key matters. In 1971, George Meany could threaten to defeat Richard Nixon when he disapproved of his wage-price control program. A year later, Meany was working to bury Nixon's opponent. After the election, Meany apparently was key in persuading the Nixon Administration to scrap Phase II. Nixon, in turn, saw the possibility of forging with Meany a new alliance that would produce a "new majority" in American politics.

The plain fact was that George Meany was playing presidential politics with a relatively free hand, but in a game where he could look behind his back one day and find his troops have headed in another direction. For the state of mind of the rank and file of labor had been sorely misread. There was a tradition among union members to care about the social reform of the New Deal. The hard-hat syndrome badly libeled what they indeed stood for. There was little evidence that union members were porkchoppers who cared only about their own share of the pie, and went down the line on all the Archie Bunker stereotypes on the issues of the day. They were genuinely concerned with the lot of the poor, were not at all America fortress isolationists, were deeply worried about deterioration of the quality of life, held high respect for Ralph Nader, and had more than average concern for human and civil rights.

In short, it appeared that George Meany was playing status quo politics, while his own members were far more inclined to opt for change. It would be important to know the answer for the rest of the 1970s to the key question: Who speaks for labor? A key to answering that question would be to understand that labor was *part* of the American political scene and not an entirely separate force.

X

BUSINESS

Public Expectations Up But Social Performance Down

At a closed meeting of thirty chief executives of major companies in late March 1973, the head of a large oil company remarked, "You can forget winning the battle with types like Nader. People only pay attention to the bad news about you." The president of an airline replied, "If that's so, then, either there's something damned wrong about the way we're doing our jobs or we don't know how to communicate the changes we are making."

By the decade of the 1970s, it was dawning on some of the more sensitive and perceptive top business executives that the ways of running business in America would probably never be the same. To be sure, chief executives would still be judged mainly on the degree to which they made their companies grow, both in volume and in profits. And there was no doubt that private ownership and operation of business would remain a cornerstone of the American system. But new intrusions into the sanctuaries of board rooms were beginning to be made by new voices with new and different demands. The thrust of consumerism and the persistent questioning of the quality of products and services somehow grew in strength. Those companies, such as Union Carbide, who thought Nader charges against them were a passing fancy that would go away, soon found out they were mistaken. Electric power companies also discovered that the air and water pollution issues were serious enough for them to commit to an estimated $30 billion investment on antipollution devices.[1] Detroit's auto industry knew early that the demands for more auto safety and pollution control could be ignored only at its peril.

One of the first businessmen to recognize the massive impact of social change on the way business was going to have to operate was Walter Straley who, in 1970, was a key vice-president of AT&T and who had spent most of his work life in the Bell System, including a remarkable stint as president of the Pacific Northwest Telephone Company. Straley told this writer of the dilemma AT&T faced. "Some companies think they can escape from the cities by moving out. They were deeply worried about the crime and pollution in the big cities, the racial tensions that concern their white employees, and the fact that to operate in many cities these days, you have to train up a substantial number of blacks and other minorities. There are some executives right in our own company who have toyed with the idea that AT&T can escape it all and move out."

Straley then added, "But there is no way the Bell System can escape. In New York City alone, we have $7 billion invested in capital equipment, in Chicago $4 billion, and in Los Angeles $3 billion. Whenever a new skyscraper is built, we have to wire it for telephone installations. We cannot get back that investment for twenty to thirty years. So what happens to the cities dictates what happens to us. What happens to blacks in the cities happens to us. What happens to the quality of life in the cities happens to us. The old community chest days, when we could give some money to the poor, volunteer to serve on a few hospital boards, be good citizens in a noblesse oblige way, all this has come to an end. Now we must be involved with all the miserable problems of the poor, the tough questions of pollution, the fate of the cities. If they perish, if America is ungovernable, we perish."

Straley and a number of other business executives represented a new breed of corporate executive. They saw good corporate citizenship not as a clever public relations device to put a wholesome face on modern business. They equated the well-being of the larger society with the survival of the corporation itself.

Not many businessmen shared the total connection Straley made. In 1971 the president of a substantial chemical company astounded this writer by saying, "We are not worried over Ralph Nader and his ilk. Almost nobody in the public knows us, even if we are a huge company. We have maintained low visibility and will continue to. Then if they accuse us of polluting the streams where we operate, it won't make much impression, because no one will be familiar with the company being attacked." The fact that his company could and, indeed, did achieve instant visibility in the next year as a prime pollutor of streams was beyond his belief.

Another experience took place in Cleveland, the home of probably the most conservative business establishment in the country. This writer visited with the chief executive officer of a steel company which has mills along the banks of the Cuyahoga River in Cleveland. I recalled that the Cuyahoga had been called "the most polluted river in America" by Stewart Udall when he was secretary of the interior. Mention of this charge of a few years earlier triggered a violent reaction from the steel executive, "Well, just let me tell you a thing or two about that. Yes, we do pollute the river and it does smell to high heaven. But if those people want jobs, then they're going to have to put up with pollution. They can either take our pollution or we'll move elsewhere and get other help. One goes with the other. They'll regulate us into socialism on this pollution issue before we are through."

Even in the 1970s it was not hard to find among top business executives unreconstructed advocates of an end to such "social-istic" measures as social security, unemployment insurance, medicare, and other state programs of assistance to the disadvantaged. In modern politics, no man more symbolized this extreme conservative view than Senator Barry Goldwater of Arizona, the Republican standard-bearer in 1964. Goldwater honestly felt that the central issue in the country was to stop the growth of "creeping socialism." In his view, as in that of many business executives, any kind of federal intervention in the affairs of business was an abridgment of freedom of enterprise and was a step down the road to a federal take-over. In the field of housing, this meant depending on the "trickle down" theory, under which middle- and upper-income families bought all of the new housing each year. The less fortunate at the bottom of the income scale then would be left to occupy the older accommodations abandoned by the well-to-do. Public housing for the poor, in this view, paid for or subsidized by government, was socialism—an incursion of the state into the private domain. Unemployment insurance was looked upon as an encouragement for the indigent to remain idle.

The clash between the free world and communism was seen by these conservatives as an extension of the struggle at home between free enterprise and socialism. The fact that communism had largely been aborted in precisely those states of Western Europe which had long traditions of social reform was conveniently ignored, as was the additional fact that communism, without exception, had succeeded in the most backward, autocratic, feudal, and most conservative countries.

For a long time, from the 1930s to well into the 1960s, a major activity of many big businessmen in America, besides running their own companies, was to give money and vigorous moral support to organizations such as the National Association of Manufacturers (NAM) and the National Chamber of Commerce, which were viewed as defenders against the "creeping socialism" that was presumed rampant in the country. Even in the 1970s, many businessmen and conservatives were still waging the struggle against government incursions into the divine province of business.

As late as 1973, the National Chamber of Commerce was organizing an educational campaign designed to rally business troops once again behind the clarion call to defend against the "attack on the American free enterprise system." The bible for the strategy was contained in a remarkable confidential memorandum [2] written in August 1971 by a Richmond attorney to his friend who was then chairman of the Education Committee of the Chamber. That lawyer was Lewis F. Powell, Jr., who has since been elevated to the U.S. Supreme Court, as one of President Nixon's appointees. Powell wrote his memorandum two months before his court nomination. Although labeled "confidential" when written, Jack Anderson, the Washington columnist, wrote several columns about the Powell memorandum, and, finally, in late 1972 it surfaced in its entirety. In a reprint of it, the Chamber of Commerce stated "Anyone reading the Powell memorandum will easily conclude that it objectively and fairly deals with a very real problem facing the free enterprise system."

The thrust of the memorandum is that "the American economic system is under broad attack . . . not from a relatively few extremists or even from the minority socialist cadre. Rather the assault on the enterprise system is broadly based and consistently pursued. It is gaining momentum and converts." Powell explained that the sources of the attack "include, not unexpectedly the Communists, New Leftists and other revolutionaries who would destroy the entire system, both political and economic. These extremists of the left are far more numerous, better financed, and increasingly more welcomed and encouraged by other elements of society, than ever before in our history." He then went on to point out that "the most disquieting voices joining the chorus of criticism come from perfectly respectable elements of society: from the college campus, the pulpit, the media, the intellectual and literary journals, the arts and sciences, and from politicians." In addition, the spokesmen for this criticism, he claimed, are "often the most articulate, the most vocal, the most prolific in their writing and speaking." Justice Powell then added, "Moreover, much of the media—for varying motives and in varying degrees—either voluntarily accords unique publicity to these 'attackers,' or at least allows them to exploit the media for their purposes. This is especially true of television, which now plays such a predominant role in shaping the thinking, attitudes, and emotions of our people."

Singled out in the Powell memorandum as examples of the attack were William Kunstler, the radical lawyer, Yale university students, a poll of students on twelve campuses in which "almost half the students favored socialization of basic U.S. industries" (quoted loosely from an editorial in the Richmond *Times-Dispatch*), Ralph Nader, and Charles Reich, the author of *The Greening of America*. Among Justice Powell's specific recommendations was that companies designate an executive vice-president with a large budget and at a higher level than public relations to devote full time to countering the attack. He also suggested that radical professors such as Herbert Marcuse be "balanced" by defenders of the system, that textbooks now out of balance be "balanced," that communist speakers on campuses be "balanced" by those who "believe in the American system." He went on to urge that the present imbalance of groups such as the American Civil Liberties Union in the judicial system be tempered by counterattack activity in the courts, and that twenty million stockholders be mobilized in a vast political action program. Finally, he urged that the same kind of antibusiness bias in the mass media, especially television news, be "balanced" as well, a charge echoed many times since by Vice-President Spiro Agnew in rousing and controversial speeches.

How the U.S. Chamber of Commerce fares in trying to counterbalance the attack remains to be seen. In one sense, the issue was not in doubt from the outset: By 88% to 4%, most Americans endorsed the system of "having industry and business under private control." By an even higher 97% to 1%, almost everyone believes in a system under which people are allowed to own private property." Given these staggeringly lopsided endorsements of the private ownership, or capitalist, system, one must ask, What kind of Don Quixote, windmill tilting exercise was Justice Powell exhorting businessmen to undertake?

Or take another example. In most countries of the world, airlines exist either as wholly owned government subsidiaries or as outright arms of government itself. Yet, in 1972, the U.S. public opposed nationalization of airlines by a thumping 87% to 6% and even opposed nationalizing a sick industry—the railroads —by over 10 to 1. In fact, the public was opposed to federal grants to keep the ailing aerospace giant Lockheed alive by government subsidy, even when the company wanted it. The compelling fact in the early 1970s was that governmental solutions to problems had become so unpopular with nearly all groups that the thought of socialism was repugnant across the land.

In the real world, which is not always reflected by corporate ideology, the dialogue over free enterprise versus socialism appeared sadly dated, perhaps as much as forty years out of date. The minions Justice Powell presumably inveighed against might be stirring up public opinion, but they produced no more than 2% or 3% of the people who wanted to replace capitalism in the U.S. Half of the 5% who classified themselves as "radicals" believed in private property.

The challenge to the business system was far different from Justice Powell's interpretation. Many businessmen were preparing to fight an imaginary battle against an enemy who was nearly nonexistent. In the simple terms of preserving a privately operated economic system, that battle was won in the 1970s before it even began.

But, if the private ownership and operation system was not in dispute, why then did a Harris Survey in early 1973 report that 77% of the American people thought the second Nixon Administration should be "tougher" on business. The public's concern was underscored by the fact that only 23% thought Nixon would be tougher, leading to the conclusion that over 1 in 2 adults in the country felt that many business abuses were unlikely to be curbed in the second Nixon term.

As reported earlier, the number of Americans who expressed a "great deal of confidence" in business leadership in the country had dropped precipitously from 55% to 27% in the period from 1966 to 1971. By 1973 business still could muster no more than 27% confidence. By any objective standard, business was in the eye of a storm of substantial criticism.

Of more direct concern to those companies which depend on consumers to buy their products was the sharp fall from grace of public confidence in the quality of products and services being marketed: from 75% to 47% [3] from 1966 to 1971. Then from 1971 to 1973, the quality reputation of business dropped off another 5 points to 42%. The trend was downward and gave little sign of leveling out. Looked at in reverse, the number of people who gave business negative marks on product quality jumped from 19% to 58% [4] in less than a decade.

Coupled with the 84% to 10% margin who gave business a low rating on "keeping down the cost of living," it is little wonder that the almost automatic reaction of consumers to the marketplace of the early 1970s was that they were "paying more and receiving less for my money." Restoration of confidence in quality had to be a high priority for any business. Without it, the rest of business efforts would come to naught.

The other major area of business slide was the human dimension. On "providing enough steady jobs for people," business in 1973 achieved a 48% to 45% positive rating. This marked a turnabout from 1971, when business came up 51% to 43% negative. But the recession had left its scars all the same, since, back in the relative boom days of 1966, business had received credit for providing steady work by a massive 76% to 21%. If employment could continue to pick up, there was hope for business to come out of the doldrums in its reputation as a supplier of regular work.

However, in other measures of how business treats employees, the signs were all negative. Traditionally, as a people we have always been on the look-out for unusual opportunities for young people. Leaving school and finding work opportunity is at one and the same time one of the most traumatic and exciting experiences for young people, their parents, relatives, and friends. In 1966, 73% gave business high marks on "offering young people a chance to get ahead." By 1973, no more than 41% could look to business as a hopeful place for the young to work, least of all young people under 30 themselves. Business had never had much reputation for "really caring about the individual," but by 1973 only 22% could credit the corporate world with this basic attribute of good will, down from a 1966 high of 39%. Again, the trend was downward.

But perhaps the most serious challenge to business on the human side of the equation could be found in the area of "allowing people to use their full creative abilities." There was little doubt that, to massive numbers of Americans, the jobs they held were merely rather drudging necessities to win the bread with which to live. In the growing mood of placing higher emphasis on self-expression, use of creative talents had taken on added importance. Business performance in finding ways to turn loose creative abilities had dropped in the public's estimation from 62% to 34% positive from 1966 to 1973. And there was little sign of a reversal.

In one area, the otherwise massive fall from grace of business was of only minor magnitude: "providing job openings for blacks and other minorities," down from 57% to 49% in 7 years. During this period, of course, new federal, state, local, and private programs had been launched to improve minority employment status. The facts did show income for blacks rising faster than that for whites, but a wide disparity still existed: $6,714 for blacks and $10,672 for whites. There were also signs that the dominant white community did not give the same urgent priority to improvement of the lot of blacks as was the case in the 1960s. Finally, the federal government under Richard Nixon was not prodding the business community to employ blacks the way it did under Lyndon Johnson.

All of these results added up to a powerful message to the business community that it simply was not delivering in the main task of running business the way people expected in a capitalist society. Although faith in know-how still hovered above the 50% mark, the erosion of confidence in technological skills was showing. The two clear and urgent areas in which business was in a make or break crisis were its ability to restore shattered confidence in product quality and in its ability to demonstrate compassion for human beings.

Although in general, corporate executives spent most of their work lives trying to run a successful business, for many years companies had also been aware that they must make a contribution to the local communities in which they operated. The highly practical problem of recruiting the best local manpower as employees dictated that any substantial company engage in community activities. The threat of local regulation and lack of cooperation could also be a difficult matter in countless ways. On the positive side, corporations, much as people, simply tended to feel better when they were liked by neighbors where they lived.

By the early 1970s, the decline of respect for the role of business in the local community had been every bit as sharp as in the mainstream operational areas. On the general notion of "building up the community," business emerged with a majority of 59% on the positive side. However, in 1966, a much higher 80% felt that way. On supporting local education, business fell from 73% to 48% who felt it had been helpful. Corporate credit for support of cultural activities dropped from 62% to 45%. One of the oldest areas of business generosity in the community, support of hospitals, went down in reputation from 64% to 43%. Business help for the needy fell in public esteem from 61% to 39% from 1966 to 1973.

In one area, business's reputation in the community remained essentially unchanged: in helping control air and water pollution. In 1966, 26% gave business high marks on the environmental issue. By 1973, 25% said the same. At least it could be said that business had apparently just about reached rock bottom in the eyes of its local neighbors in the reputation for helping clean up the environment.

Two other areas of community involvement were able to muster just over 4 in 10 backing of those willing to give business high marks: "working for good government" and "setting an example of good citizenship for the young." But both were far off the high point of 1966. Efforts to support local government had dropped in esteem from 70% to 42% and setting a model for the young dropped in reputation from 66% to 42%. These areas were particularly important, for they strongly implied that in the local community, business was believed to be guilty of serious errors of omission. Compared with over 2 in 3 people who in 1966 felt businessmen were pillars in the community, standing for good government and as examples for the young to follow, by 1973 less than half the public felt this way. Whatever moral force business might have provided locally had rapidly begun to run out.

A pivotal question that must be answered was whether this wholesale decline of confidence in business stemmed from the massive attack on the system from the left which Justice Powell warned about in 1971 or whether it resulted from a conviction that business had actually performed in disappointing fashion. The answers could be found indelibly clearly from the facts— which were vastly different than might have been anticipated.

In addition to probing in considerable depth to determine business's reputation in the areas of corporate operations and community activity, from 1966 on, the Harris Survey also asked about business performance in broader national and international areas. Besides asking about business's record on these broader dimensions, the survey also asked whether business *should* "take special leadership" in each area. If the American people were turning their backs on the capitalist system, then one would expect that the last thing they would demand would be greater involvement by business in helping solve the nation's ills. If socialism were on the march in the U.S., then predictably the public would want less business leadership in areas such as cleaning up the environment, wiping out poverty, rebuilding cities, controlling crime, eliminating economic depressions, and other key problems.

But exactly the opposite was the case: Since 1966, in area after area, the American people had escalated their expectations of what they would like to see business "take special leadership" in. Precisely because people were so turned off by governmental solutions of nearly any kind, they came to believe that only strong leadership from the private sector could provide the thrust to find themselves to the pressing problems of the day. In mid-1972, the Harris firm conducted a survey about bankers and probed this dimension.[5] Among the groups surveyed were leaders of ethnic and dissident groups, mainly the types singled out by Justice Powell as the heart of the cabal to undermine the system. When asked if bankers should take the lead in helping solve community problems, 88% of these dissident leaders, more than any other leadership group, said they should. When probed for why they felt this way, their main answer was, "Bankers and big businessmen have the money and the clout to get things done."

The rise in the number of Americans who felt business should take special leadership in the broad issues of the day was interesting. One set of problems obviously and directly was related to business operational areas: "controlling air and water pollution," up from 69% to 92% from 1966 to 1973; "eliminating economic depressions," up from 73% to 88% over the same period; "enabling people to use their talents creatively," up from 73% to 85%; "cutting down accidents on the highways," up from 50% to 72% (especially applicable to the automotive industry). In these areas, the public was saying it would like to see business take more leadership by setting an example in their daily operations and planning.

Even more sizable increases in public desires for business to take "special leadership" could be found in problems that business obviously could not solve itself. In these cases, the public was indicating in strong terms that it wanted business leaders to speak out and support change. Among them were: "eliminating racial discrimination," up from 69% to 84%; "wiping out poverty," up from 69% to 83% since 1966; "rebuilding cities," up from 74% to 85% over the same period; "controlling crime," up from 42% to 73%; "raising moral standards," up from 48% to 70%; "eliminating religious prejudice," up from 37% to 63%.

The strong implications of these results were that the American people had come to believe that business should take the lead, not only in its daily behavior but also as advocates for raising moral standards, for curbing crime, for wiping out poverty, and for rebuilding cities. Certainly this was not a mandate from a people who were spoiling to overthrow the private business system. Instead, it was a blunt statement that, given their disenchantment with government, their skepticism about union leadership, if the most powerful elements in the private sector did not step forth with leadership, who else could?

Business's troubles, however, were further compounded by the fact that, in the face of rising expectations for *more* leadership, the public's assessment of actual business performance in all of these broader areas of concern had fallen sharply since the high-water mark of 1966. The impact of the recent recession was evident in the fact that in 1973 no more than 41% of the public thought business had been "helpful in eliminating economic depressions," far off the 1966 high of 75% who felt that way. On "enabling people to use their talents creatively, business's positive marks had fallen from 63% to 41% over the same period.

However, in three other areas directly relating to their operations, business did not show signs of major slippage. In the area of "eliminating racial discrimination," the fall-off from 1966 was only from 58% to 50% that business had been "helpful." As reported earlier, apparently there was some public recognition that business was trying to do better in employing minorities. In "cutting down accidents on the highways," the relatively low level of 29% who said "helpful" in 1966 was still at the 29% mark, an indication that in the spate of measures taken to improve auto safety, business at least had hit bottom and had stopped slipping to new lows. In "controlling air and water pollution," business's marks were never high, with only 35% who in 1966 said companies were being "helpful." By 1971, the number who credited business on environmental control had dropped to 28%, but by 1973, public praise had risen to 36%. This was still not good for business, but was at least a sign that the worst may have been behind it on the ecological issue.

In the broader areas, beyond business's control, the trend was even more uniformly down on business performance. On the poverty issue, business's standing for being "helpful" had fallen from 63% in 1966 to 35% in 1973, a drop of 28 points. On "finding cures for disease," the results showed a decrease from 71% to 47% over the same period. On "raising living standards around the world," the decline was from 61% to 52%; on "eliminating religious prejudice," from 34% to 28%; on "controlling crime," from 32% to 23%. On "raising moral standards," business was held in low regard in 1966 with only 29% according the corporate establishment positive marks. By 1973, the number had dropped to 21%.

The unsettling part of these results was not simply that business was believed to have done a poorer job in taking leadership, but that the corporate world was deteriorating in reputation at that very time when people expected more from it. Here was the ludicrous situation of the American people wanting to thrust leadership onto the shoulders of businessmen, probably more than ever in history, but the same people were also criticizing business more severely for not having taken that leadership.

If ever there was an opportunity for business to rise to a new position in society, surely this was it. After being saddled for years with the charge of standing too much for the status quo, of being too insensitive to the quest for change, now business had a chance to strike out in the direction of advocating change in its day-to-day operations, of achieving a new place of respect in American society. Business was indeed under attack, not from enemies of the system, but rather from those who wanted the system to work better and who were now demanding from the corporate world a new type of business leader.

In a strange way, there was every indication that business and labor leadership could well be changing their traditional roles in society. By 1973, George Meany had shown real signs of playing status quo politics. He appeared to have achieved a position in a relatively conservative Republican Administration in Washington that few business leaders could match. For their part, big businessmen privately found it highly ironic that they were pilloried for being too great an influence on the Nixon Administration when, in fact, many felt little consulted on the decision making. In December 1972, the top governmental advisory body drawn from business, the Business Council, had to cancel its meeting because no top people from the Administration were available to participate. Privately White House aides said that the president did not have much confidence in such business groups, especially when organized as a formal arm of government.

For business, this development could be an opportunity to reassert its role of leadership in a new and different way from the past. Instead of being an adjunct of a GOP regime, they could now be an independent force, pressing for positive change in society, setting a new kind of example. The public mandate was there.

In early 1973, this writer tested the waters among top business executives in the country to see if there were much appetite to assume a new mantle of leadership. In January 1973,[6] I presented many of the findings reported in this chapter to about twenty-five top business, educational, and citizen leaders who make up the Senior Executives Council of the Conference Board. The session proved to be highly stimulating to the group and ran a full hour and a half over schedule. It was no surprise that nonbusiness affiliated men such as John Gardner of Common Cause and Martin Meyerson, president of the University of Pennsylvania, immediately saw the opportunity as well as the challenge for business. Some of the top businessmen present indicated by their questions that they were still bogged down in the old rhetoric: Any criticism of business must be hostile and must be designed to undermine the system; ergo, the struggle was between those who would preserve free enterprise and those who would put the country on the road to statist socialism. While stimulating, the session had some of the familiar overtones of a Sunday prayer meeting in church, where the congregation can purge itself of its guilt and then wake up on Monday to go back to all the old ways of doing things, including sinning on occasion.

At about the same time, this writer also had occasion to spend time with David Rockefeller, the chairman of the Chase Manhattan Bank, and the youngest of the Rockefeller brothers. Rockefeller was disturbed by the results of the Harris Survey. He privately contemplated that the kinds of acts of good will he did back in the early 1960s somehow were met with hostility in the early 1970s. In late March 1973,[7] he wrote an article on the Op Ed page of the New York *Times*. In it he advocated that and urged capitalism "to keep up-to-date." He wrote, "It is a matter of particular urgency that we find the means to overcome the alienation perceived by many people between our economic progress and the attainment of our other social goals." He urged his fellow businessmen, "It is vital that social accountability become an integral part of corporate conduct, rather than a philanthropic add-on." He went on to point out, "Problems such as pollution abatement, provision of good housing, and the need to supply adequate sources of energy are exceedingly complex and require concerted and dedicated action. Unless business takes a leadership role in creating workable solutions, it will only suffer with its environment. It will also abdicate to government and others much of its potential for a more positive position in society." Then he made his major point, "Finally, we must press forward on the national level to create broader and more viable long-range goals, to assess what business can and cannot do to meet those goals, and to set more comprehensive strategies to combine the strengths of public and private resources. . . . Government, business, private citizens, and the academic community must strive to come up with mutually agreeable long-range objectives."

Rockefeller put much of the problem and the challenge in perspective when he wrote, "We must also strengthen our general understanding of who is responsible for what. Listening to some commentators, you would think business could solve all problems, while others suggest that government is the only hope. The truth is somewhere in between, with many areas, such as environment or employment or housing, requiring joint efforts. Family assistance and education, on the other hand, are primarily public problems, though some joint efforts to improve administration have been very fruitful. If government, business, labor, and non-profit groups could sharpen their sense of respective resources and responsibility, progress could be much faster."

Men such as David Rockefeller were getting the message. So was Henry Ford, II, the scion of another famous family. He was at the Conference Board meeting; afterward he obviously was interested by what he had heard. Ford is an impulsive man who has learned after years of being surrounded by all kinds of layers and buffers of advisors to trust his own instincts and to detest fakery, puff, and cant. When he commits to something, he believes it wholeheartedly. He asked this writer to address one of the rare meetings of his top 150 Ford Motor Company executives at Boca Raton on the subject of where business stood with the public and "to lay it on the line." I delivered the message once again in early February. Afterward, in a discussion with top Ford executives, the dilemma for modern businessmen emerged. No industry has been more beset by consumerism (cars that wear out, poor repair and maintenance service), by the pollution issue (development of pollution emission control engines by 1975), by a basketful of operational problems all close to home. "How," Vice-President Will Scott pleaded, "can we move out to stake out positions on the energy crisis or foreign trade, which affect us in the long run, let alone such sweeping issues as raising moral standards, raising living standards in the world, eliminating racial and religious discrimination, which are well beyond our control, when we have so much of our own house to put in order in the automobile business?"

The answer is not easily forthcoming. In fact, the odds are heavily against business struggling through the maze of its own parochial problems to rise to new leadership for positive change. As another enlightened businessman, J. Irwin Miller, head of Cummins Engine, skeptically put it to this writer, "The only time you ever see a top businessman before a congressional committee is when his own ox is being gored."

Yet there was that outside chance that the years ahead would see some very basic and traditional roles reversed. Big labor leadership was hugging the mythical center as hard as it could and was rapidly backing into a status quo position. Some big businessmen, such as David Rockefeller, Henry Ford, II, Robert Lilley (president of AT&T), and Frank Cary (president of IBM) were beginning to bite the bullet in pursuit of social change. As Rockefeller put it, "Social objectives can be formally incorporated into regular business planning. Managers can be evaluated, in part, on their social productivity." It was a far cry from William Henry Vanderbilt's "The public be damned." The proof of the pudding was not yet near at hand. But the stirrings were there all the same, Justice Powell and his fears about a leftist attack that would destroy free enterprise notwithstanding.

XI

FEAR AND
VIOLENCE
A New Way of Life

By the early 1970s, 62% [1] of all the women in the country 18 years of age or over whom we surveyed admitted they were deeply worried about violence and safety on the streets when they went out of their homes in the day or night. In a big Eastern city, Baltimore, 1 in 6 people reported "keeping a loaded gun nearby at home" at all times, 1 in 5 found themselves "watching out the window for suspicious strangers," 1 in 4 regularly went to bed with a protective weapon nearby, 4 in 10 had taken to "walking faster at night," over 4 in 10 posted a police call number around the house, nearly 1 in 2 talked to callers through the door instead of opening their doors, 1 in 2 deliberately "stayed at home in the evening rather than going out," almost 6 in 10 had taken to "looking over my shoulder when I hear footsteps behind me," the same number kept their doors locked "even when people are at home," 6 in 10 parents felt "worried about their children's safety when they were out at night," and more than 6 in 10 worried about the safety of their husband or wife "when out at night."

Given this apprehension over crime and safety, it was hardly surprising to find in 1971 that, by 70% to 26%, a big majority of the people surveyed nationwide felt that "law and order had broken down in the country." The state of siege that had taken over in many cities and suburbs was so endemic that majorities said they "welcomed" such remedies as "bars on windows" (51%), "floodlights around the house" (56%), "burglar alarms" (65%), "use of private police" (61%), "extra locks" (60%), "having a gun in the house to protect against intruders" (62%), and a "watchdog" (80%).

Still, when asked if violence were part and parcel of the pioneer tradition of America, by 66% to 22%, a 3 to 1 majority denied it. Fully 99% expressed as one of their fondest hopes that there could be a decline in violence in the country. Yet by 57% to 33%, a majority also expressed doubt that they would see an end to violence on a large scale during their lifetime.

The facts showed that, although we could not admit that violence ran deep in the national grain, indeed in many ways some of our basic attitudes condoned it. For instance, majorities agreed that "justice may have been a little rough-and-ready in the days of the Old West, but things worked better than they do today with all the legal red tape," that "human nature being what it is, there always must be wars and conflict," and that "when a boy is growing up, it is important he have a few fist fights," a view held by 70%.

All of these facts could be reported without much shock by 1973, although only a short decade before, the number of people who volunteered concern about crime and violence as one of the most important issues was no more than 2%. By 1964, 8% mentioned the subject. By late 1968, a dramatic 65% volunteered that crime and violence was the most important issue facing the country. In 5 short years in the 1960s, fear for one's personal safety grew from almost nonexistence to a pervasive, dark shadow that followed 2 in every 3 citizens through their waking days and their troubled sleeps. By 1968, apprehension over crime reached such proportions that a high of 81% [2] reported "all law and order in the country had broken down."

Fear grew in waves throughout the 1960s. It began with the

nonviolent civil rights demonstrations in the early part of the decade, most symbolized by the Birmingham, Alabama, confrontation between protesting blacks and the hoses and dogs set loose by Police Chief Eugene "Bull" Connors. Perhaps the most shattering blow came on November 22, 1963, when youthful President John F. Kennedy was shot in cold blood in a motorcade in Dallas.

The JFK murder shook the country to its roots. Later, in 1968, people would still tell of their reactions on that fatal day. A substantial 44% reported they were struck by fear. As a housewife in Menlo Park, Illinois, put it, "I felt as though my whole world had come apart, like falling into a huge crack in a human earthquake. I was frightened for myself, my family, my children." But 60% reported they reacted in anger. A machinist in Lorraine, Ohio, said, "I was mad, blind mad. I wanted to hit somebody, something with my fist but there was nothing there." An even larger 64% said they felt "hopeless." A retail merchant in Somerville, Massachusetts, put it this way, "I felt like I had everything that meant anything wrapped up in him. When it went, I felt it all went." Almost 3 in every 4 people, 73%, expressed their emotions as "at a loss." An even higher 86% reported that they felt "sad." A student at Manhattan College in the Bronx put it for many, "I cried that night for the first time since I was 11 years old. I felt better and then started to cry all over again." The morning after the assassination as thousands whose lives had been intimately intertwined with that of the slain young president wended their way to Washington, this writer made the sad trek to the White House. Old friends from the bright campaign days of 1960 gathered in the anteroom of the East Wing. I recall well the words of Theodore H. White who had written the landmark account of the Kennedy campaign three years earlier. Unashamed of his grief, back to chain smoking the cigarettes he had quit a few months before, Teddy White shook his head incredulously, "How could it happen in America? A banana republic, yes. But in this full, rich, good country so full of hope, oh no!"

The first Kennedy assassination broke the heart of the country, but it also gave rise to a myth that would not die: Despite the conclusion of the Warren Commission that the murder was the act of one man, Lee Harvey Oswald, a sizable majority of 65% continued to believe "it was not the work of one man," a conspiracy. In turn, this gave rise to a mass suspicion that nameless, vague, unidentified forces were set loose in the country, bent on a course of violence and assassination.

Murder of other mass leaders was to strike again in 1968, when Martin Luther King was shot in Memphis in April and Robert Kennedy was shot in Los Angeles in early June, the night of his victory in the California Democratic primary. In both cases, millions of Americans reacted with shock and sadness, angered, fearful, horrified, and dismayed. In the aftermath of both killings, most people refused to believe one man was the cause. The conspiracy theory was reinforced.

Just after the assassination of Robert Kennedy, we asked a cross-section of the American people if they thought "something was deeply wrong with America" or if "we always have a crisis of some kind or other." In March 1968, the identical question had been asked and by 55% to 39% a majority had in effect said whatever the crisis, as a people we could ride it out. But, after the killings of King and Kennedy, the riots which ignited the black ghettoes in April and May, the upset, horror, and shock of the assassinations, by 55% to 41% [3] a majority now said "something was deeply wrong in America." When asked why they felt this way, the majority chorused back that "all semblance of law and order was gone," "the land was filled with unrest," "the police seem incapable of protecting and keeping order," "crime is on the increase," "assassinations of leaders can't be stopped."

The turning point could be pinpointed in the aftermath of the bloody spring and early summer of 1968. The number who worried about "law and order" rose to 65%.[4] Even though 2 in every 3 people were not prepared to say that violence was an integral part of our national heritage, it was fair to judge that for the first time since the bloodbath of the Civil War a century before, a majority of Americans doubted that we could avoid a legacy of violence in the days and years ahead.

In the fall of 1968, 51% of the public was to respond to the

Harris Survey that "if people go into politics, they have to accept the fact they might get killed." More startling was the 55% to 30% majority who said, "A lot more people in government and politics will probably be assassinated in the next few years." Now there seemed to be an inevitability of violence, of a sustained breakdown of law and order, of a continued slaughter of the best in our leadership. No one could be immune any longer. The average citizen could not rest easy in his house, but rather needed armed protection, on the streets one walked in peril, and the high and the mighty were more likely to be victims of the carnage than anyone else.

If the triggers for the believed breakdown of law and order were the killings of John and Robert Kennedy and Martin Luther King, then the racial disorders of 1968, the rising crime rate, and the deepening U.S. involvement in Vietnam locked the national terror in tight. A majority of 59% expressed the view that "racial conflicts" were a real contributor to the wave of violence. A mark of the personal impact was the 54% of the people nationwide who felt "uneasy" about their being personally affected by race riots on their own neighborhood streets. Blacks in the big cities notably expressed the most fear. But nearly half the whites in rural and small-town areas where few blacks lived also expressed apprehension.

By a 3 to 1 margin, most whites felt that most blacks favored "nonviolence instead of violence." But 69% believed that "radicals on the streets" were stirring up the trouble. Somehow, the American people preferred to explain the riots in conspiratorial terms, as they had the three shattering assassinations. Although the riots caused antiblack feeling to rise, the terror over the breakdown of law and order was not so great that the guilt feelings of the white majority about the treatment of blacks were blotted out. To the contrary, by 63% to 27%, a sizable majority expressed the view that "until there is justice for minorities, there won't be law and order."

The escalation of the Vietnam War in 1968 also took its toll of public confidence in the nation's ability to maintain law and order. A majority of 57% said that "pictures of killing in the war in Vietnam" were a contributor to violence in the country. A minority of 38% saw antiwar demonstrators at home as a "major" cause of the breakdown of law and order. The war was coming through loud and clear every night on the television tube and the dominant message was "bloodshed" and "horror." A majority of 54% volunteered that the most troubling thing about the war was the "loss of human life." Never had the consequences of a war been brought home so graphically to a people.

Copying the example of the blacks in the earlier part of the decade, antiwar protesters took to the streets. They marched, they picketed, they chanted, they tore up trash baskets, they sat down and stopped traffic, they disrupted the cities where they demonstrated. Most of the young in the protest marches were dedicated to nonviolence, as the blacks and white liberals who had taken to the streets behind Martin Luther King, had been earlier in the decade. But the militants and revolutionaries, always a minority, invariably captured the major share of attention with their violence. Not only did the instant medium of TV contribute to this impression, but, in the end, when violent incidents triggered a confrontation with the police, the nonviolent would be arrested with the violent.

The antiwar demonstrations reached their high point in October 1969 when massive marches were held across the country on behalf of a "moratorium" in the war. By now, the youthful protesters had been joined by many of their elders. When asked how they felt about the tactic of taking to the streets to demonstrate, by 51% to 36% a majority of the country said they disagreed with the protests. Yet when asked how they felt about the goals of the demonstrations, by a narrow 46% to 45% margin, most Americans expressed sympathy with their cause. The popular rhetoric presumed to be echoing out of Middle America that "the protesters are just a bunch of hippy, long-haired, irresponsible young people who ought to be cracked down on" in fact met with 58% to 31% rejection by the American people. Instead, by 81% to 11%, a big majority summed up reaction to the substance of the protests by agreeing with the statement, "the antiwar demonstrators may not be entirely right, but they are raising real questions which ought to be discussed and answered."

Despite this highly tolerant and even sympathetic view of the antiwar protests, the American people nonetheless could never bring themselves to condone the tactics of the protesters. Much the same pattern prevailed in the race riots. After the wave of burnings, lootings, the conflagration of the black ghettoes in 1968, large majorities of the people could find sympathy with the desperate plight of the blacks and over 80% favored a "domestic Marshall Plan to rebuild the ghettoes of the big cities." Particularly revealing was the roster of what whites and blacks viewed in 1968 as the major causes of the riots: lack of good education for blacks (53%), lack of decent housing for blacks (47%), lack of progress in giving blacks equality (41%), lack of jobs for young blacks (41%), hatred of whites by blacks (41%), lack of firmness by local and state officials (35%), desire of blacks for violence (24%), desire of blacks to loot stores (21%), police brutality against blacks (14%). Clearly, the dominant causes for the riots were seen emanating from genuine black grievances rather than an innate violent strain in blacks themselves. Yet by 73% to 18%, a big majority also condemned the tactics of the riots.

The most unnerving part of the breakdown of law and order was its impact on the streets of the country. Somehow, almost overnight, the entire hierarchy of orderly communications in a democracy was being by-passed. An era of fear in the streets had taken over. The result was not only inevitable violence, but suddenly the streets had become a battleground, no neighborhood was immune. Life had been reduced to the raw and primitive proposition of physical survival right outside the house where one lived. By mid-1968, a majority of 51% reported owning a gun in their home. And, although 71% favored strict gun control legislation, nonetheless 51% said they "would use a gun to shoot people in a riot if they were threatened personally." A majority, 53% nationwide, openly admitted they were afraid to walk on their own streets.

The assassinations of the Kennedys and King, the nightly TV reports of killing in the war in Vietnam, the riots in the ghettoes of the cities, the violence that marred the antiwar protests, each alone might have been enough to set off near panic among the ordinarily peaceful and law-abiding citizens of the republic. But the last straw was the hard fact that crime itself seemed to be increasing rapidly. As early as 1964, 73% of the people of the country felt that crime was increasing in their home area. Crime of all kinds seemed to be on the upswing, both of a physical and white collar variety.

Street crime, mostly believed to be caused by young muggers and marauders, was particularly personal. Women and older people felt more vulnerable than others. As one woman office manager in New York City told her story, "I've had my purse snatched. I've been pushed around in my elevator by gangs of kids. Every time I go out alone, I feel it might be my last trip. I tremble at setting foot outside my door, even to go to work." Nor was small-town America immune. In Rocky Mount, North Carolina, a 68-year-old man added, "We've been robbed and our car has been broken into twice. It's terrible what's happening. You have to fear for your life."

Even in the midst of the race riots, a substantial 63% of the public blamed the breakdown of law and order on "too many criminals loose on the streets." When asked what made people turn into criminals, most Americans laid the cause at the doorstep of the kind of upbringing a person has had, although social elements such as poverty, unemployment, lack of education, broken homes were also cited. "Lack of parental guidance and discipline," however, was viewed as the root cause. A doctor in Sonoma, California, said it for many, "I believe it's basically the parents' fault. They don't love and give their children any moral education. The family should communicate and do things together." A skilled worker in Johnson City, New York, touched on almost all the major reasons when he added, "Environment has a lot to do with it. If you live on the wrong side of the tracks, no money, no food, sometimes you can be driven to crime. Mental disturbances contribute to a higher crime rate, too. No home life, no spiritual life to speak of, no discipline in the home. They all help to make people turn to crime."

Coupled with these broadly based roots for criminal behavior, people also simply did not feel that the system of law enforcement really discouraged crime. As far back as 1967, a sizable 62% [5] felt that law enforcement just did not work in dampening the crime rate. At the same time, the public has been highly sympathetic and supportive of law enforcement officials at the local, state, and federal levels. Consistently, majorities of 2 to 1 have given state and local police positive ratings on the jobs they have done. The prevailing view of police officers was that they were "dedicated" (50%), "hardworking" (48%), "want to help their fellow men" (42%), courageous" (38%), "intelligent" (39%), and "kind" (21%). Commonly leveled criticisms of the police simply did not draw much backing: "not too bright" (11%), "corrupt" (9%), "incompetent" (9%), "lazy" (8%), "violent" (6%), and "sadistic" (3%). Only among blacks and the young did criticisms of the police mount during the late 1960s and early 1970s. Pluralities of both groups were inclined to charge the police with "excessive brutality."

Despite this rather temperate and balanced view of the police, the public found a certain amount of solace in rallying behind certain catch phrases and popular slogans and notions. One of these which caught on was "Back Your Local Police," almost inevitably found as a bumper sticker on the private cars of the police themselves. Thus, the claim "law and order would improve if more people backed up their local police" was agreed to by a massive 87% to 8% majority. In nearly any local community, the demand to "put more police out on the streets" met with 8 to 1 public support. The proposition that "not enough money is provided for the police and other law enforcement agencies; they need more men and better equipment" met with 84% to 11% nationwide agreement in 1971.

Yet, even after police forces had been increased, after local police had been backed up, as America approached the mid-1970s, an even higher than ever 72% of the public felt that "activities of law enforcement officials did not discourage crime." Somehow, people were willing to extol the local cop on the beat, but the net result of the system of law enforcement did not improve appreciably simply by "backing up your local police."

Another favorite theme which was repeated over and over was the complaint that "violation of law and order has been encouraged by the courts." As early as 1966, 44% of the public felt that judges had been handing down "too lenient sentences." By

1970, the "too lenient" charge against judges had grown to 64% of the people nationwide. Unquestionably, the U.S. Supreme Court in its landmark decisions beginning with the Miranda case had led a majority of 74% of public opinion to believe that offenders at the time of their arrest were being given so many rights that the system of law enforcement was being impaired. A substantial 64% said they felt there was "too much mollycoddling of hardened criminals."

An urgent cry to the courts to "get tough" boomed across the land in the early 1970s. In fact, President Nixon himself was leading the rallying call. Yet, when the people themselves were asked to state the kind of sentences they would impose on convicted criminals, their punishment was not much different from the prevailing practices of the much-maligned judges themselves. For example, "a grown man, convicted of murder," according to 90% of the public, should be given a "long sentence;" "an adult drug pusher" should be given "a long sentence," according to 94%; and "a grown man convicted of armed robbery" should be given "a long sentence," in the view of 86%. But "an accountant guilty of embezzlement," according to 50%, should be given a "short sentence and then paroled and put on probation;" "a 22-year-old caught looting in a riot" should be given "a short sentence, paroled, and put on probation," in the view of 67%; "a convicted prostitute" should be similarly given "a short sentence, paroled, and put on probation," according to 62%; and, finally, "a 25-year-old convicted of burglary" should be given a more lenient than harsher sentence, said 77%.

The public was even more charitable toward youthful offenders, with majorities recommending shorter rather than longer sentences in reform schools for "15-year-old muggers of old men" or "16 year olds convicted of stealing cars." In the cases of "a 14 year old caught looting in a riot" or "a 16 year old caught breaking school windows" or "a 17 year old caught shoplifting for the first time," sizable majorities said they would oppose reform school sentences, but instead would recommend "probation."

By any standard, there appeared to be a wide gulf between the popular rhetoric on crime and what people would do if they were running a police force or were sitting in judgment. Indeed, there were other admissions from the public that ultimate solutions might not be forthcoming from the sloganeering, but instead from some major overhauls of the system of criminal justice. For example, in 1971, 61% of the public had come to hold the view that "many of the problems in controlling crime lie in overcrowded courts" and 78% now believed that "too long a time passed between the time someone is arrested for a crime" and "when he is brought to trial." Such pressing administrative problems as overcrowded court calendars and the accused rotting away in jails awaiting trial and finally begun to dawn on the American public.

Added to the recognition that the court system was not working because it could not plow through the enormous backlog of cases was the firmly grounded conviction that "jails are the real breeders of crime," a view held by 64%. No more than a third of the public was convinced that "when a man gets out of prison he is likely to be under the control of the authorities instead of organized crime." As the mid-1970s approached, the American people were beginning to realize that perhaps two of the most important targets were the need to crack down harder on organized crime and that the country simply had no effective system for rehabilitation of offenders who had served their debt to society.

An indication of this more subtle but highly significant shift of emphasis by the people themselves on the crime issue could be seen in a comparison of results to identical surveys conducted in 1968 and in 1971. In 1968, 51% named "the courts" as a major cause of crime. By 1971, the number who felt that way had declined to 42%. By the same token, in 1968, 61% had named "the growth of organized crime" as a major cause of crime. But by 1971, those who felt this way had risen to 74%.[6]

The growing public awareness of the role of organized crime reached the point by the early 1970s where 62% of the public felt "organized crime such as the Mafia is behind the big increase in crime." The fact that illegal drugs were manufactured, smuggled into the country, and sold on the streets by organized mobsters undoubtedly escalated public attention. Films, such as

"The Godfather," made millions who had an otherwise vague association of the word *Mafia* with organized crime take a much harder look at the subject.

When asked about it, 78% of the public acknowledged that "there is a Mafia." Contrary to the claims of the Italian-American Civil Rights League, organized by mobster Joseph Colombo, that "there is no Mafia" and reference to it is a "slur against people of Italian origin," by 57% to 24% the public thought there was indeed a Mafia, but that it was *not* "mostly run by Italians," suggesting instead that its ethnic make-up was drawn from "many different nationalities." The fact is that many people of Italian descent have been deeply offended by the efforts to automatically label any attack on the Mafia as an anti-Italian prejudice. The Italians have suffered much discrimination, particularly at the professional level; but it is doubtful the reason was because they had been "smeared" with the brush of the Mafia charge.

The American people by 1971 had become convinced by a massive 87% to 6% that "there is an organized crime syndicate that runs most of the rackets, drug smuggling, and illegal betting in the United States." Indeed, by all the evidence accumulated over the past two decades by honest federal, state, and local investigators, the public was entirely correct in that conclusion.

Another widespread belief was that "organized crime has corrupted and controls many politicians in this country," a view held by an 80% to 9% majority of the public. In well over a quarter-century of rather intimate association and involvement in American politics this writer could vouch for the fact that organized crime is active in politics at all levels. In New York City, where in the 1950s public evidence was uncovered that the late Frank Costello had dictated the designation of judges, there was ample evidence from my own experience not to doubt for a moment that a "shadow crime government" operated around the clock to influence government at many levels. In one campaign in the 1950s, a lawyer who had once been so indiscreet as to confess that his real "boss" was Joe Adonis, onetime vice-czar for the underworld, braggingly proved his influence by calling four judges off the bench during court hours, "just to prove" his and his higher-ups' power over the judiciary. The mob seeks to infiltrate the court system for an obvious reason: to be able to fix cases against their own or to temper sentences when members of the mob are indicted and convicted. When he was U.S. attorney for the Southern District of New York, the able Robert Morgenthau told this writer he could consistently predict a pattern of leniency among three sitting federal judges on any narcotics cases which came before them. He couldn't prove they were "owned" by the Mafia, but he tried to avoid trying drug cases in those judges' courts.

In the early 1960s, this writer had a bizarre offer one day that, until years later, I didn't realize must have involved the Mafia. A public relations man who had been involved in questionable matters in New York City politics called from Grand Bahama Island to say he had "a new political client for me." He said he was calling at the behest of his partner who was a Canadian businessman, a financial contributor to President Kennedy's campaign of 1960, who wanted to build new resort hotels in Grand Bahama, a large island in the Bahamian chain west of southern Florida. The rub was that the hotels needed government approval, for a very good reason: They would have gambling casinos in them and gambling was not yet legal in the Bahamas. His problem centered on the upcoming elections in the Bahamas, in which the "white party" was pitted against the "black party." The "white party" represented the "in" group in island politics and indeed was run by white colonialists. The "out" party was the "black party," which was led by native blacks.

The public relations man's scheme was no more and no less than an attempt to steal and to buy the election. The rules of the election to the local parliament were that anyone could run in the election if he had twenty signatures behind his candidacy. Then, in the election itself, if no candidate received a majority for any particular seat, a candidate could throw his vote to another man until someone finally achieved a majority. The plan was simple: Hundreds of candidates would be persuaded to go into the races and they, in turn, would be bought off for $1.00 a vote. He wanted our firm to "run the election."

This writer was startled at the scheme, to say the least, and immediately turned down the offer. Because the top man the public relations man represented had been a contributor to the Kennedy campaign, I called then President Kennedy to tell him what his "friends" were up to in the Bahamas. His reply was cryptic, "Well, I'd take a pass on that one. I'll have to look into that." The public relations man pressed hard for at least a half-dozen more calls until I stopped taking them and he gave up calling.

The Bahama elections were won by the "white party," in all probability using some of the means just described. Gambling was authorized in Grand Bahama Island and flourishes there today. Years later, the U.S. Department of Justice investigated the casino resort development on Grand Bahama and found that the moving hand behind the scheme was Meyer Lansky, the boss of the old Purple Gang in Detriot, who in 1973 finally was indicted in Miami for "skimming" gambling profits illegally in Las Vegas in earlier days. Purely and simply, Lansky for many years had been the gambling genius of the Mafia in the U.S. and in the Carribean.

How deeply the public relations man and the Canadian were involved with the Mafia is beyond this writer's knowledge. However, a partner of theirs in another Canadian business venture, a publicly listed company, and an aspiring New York City politician, ran into this writer a year later in a restaurant in downtown Detroit. My host was one of the top executives of the Detroit *Free Press*, the Knight newspaper. The New Yorker came up to our table to greet me and then left. My newspaper friend said, "I don't know who that fellow was, but the guy with him is one of the top hoods in the Purple Gang here." Both the public relations man and his political friend from the Detroit encounter have risen to positions of prominence in New York City politics. Both are eminently respectable to this day, one has held a seat in the City Council and the other has held high Democratic party positions.

But the mob is not partisan to one political party. In the Lindsay Administration a few years back, a licensing inspector was doing his job in a routine way and decided not to renew the license of a cabaret which had had many violations and which was suspected of Mafia ties. The inspector notified the cabaret owner his license was being revoked. The next day the department head to whom the inspector reported was called by a higher ranking official at City Hall to be told that the inspector was being overridden "because the cabaret owner was a friend of a prominent Republican party leader in town." The Republican leader in turn was a director of a bank which reportedly was controlled by Mafia interests.

By the 1970s it had finally dawned on large numbers of Americans that much of the increase in crime could be laid at the doorstep of organized crime. The same official of the Lindsay Administration who had overruled the inspector once told this writer with a straight face that "there may be small gangs of crooks, but there is no national organized crime syndicate called the Mafia in the U.S." When a cross-section of the American people was asked about this preposterous notion in 1971, it was rejected by a 78% to 7% margin. Similarly, by 61% to 26%, a majority also rejected out of hand the claim that "organized crime is not nearly as serious a problem as muggers, teen-age dope peddlers, and other individual criminals."

The question, of course, remained how to legally root out organized crime from the holds it had dug within both illicit and legal business. At the end of the first Nixon term, the public doubted by close to 2 to 1 that "the Nixon Administration is making real progress in catching and convicting leaders of organized crime." At the end of his first four years in office, Nixon received negative marks of 55% to 38% in handling "crime and law and order," despite some spectacular successes such as the cases successfully prosecuted out of the northern New Jersey U.S. attorney's office and the metropolitan strike force, along with literally reams of rhetoric from the Justice Department pledging a war on crime and a clean-up of organized mobsters.

The tentacles of organized crime still reach into all major avenues of illicit traffic in the country, and the Mafia is far from broken. This writer has yet to go to a major U.S. city and talk to a knowledgeable editor or reporter who could not readily identify the leading mob and Mafia characters in town. The simple truth is that, until organized crime and all its connections with legitimate business, organized labor, and politics is frontally assaulted, crime, its major business, will fall under the control of a "shadow government" and the safety of every citizen will be in jeopardy. In late 1961, when he was attorney general, Robert Kennedy asked, at a time when I was deeply involved in New York City politics, why I took the trouble to spend so much time in local politics. I said I wanted to drive the mob out of politics. Typically, hair awry, in his shirt sleeves and with his collar opened at the throat, he straightened up from his cluttered desk, pointed his finger at me, and said, "Good luck, I wish you well. But you'll never make it." The job still remains undone.

The manpower pool of organized crime is drawn straight out of the prisons of the country. The problem of recidivism, of men who have served time as offenders who come back to ex-prisoner status, to a life of crime, is massive. In 1967, under the direction of Michael Edison, the Harris firm undertook a series of groundbreaking studies over the next two years on the entire question of public attitudes toward crime, offenders, and rehabilitation for the Joint Commission on Correctional Manpower, a combined study effort of the federal government and the fifty states.[7]

One of the key series of questions we put to the public back in 1967 was how people viewed the prison system. We asked what they thought the main emphasis in most prisons was: to punish the offender, to put the individual criminal away to "protect society" from his ravages, or to rehabilitate those serving time so they could go straight upon their return to civilian life. No more than 13% said "punishment" was the main emphasis of prisons and no more than 24% picked "protecting society." Most, however, thought prison emphasis centered on "rehabilitation," cited by 48%. Then we asked what the emphasis in prisons *ought* to be. The results: 7% picked "punishment" and 12% "protecting society." A thumping 78% said "rehabilitation" should be the main business of prisons. There was an obvious

gap between the 48% who said rehabilitation was being empha-
sized and the much higher 72% who thought it should be. Here
was the basis for a broad public mandate to strengthen rehabilitation work in the prison system.

Specifically, the public expressed the view that not enough
"psychological help" was given to ex-prisoners, nor were they
assisted adequately in finding a place to live, nor trained properly
for useful work, nor helped in obtaining "decent jobs," nor
guided on "how to keep out of trouble." By a narrow 43% to
40%, the public opted for spending more federal money on
prison systems and criminal rehabilitation programs, although
by nearly 2 to 1, people were unwilling to see their taxes raised
for this purpose.

Then people were put to the test personally to see how willing they might be to work next to an ex-convict, hire one if they
were an employer, or come into contact with someone who
served time. Although the public expressed a fair degree of tolerance for working with convicted white collar criminals (people caught for evading income taxes, shoplifting at age 16) substantial minorities said they would feel "uneasy" working with
someone convicted of stealing an auto, passing bad checks, or
embezzling from a charity. A majority would feel a sense of
unease at working with an ex-convict who "shot someone in an
armed robbery."

As employers, people would be even harsher on the person
who had paid his debt to society. Minorities of from 35% to
43% would not hire someone who had served time for armed
robbery as a janitor or production worker. Majorities would not
hire an ex-convict as a salesman, a supervisor, or as a clerk handling money. Majorities reported they would be "uneasy" having
someone convicted of armed robbery as an insurance agent, as
their employer, as their "son's best friend," or a "new close personal friend." Even a young person who spent time in a reform
school for robbery would make 4 in 10 uneasy as a "boy in my
son's high school class" or as "someone my son knows in a social
club." Majorities of adults said they would feel unease if a
former juvenile delinquent were "a close personal friend of my

child" or "a boy seriously dating my teen-age daughter" (which would make 84% "uneasy").

It was patently apparent from these results that in the mid-1960s the American people had glimmerings of recognition that the rehabilitation problem was an important key to controlling crime, but that the people themselves were far from ready to become personally involved in bringing an ex-convict back to society. Obviously, rehabilitation was a "style" question to be talked about in the safety of one's parlor, but live ex-cons were people to be avoided in one's daily life. Indeed, no more than 29% in the sixties could say that "lack of public support for programs to rehabilitate ex-offenders" was a major cause of crime in the country.

But by the early 1970s, things were to change. Much as organized crime would become far more a reality, so the public would be far more willing to come to grips with recidivism. When, in 1970, the Harris Survey asked people again what the emphasis in prisons was and what it should be, the number who thought in actual practice "rehabilitation" was the main thrust of prisons had dropped from 48% to 27%. Yet the number who thought rehabilitation *should be* the principle business of correctional institutions remained a high 73%. The gap between the job being done to rehabilitate criminals had just about doubled in only a few years. By 2 to 1, people labeled the rehabilitation of ex-prisoners as "inadequate."

When in 1971, people were asked their willingness to work with, live on the same block, or hire an ex-convict if they were an employer, majorities ranging from 77% to 85% said they would indeed be willing. Even the touchy area of "having a center for the rehabilitation of convicts in your own neighborhood" found a public willingness by a margin of 56% to 34%. By 1972, a 66% to 23% majority would favor spending more federal funds for "rehabilitating criminals to normal life."

In September 1971 the most violent and most publicized prison riot broke out at the Attica Prison complex in Auburn, New York. The Attica episode followed a growing pattern, with black militant prisoners taking the lead in demanding prison reform and inmate rights. The outbreak did not consist so much of an escape attempt as a seizure of hostages and an encampment in sections of the prison until the full list of inmate grievances had been heard and acted upon. At Attica, panic took over and twenty-eight prisoners and nine guard hostages were dead by the time the outbreak had subsided. A tough approach had been taken, and, by all accounts, had only ended in bloodshed and little correction of prison conditions. Shortly after the Attica affair, similar riots broke out in two prisons in New Jersey. But instead of taking the "tough" approach that may have sounded good, but ended in bloodshed at Attica, Governor William Cahill took a patient approach, without using force, the outbreak was quelled, and there was no bloodshed.

In early 1972 we polled the country on the prison riot issue. When asked to give their estimate of why the prison outbreaks and take-overs had occurred, only 23% said "the authorities were too easy on the inmates." Better than twice that number, 58%, answered, "The authorities don't understand inmate needs." Further probing revealed a surprising degree of sensitivity to the status of prisoners. While 66% thought prison authorities had to be "tough" and a majority agreed that "prisoners are people who have committed crimes and do not have rights like other people," by a 3 to 2 margin the public also thought that "the recent prison outbreaks are a sure sign that conditions in prison are inhuman and unfair to the inmates." In addition, a massive 86% had come to the conclusion that "the way to keep peace in prisons today is to establish real communications with the inmates and to satisfy their legitimate needs as people." An even higher 93% said, "While serving in prison, prisoners are right to feel they should be treated as human beings." By a 6 to 1 margin, the American people advised other prison authorities, "Don't use force, as they did in Attica, but follow the course of reason and calm, as in New Jersey."

The public had changed considerably on the subject of the treatment and rehabilitation of criminals. Part of the reason was that the old shibboleths of a "tougher crackdown," "stiffer sentences," "an end to mollycoddling," "more cops on the beat," sounded emptier and emptier. This sense of suspicion would undoubtedly be heightened by the widespread abuses of the law enforcement process by a "law and order" Nixon Administration in the Watergate affair. Ringing rhetoric seemed to be followed by few answers, even when ex-policemen were voted into office as mayors of big cities or hard-liners on crime were put in the White House. Part of the reason also lay in the fact that, as the American people became more sophisticated about it, as they lived with crime as virtually a permanent appendage to modern life, they realized that professional law enforcement efforts directed against organized crime and a major overhaul of the system of rehabilitation of ex-prisoners would provide far more answers and would one day end the long night of siege on the nation's streets.

Yet, as the 1960s grew older and as the decade of the 1970s began, another scourge descended on the security of an American people already plagued by assassinations of their most vibrant young leaders, by race riots, by protest marches, by nightly killing in the news from Vietnam, and by rising street crime: the miserable problem of drug abuse. By 1971,[8] early in the decade, a massive 81% of the public put "increase use of illegal drugs" at the top of the list of causes for the breakdown of law and order.

The use of illegal drugs spread rapidly during the latter part of the 1960s, with our Harris Survey showing the number of people who had tried marijuana rising from 3% to 5% to 10% to 17% in the population 16 and over. But drug experimentation had penetrated to even younger ages, with grade-schoolers eager to try the forbidden fruit.

The reaction of adult America to the sudden outbreak of drugs was deep shock, chiefly for two reasons: (1) because drug abuse was prevalent among the young, and as a country we had always worshipped at the shrine of the precious young; and (2) because in big cities it soon became evident that the only way junkies could feed their habits was to steal, mug, and rob people on the streets or in their houses to find the money to buy the drugs. The sight of teen-agers freaked out on acid, of 16 year olds dying from overdoses of speed or heroin literally terrified the country in the late 1960s.

Fear of illegal drugs took over. When the young compared the use of grass to the use of liquor by their parents, the older generation answered back, by a 5 to 1 margin, that "smoking marijuana was a more serious problem than excessive drinking." The reason for this conviction was not hard to find. The popular theory, buttressed by the testimony of many doctors, was that young people started out experimenting with "soft" drugs, such as marijuana and hashish, and then soon graduated to LSD, speed, barbiturates, cocaine, the dreaded heroin, and other exotic mixtures of opium-derived drugs.

Throughout the early 1970s, sizable majorities of the American people stuck rigidly to their position that none of the illegal drugs should be legalized. The drug abuse plague was not confined to the children of the ghetto or the disadvantaged, although it reached deep and extracted a heavy toll among the minorities. This plague hit the houses of the most affluent, the rich, and the famous. It seemed to spread through a whole generation of young people growing up. With the mobility of the automobile, with access to money that would have boggled the minds of young people who grew up in the Great Depression, it was relatively easy for nearly any young person to obtain nearly any variety of drug—hard or soft.

After the first wave of panic in the latter part of the 1960s, the country began to recognize the need for drug clinics, halfway houses, information programs, and federal, state, and local law enforcement designed to curb the drug abuse. The problem seemed most intense in the sanctified confines of the colleges and universities with the best reputations. The better the education, it seemed, the higher the incidence of drug experimentation and usage. Ex-Harvard professor Timothy Leary adorned student protest meetings and captured headlines, if not a mass following, with his incantations to "tune in, turn on, drop out" —all to the tune of psychedelic music, dress, and acid drug experience.

As the middle of the decade of the seventies approached, at times, it seemed that the nation's communications media had become flooded with drug warnings, information, exhortations. Pro football players would urge the young to "turn on" with a fit body and mind. CBS radio would produce a distinguished series of as many as ten broadcasts a day on the drug problem. Pamphlets, special school programs and courses, parent training sessions, and a whole host of professional and ad hoc weapons were brought into the battle against drug abuse.

By 1972, a 68% to 25% sizable majority could be found in support of "stiffer penalties for hard drug users," including life imprisonment. The federal government negotiated with Turkey and other nations to try to dry up the supply of heroin. A furious debate was carried on over the use of methadone, the drug purposely given to heroin addicts, in an attempt to satisfy their cravings for a stronger drug—but which was addictive in itself.

Further studies began to sort out some fact from fantasy in the panic. In 1973,[9] a special Presidential Commission on Drug Abuse, headed by former Governor Raymond Shafer of Pennsylvania, came up with findings which indicated that soft drugs were probably less harmful than the compulsive use of alcohol. In fact, the Shafer Commission named alcohol as the nation's number one problem. It further recommended that criminal penalties for use of marijuana be eased. The day could be foreseen when the sale and use of marijuana might be legalized, probably much sooner than most people imagined in 1973.

Public opinion nonetheless appeared to be standing firm in its tough, intractable stand on the use of marijuana. In 1969, the American people opposed legalizing the sale and use of marijuana by a massive 78% to 16% margin. By 1972, there was no change on the subject at all: A 79% to 15% majority was against legalizing the use of grass. And 1973 saw little change again: 79% to 16% opposition. The basic cause of adult America's unbending views was the deep-seated conviction that marijuana use among the young would lead to other illegal hard drug usage. Nearly everyone knew that speed could disintegrate the brain and an overdose of heroin could kill instantly. Until the hard drug epidemic had been brought under control, the public would be unwilling to condone use of soft drugs, even though mounting evidence indicated there were no perceivable addiction or health problems from moderate use of marijuana and that experimentation with the drug did not lead inevitably to hard drug experimentation or use.

The number of people who were willing to see an easing of stiff penalties (up to twenty years in prison) for possession of marijuana rose to 40% in 1972, even though no more than 16% would agree to legalize the drug. A majority of 61% of people under 30 wanted to see the criminal penalties on "grass" eased, but an even higher 65% of people over 50 did not. At the same time, there were reports of a fall-off in the use of the hallucinogenic drug LSD, a decline in experimentation with amphetamines (speed), and the number of heroin addicts now coming in for treatment was mounting rapidly. The drug problem was far from being solved, as any terrified parent with a child in school who was experimenting could testify. There were signs, however, that the combined powerful warnings of the mass media, the schools, and parents were beginning to take hold among the young.

But the use of marijuana did not appear to be tapering off. There were indications that as many as 22% had tried it by 1973 in the 18-year-old and over adult population and among the under 30 group, sometimes usage had swelled to an estimated 4 in 10. There was every indication that the issue of how to handle the use of grass would continue to plague the establishment. Unless further evidence were soon furnished that marijuana had some greater deleterious effect than medical studies had shown up to 1973, the drug appeared on its way toward legalization. The alternative of not legalizing grass would then have to be faced: of enduring a permanent illegal structure for the production and distribution of a soft drug which literally millions of people used, but who violated the law whenever they purchased it.

The drug problem was not confined to the young in civilian life. One special problem particularly shocked people in a war that produced many shocks: the disclosures in the early 1970s that many men in the armed services were using illegal drugs. The first signs of public alarm and even guilt over the Army,

Navy, Marines, and Air Force being inundated by drug usage could be seen in a massive study our firm conducted in late 1971 for the Veterans Administration: 74% of the public felt soft drugs were "very accessible" in the armed forces and 54% felt the same about the availability of hard drugs. Interestingly enough, a lower 60% of Vietnam veterans themselves felt soft drugs were "very accessible" and a much lower 30% testified to the easy availability of hard drugs in the service.

When asked for a generalized estimate of why servicemen used drugs, the public was inclined to attribute the causes to "the pressures of war," "feelings of opposition to the Vietnam War," and a "feeling of loneliness and homesickness." Veterans themselves were more inclined to trace the causes of in-service drug use to "boredom and the desire to have something to do," the desire to "try something different," and as a "means of escape."

The veterans were frank about their use of both hard and soft drugs. The following table shows the pattern of their usage of illegal drugs before, during, and after their years in the armed forces. The results were obtained by a secret ballot technique, under which no user could be identified individually:

Veterans Use of Drugs [10]

	PRE-SERVICE %	IN-SERVICE %	POST-SERVICE %
Marijuana	14	29	23
Hashish	15	10	9
Amphetamines	2	10	8
Barbiturates	2	4	3
LSD	2	4	4
Opium	1	5	2
Heroin	1	2	2
Used illegal drugs	17	32	26
Did not use	83	68	74

The pattern showed much increased drug usage during their service experience. It also indicated that most of the drug usage centered on the two soft drugs, marijuana and hashish, all through their history of drug usage. The results also indicated that the vast majority never used illegal drugs at all.

The pivotal question, however, was: What kind of punishment ought to be meted out to servicemen caught using drugs? Massive cross-sections of both the public and veterans were asked about hard and soft drugs separately. In the case of hard drugs, the same public, 68% of which could support up to life imprisonment for civilian hard drug users came forth with only a 50% to 37% division in favor of some punishment of servicemen caught using hard drugs. In the case of soft drugs, by 47% to 39%, most adult Americans held the view that servicemen found to be using marijuana should receive *no* punishment at all. It was no surprise to find the under 30 group in the public opposed to punishment for use of marijuana, but striking indeed was the 45% to 38% plurality of people over 50 who opposed punishment.

The ultimate irony was yet to come in the survey. When veterans were asked the same questions, by 64% to 29%, they favored punishment for servicemen caught using hard drugs and, by 49% to 42%, they also favored punishing users of soft drugs. The men who had lived through Vietnam took a tougher stance on punishment for illegal drug usage than the adult American public as a whole. The inescapable conclusion was that *under certain conditions,* most Americans could indeed be rather flexible and quite bending in their previously intractable opposition to easing penalties for soft drug usage particularly.

There was also a growing awareness that, not only did American society in the 1970s have an illegal drug problem, but that the country might also have to face a legal drug problem of perhaps more massive proportions. The documentation for this discovery emerged in a Harris study as far back as 1969. A cross-section of the public was asked about the usage of four legal drugs and how dangerous each was believed to be. The results produced an admission of usage of tranquilizers by 37% of the public 18 and over, with 41% of the public labeling these pills as could be "dangerous;" 32% who used pain-killing drugs, admitted to be "dangerous" by 43%; 28% who used sleeping pills, admitted by an even 50% to be "dangerous;" and 11% who used pep-up pills, thought to be "dangerous" by 73% of the public. Illegal drug penetration at the time showed 10% who reported using marijuana, labeled "dangerous" by 69% (less than pep-up pills); 4% who used LSD, labeled dangerous by 89%; and 1% who admitted using heroin, viewed as "dangerous" by 97% of the public.

The vast bulk of the use of the legal drugs was by people over 30, while the illegal variety were mainly used by people under 30. This made possible a fascinating research experiment to measure the affinity between adult usage of legal drugs and the likelihood of their off-spring using illegal drugs later on. The following table summarizes the relationship between heavy illegal drug usage and heavy legal drug usage:

Relationship of Legal and Illegal Drug Usage [11]

Use Illegal Drugs
(Mainly the Young)

Use Legal Drugs (Mainly over 30)	LIGHT USERS	MODERATE USERS	HEAVY USERS
Light users	29	12	7
Moderate users	58	56	38
Heavy users	13	32	55

The results were startling, for they indicated that if a youth were a light user of illegal drugs (i.e., marijuana once a month or less, but no hard drugs), then the chances were his parents are moderate users of legal drugs (tranquilizers, sleeping pills, pep-up pills, pain-killing pills). If a young person were a moderate user of illegal drugs (marijuana, some experimentation with hard drugs), the chances were that parents would be moderate to heavy users of legal drugs. The most telling finding, however, was that if a young person were a heavy user of illegal drugs (the whole gamut of soft and hard drugs), then there was every likelihood his parents have been heavy users of legal drugs.

This finding, of course, shed some quite different light on how to attack the problems of drug abuse. The clear implication was that unless there were tighter controls over the dissemination and use of legal drugs by parents, there was every reason to expect the children of heavy legal drug users to become heavy users of illegal drugs. These results also blurred considerably the question of what drugs should be and should not be declared legal or illegal. Indeed, much of the public saw real danger in many drugs which no one can go to jail for using, if one simply had a doctor's prescription. These facts tended to buttress the finding of the Shafer Commission that "one of the most serious problems in drugs in the U.S. concerns many respectable housewives who are regular users of barbiturates [sleeping pills]."

One of the signs of a change in the drug problem in 1973 appeared to be emerging in a shift at the high-school level from use of illegal soft or hard drugs to increased usage of alcohol. Of course, alcohol was perfectly legal in most of the country, although use by minors can be illegal. However, there were few cases of young people serving out twenty-year sentences for illegal use of gin, vodka, bourbon, or beer. What is more, many parents were reported to be highly relieved that their off-spring had taken up liquor rather than the dread illegal drugs. A young person in the 1970s had real incentives to turn away from illegal drugs and to take up drinking alcoholic beverages: no hassle with the law, no problem of availability, and even tacit parental approval.

The only trouble with this development if indeed alcohol was supplanting illegal drug usage among the young, was that the number of families admitting to having a member with a "drinking problem" had literally leaped forward over the past eight years:

Families Reporting "Someone Close to Me" with a Drinking Problem [12]

	SOMEONE WITH DRINKING PROBLEM %
1972	36
1971	27
1970	23
1968	22

	SOMEONE WITH DRINKING PROBLEM
	%
1966	20
1965	19
1964	16

On the assumption that there was some direct relationship to what people reported and the actual reality of a "drinking problem," and even discounting a greater candor by people in 1972 than in 1964, nonetheless the indisputable fact was that alcoholism was a major and monumental problem in affluent, prosperous America in the early part of the decade of the 1970s. If the deaths on the highways each year were a form of serious, violent crime, most of it stemming from drunken driving, then alcohol could be viewed as a major cause of the breakdown of law and order.

The fact was that, by 1973, almost as many people had come to view alcohol as a "very serious problem" (69%) as felt the same way about "smoking marijuana" (72%). Ironically, this was not because the public had grown more tolerant of smoking marijuana. Rather, people were becoming more alarmed about the use of alcohol and its dangers. There were differences, of course. Alcohol was legal in most places and the mobsters dealing in it had by and large long since gone legal themselves. Marijuana was illegal both in its purchase and in its use. And illegal by any definition meant opening the door to those who thrive on illegality: criminals and organized crime.

As was the case with labor leaders who misread their constituency or businessmen who misread the opportunities to take broader leadership, there was ample evidence that public officials were sorely misreading the crime and drug issues. The confusion among politicians, public officials, journalists, and even political analysts in reading the political meaning of the crime issue stemmed directly from the experience of the 1968 presidential election and some select mayoral contests in big cities since. The prevailing wisdom had suggested that the "law and order" issue was decisive in determining the outcome of the 1968 race for the White House. Further, it was argued, the so-called social issue (fear of crime, pornography, drugs, youthful excesses) had become a dominant determinant of political power in the 1970s. That proposition is worth examining in some detail, only because rarely have so many men in high places who should know better been so taken in by an unfounded and ungrounded contention.

In 1968 the issues of Vietnam, law and order, race, taxes, and the economy were dominant on the minds of the voters, from August right through election day. In August, Richard Nixon held a 40% to 34% lead nationwide over Humphrey in the Harris Survey. But he held a much wider lead on all the issues. Nixon was preferred to Humphrey in August as "better" on "keeping the economy healthy" by 11 points; on "handling taxes and spending" by 17 points; on "handling Vietnam" by 14 points; on "keeping down the cost of living" by 14 points; and on "maintaining law and order" by 12 points. In September the Nixon lead achieved its widest margin in the entire campaign, a 39% to 31% lead, or 8 points, with Wallace at his highest point at 21%. Both Nixon and Wallace were pounding away at the "law and order" issue daily. Listening to the two "out" candidates and watching the widening Nixon lead and the Wallace surge might lead a superficial observer to conclude that the social issue had taken over and was decisive.

But something happened to the social issue on the way to the election between mid-September and late October 1968. In August, the number of voters who named the courts as a "major" cause of the breakdown of law and order came to 68%. By late October, no more than 51% singled out the courts for such blame, a decline of 17 points in the intensity of the issue. More important, the 12-point lead Nixon had over Humphrey on "law and order" in August shrank to no more than a 4-point (42% to 38%) edge by late October. Indeed, in the same period, Nixon's lead in the voting preference went from 6 points ahead (40% to 34%) to 3 points ahead (40% to 37%). Analytically, the test, then, was whether "law and order" as an issue was merely symptomatic of the overall trend or whether it was the determining element. If other issues behaved much as "law and order," then one might conclude "law and order" was working for Nixon.

But the other issues did not close as "law and order" did. Vietnam, under the impetus of the flurry of activity that a cease-fire might be won, rose to become the dominant issue. The high cost of living also was high in voters' minds, and Nixon was pounding away at that issue, too. On Vietnam Nixon kept a 6-point lead (36% to 30%) to the end; on "keeping down the cost of living," he maintained an even wider 11-point lead (38% to 27%). On the related economic issue of "taxes and spending," Nixon also maintained an 11-point lead (40% to 29%).

Thus, the evidence showed that by the end of the 1968 election, it was Vietnam, inflation, and taxes and spending which were working for Nixon rather than the law and order issue. Law and order, although on the minds of voters, was far less a cutting edge in the election than it had appeared in August or September. Another proof of this could be found in the Wallace vote. By late October, Wallace still could corral 24% of the voters who thought he could best "maintain law and order," up from 21% who felt that way in August. Yet the Wallace vote preference was dropping steadily from 21% to 18% to 16% to 13% of the vote during this same period. Wallace was winning the battle on who could best handle crime and unrest, but was losing the election in the process.

In the 1970 election, Nixon and Agnew tried to exploit the social issue, with heavy emphasis on student unrest and antiwar protests. The record in the results of that election clearly showed the effort backfired. The Nixon people admitted privately to this writer that their effort to exploit the issue was a failure two weeks after the 1970 election was over. By the time the 1972 election rolled around, the social issue had almost totally lost whatever thrust it had had in the past. By then Richard Nixon was the "in" candidate, and was having his own troubles on the "law and order" issue. His rating on handling "crime and law and order" in October 1970 was 55% to 39% negative, by November 1971 it had fallen to a low of 67% to 28% negative, and by November 1972 was no better than 57% to 38%

negative, even though he was winning by a 24-point margin in the election itself. On the issue of "controlling drug abuse," Nixon's standing was also negative, though by a lesser 49% to 43% margin.

Early in the 1972 campaign, the public was asked who could handle certain issues better, the Nixon Administration or the Democratic Congress. On "controlling crime and law and order," 24% said the Democratic Congress, 21% the Nixon Administration, 24% said "neither," and 18% said "both equally." Then people were asked who could "control crime and law and order" best, the Republicans or the Democrats. The results: the Democrats 22%, the Republicans 20%, neither 14%, both equally 26%. Certainly there was no sign here that the crime or "law and order" issue had real cutting edges and certainly it was no Nixon advantage.

The obvious truth was that there simply was not a Republican or Democratic way to enforce the law. In fact, far more important was that people did not see violence as a political issue at all. Charges such as "soft on crime" or easy promises "to get tough" simply did not solve the crime problem. By the early 1970s such old rallying cries had lost almost all political credibility. The people were still deeply worried, still felt beset by a sense of personal insecurity, still felt crime and drug abuse had not been solved by any means. But in many ways, the people were far ahead of their political leaders on the issue. They had long since turned off the easy promises of politicians and were determined to get to the heart of reforming the criminal justice system to make law enforcement more efficient, to make crime detection more efficient, to clean up the incredible delays in the administration of the court system, to zero in on organized crime, and to sort out the facts from the fictions about drug abuse and the dangers of alcohol.

The people were beginning to see the failure of the system of law enforcement and justice more as an indictment of the establishment than as a problem which could be solved by simple crackdowns on youthful street punks and marauders. It was interesting to note that when asked to state which was "worse," by 58% to 27% the public thought "a dishonest used car dealer was worse than a teen-age auto thief;" by 54% to 32%, "a busi-nessman who cheats on his wife is worse than a young hippy who smokes illegal marijuana;" by 50% to 37%, "a factory that evades antipollution laws is worse than a house of prostitution;" by 67% to 20%, "an airline pilot who drinks on the job is worse than an airplane hijacker;" and by 70% to 14%,[13] "a banker who embezzles from his depositors is worse than a bank rob-ber." Obviously, people were not condoning criminals who could do much harm to society and to their own person if con-fronted in real life, but, after a decade of Vietnam killing on television, of assassinations of the two Kennedys and Martin Lu-ther King, of militant blacks and the young taking to the streets, of watching crime increase and drug abuse spread, the public obviously had much more knowledge, had many sober second thoughts, and was becoming fed up with those members of the establishment who still came up with the hollow scare words as an answer to the breakdown of law and order. The Watergate scandals in 1973 made people more skeptical than ever about politicians who cloaked themselves with the mantle of "law and order." The public was fed up with emotional outcries and hand-wringing at all levels and wanted real problems solved in real ways. This was perhaps the most hopeful sign in the long night of fear and violence that had descended over the land.

XII

YOUTH
When Will We
Ever Learn?

Back in the hopeful spring of 1960, late into the night of the successful West Virginia primary, candidate John F. Kennedy was musing about what it would mean if he won the presidency. He told this writer, "Everyone thinks the significance of my winning in November would be to prove a Catholic could make it all the way to the White House. But the real significance will be that we will have by-passed a whole generation. Never again will anyone from Stevenson's generation be president. I think the establishment resents our youth as much as anything else. But it is time the vigor of youth took over."

Nearly everything about Kennedy and his brief stay at the White House symbolized the American worship of things young. The striking good looks of the young president, matched by the ethereal beauty of his young wife Jacqueline, the glamorous state dinners, touch football and sailing at the Kennedy compound at Hyannisport, the walks along the beach, the touching scenes of the youthful chief executive playing with his daughter

Caroline and later with John-John, all gave a verve to the office, to the country, and even to the world. The young were beautiful and to be beautiful you had to stay young.

When Lee Harvey Oswald shattered Kennedy's skull from his perch in the Dallas Bookmart in 1963, he shattered perhaps the most powerful symbol of youth produced by the twentieth century. People all over the earth wept that late November weekend as the death of few other American presidents had been mourned. It was not simply the shock of a brutal and unexpected assassination. The identification of people everywhere with the hope and vibrance that flows from being young had been wiped out. The idol of youth worship had been shattered, physically in 1963, symbolically in the decade that was to follow.

Ten years later, in 1973, despite predictions of historians that the Kennedy magic would pass, when the Harris Survey asked the public to assess the last six presidents from Roosevelt to Nixon, JFK was credited by more Americans than any other man to occupy the White House in modern times for "most inspiring confidence," "doing the best job in the White House," "best in foreign affairs," "best in domestic affairs," and even "the best administrator" (which would have amused Kennedy). But the one area in which Kennedy literally swamped Roosevelt, Truman, Eisenhower, Nixon, and Johnson was "as the most appealing personally." On this dimension, 66% of the public named Kennedy, with Ike second at a distant 10% and FDR third at 9%. In commenting on this result, a key Nixon aide passed it off as "well, what more could you expect when a young president is martyred." But Kennedy in the 1970s was a symbol of a time when youth meant hope and when the young believed in the future, when children could grow up and earnestly believe the ringing words of the inaugural of 1960, "Ask not what your country can do for you, but what you can do for your country."

By 1973, much of adult America had come to hold a somewhat jaundiced view of the young people of that day, their new life styles, their new manners, and their new impact on life in the country. Despite the protestations of the young for many

years now that they would not rest easy until the "hypocrisy" of
their elders had been corrected, no more than 24% of the public
could say "the integrity of today's young is greater than in past
generations." In their use of illegal drugs, the young were
viewed as "immoral" by 57% of the country and by a higher
68% of all people over 50. Despite constant claims by the young
that their surge of revolt and protest was a reaction to an "immoral war in Vietnam," a deterioration of the quality of life at
home, and "injustices toward blacks and other minorities," no
more than a third of all those over 30 were willing to say young
people's problems stemmed primarily from "the times." Instead,
over 6 in 10 attributed youthful troubles to a "lack of old-fash-
ioned parental discipline." For a long time prior to 1973, majorities of the over 30 group had labeled "young people who smoke
marijuana," "homosexuals," "antiwar student protesters," "young
people at rock festivals," and "hippies" all as "harmful to America," although "blacks who demonstrate for civil rights," "members of the women's liberation movement," and "Mexican-Ameri-
cans, Indians, and other minorities who agitated for more equal
treatment" were not viewed as "harmful."

By the standards of the 1950s, the young who had been
hatched in America and had grown up in the 1960s and 1970s
were a new breed. The young no longer seemed to be the beautiful people. To be young meant to wear long, unkempt, dirty
hair, frayed jeans, sloppy sandals, and to shock with a stream of
four-letter words; above all, they seemed to be eternally defying
their elders. Spiro Agnew would call it the "price of permissiveness." The young would sharply disagree, proclaiming that they
had discovered a new liberation from the chains of the past.

One immediate explanation for the decade of youthful revolt
unquestionably had been the war in Vietnam. Not only did most
young people think the war was "a mistake" and "immoral," but
they deeply resented the fact that it fell to the lot of youth to
fight it. However, the deep cultural divisions had begun to take
shape long before the war became a dominant issue. The generational split over rock music, the horror of parents at the sight
of their offspring experimenting with drugs, the smashing of traditional mores against sex and nudity, the wild dress, and the

foul language, all had begun earlier in the 1960s. But they grew in intensity and breadth, reaching a climax in 1968–70.

A historic irony was that in the 1964 race for president, young people between 21 and 34 years of age had led the way in electing Lyndon Johnson over Barry Goldwater with 68% of their vote compared to 58% for LBJ among those 50 and over. By 1968, four years later, the young would give Johnson 62% to 38% negative marks on the job he had done in the White House. Johnson was to go from the euphoric peak of his 61% victory margin of 1964 to depths of popular disapproval rarely seen in politics. The real turning point occurred in 1967, when his overall rating on the job he was doing dropped from 54% positive, to 47%, to 43%, to an all-time low of 39%[1] positive nationally. In his handling of the war, he went to an even lower 23% and finally confidence in him personally hit a rock bottom identical 23%. That October of 1967, Johnson ran behind all possible Republican opponents in trial heats for 1968, losing to Rockefeller by 52% to 35%, to Romney by 46% to 37%, to Nixon by 48% to 41%, to Reagan by 46% to 41%, to Senator Charles Percy 41% to 40%, and to Mayor John Lindsay by 40% to 39%. The losses in the poll to Lindsay and Percy were particularly galling news at the White House, and in retrospect, this writer always felt contributed heavily to LBJ's later decision not to run in 1968.

But the last straw in that October poll was the additonal news that when Democratic voters were asked whom they preferred between Johnson and Robert Kennedy, the president ran disastrously behind by a margin of 52% to 32%. The key throughout the fall of 1967 was the fact that the young people had obviously soured on President Johnson. Against Kennedy, Johnson was behind among older voters by 48% to 42%, but among the young he was trailing by a humiliating 61% to 23% margin.

Lyndon Johnson had always had a stronger aversion to Bobby than anyone else in the Kennedy family, perhaps dating back to 1960, when Bobby was dismayed at his brother's decision to offer the vice-presidency to the Texan in the first place. This writer was with Robert Kennedy, Larry O'Brien, and Kenneth O'Donnell at the Biltmore Hotel in Los Angeles in July 1960 when the word came down that Johnson had been offered the nomination and had accepted, upsetting the previously agreed upon plan to name Missouri's Senator Stewart Symington as JFK's running mate. While in typically stoic fashion, Bobby took the decision as final, he was obviously not pleased with it. But perhaps more important, Johnson felt dogged by the shadows of the Kennedys and never seemed to feel confidence he could defeat them in a head-to-head political battle. The specter of running against Bobby Kennedy for the Democratic nomination in 1968 must have haunted Lyndon Johnson in the fall of 1967. To make matters worse, Kennedy had broken with Johnson on Vietnam, which was surely the president's Achilles heel in any upcoming campaign.

Robert Kennedy talked with this writer twice about what he should do in his relationship with Lyndon Johnson. He knew the chemistry between them was bad. In the summer of 1964, Bobby told me that he wanted to run for vice-president with LBJ. He felt he could help unify the country if he served under the new president. His problem was that he had hardly seen Johnson since the assassination even though he continued as attorney general, and he found it hard to talk to him. I advised him to go directly to the president and tell him he wanted to run, that he would be a loyal number two man, and that the gesture would make Johnson look good in its gracious generosity. The next day Walter Jenkins, LBJ's trusted aide, called and asked if I had talked with Bobby. I said I had and asked if Bobby had asked to see the president. Kennedy had called for an appointment and Jenkins said, "The boss would be ready for it." Bobby called me right after the talk and I asked him how it had gone. He said, "It was all very uncomfortable. I found it hard to say what I wanted and he didn't seem to want to listen." He was very pessimistic about the prospects. Jenkins also called to say the president didn't like the idea at all and "knew it just wouldn't work having Bobby on the ticket." A few days later, Johnson issued his statement ruling out "all cabinet officers as his possible running mate." This occasioned the famous telegram Bobby Kennedy sent to all his fellow cabinet members in which he apologized for "having taken you over the side with me."

In late January 1968 Robert Kennedy asked to see me at his United Nations Plaza apartment in New York, his official residence as the junior senator from New York, to ask my views about his running for the presidency. Senator Eugene McCarthy of Minnesota had already declared his candidacy the previous December, running on an anti-Johnson, anti-Vietnam platform. McCarthy was entered in the New Hampshire primary and his army of volunteers clearly would be drawn from the young on account of their disenchantment with the war. A December Harris Survey had shown that by 69% to 23% young people felt "antiwar sentiment is rising in the U.S. and the people have a right to feel this way" and by 74% to 19% that "the true test of our democracy is whether we allow people with unpopular views to express them without interference." The young also looked with favor by 67% to 26% on demonstrations against the war "as long as they were peaceful." In all cases, the young felt much more strongly about the war than their elders. Although McCarthy at the time was not well known, he had a cause and he was later to have a student army in the field.

If there were bad blood between Robert Kennedy and Lyndon Johnson, there was downright hostility and mutual contempt between Gene McCarthy and the Kennedys. In my former life in 1958, when polling for candidates, McCarthy had been a client in his bid to win the U.S. Senate seat in Minnesota. A congressman from heavily Catholic St. Paul, McCarthy was not well known and had an uphill fight against incumbent Republican Senator Edward Thye. The survey we conducted for him showed that his best hope for winning was to stick as closely in his campaigning to the popular Governor Orville Freeman and to work hard for the Catholic vote where he was lagging. Senator Humphrey, who held the other U.S. Senate seat frrom Minnesota and was not running that year, called to say he found the report highly useful but was having a "devil of a time keeping Gene to the tasks outlined in the poll." After the election, which McCarthy won by riding in on Freeman's coattails and by concentrating on the Catholic vote, the newly elected senator visited me in my New York office. To my amazement, rather than feeling grateful for the help, he took me to task for having the affrontery to suggest he run not on his own but in Freeman's shadow and to have suggested the demeaning experience of going to communion breakfasts to seek votes. From then on, this writer knew McCarthy would be a strange bird in American politics.

The first time I learned of the strained relations between John Kennedy and Gene McCarthy was early in 1960 when reporter Joseph Alsop told me that McCarthy was deeply resentful of Kennedy's bid for the White House. He said McCarthy felt that it was not right for Kennedy to be the first Catholic president, since Jack Kennedy rarely went to church and wasn't a particularly good Catholic, and, besides, Kennedy was just trying to buy the nomination with his money. Joe Alsop pointed out that the implication was that McCarthy was jealous and felt that he, as a more devout Catholic and as a Democrat who did not have the money to buy the nomination, ought to be the nominee. At the Democratic Convention of 1960, McCarthy demonstrated the depth of his anti-Kennedy feelings when he supported Lyndon Johnson at the beginning and then on the eve of the nominating sessions turned up as the man who placed Adlai Stevenson in nomination. Both acts annoyed John and Robert Kennedy no end, for they were convinced that McCarthy's motives were less a matter of devotion to Johnson or Stevenson, who represented quite different ends of that year's political spectrum, but instead a deep and abiding desire to stop Jack Kennedy at all cost. McCarthy's speech for Stevenson made a real impression on the delegates and overnight made him a man to be reckoned with, even though it was in behalf of a losing cause.

In my late January 1968 conversation with Robert Kennedy, easily as much time was spent discussing Eugene McCarthy as Lyndon Johnson. Bobby felt that Johnson was wrong about the war and that he was not viable as a candidate. He, too, had been impressed by the October results that showed Johnson losing to "even Percy and Lindsay," as Bobby put it. He was impressed by his latest 52% to 32% lead over LBJ in the Democratic preference test in the Harris Survey. But his strongest feelings were reserved for McCarthy. "Why should he be the one to benefit from Johnson's mistakes?" he asked. "He would just be capitalizing on the hope that we built up with Jack among the young people, and, remember, he fought us all the way on doing that. We couldn't even get him out to campaign in 1960." I advised Robert Kennedy not to run, on the ground that, if Lyndon Johnson wanted the nomination, he could get it, and even if he didn't run, he would probably do everything he could to stop Bobby. I urged him to wait to see what Johnson's move would be.

Robert Kennedy did not heed my advice, and he soon declared for the nomination. I always felt the fact Gene McCarthy was already in it was a key determinant in his decision. Our own polls were showing that by 57% to 18%,[2] the public acknowledged that McCarthy "had captured the imagination of the younger generation in politics." McCarthy also was credited by 75% as having been "courageous to run against LBJ" and by 72% as an "independent-minded man." But it was the McCarthy appeal among the young that seemed to trouble Bobby most of all.

Indeed, in his own right, Robert Kennedy had two major assets with the public going for him in 1968, apart from the fact that he was a household word. By 65% to 19%, most Americans felt he was "courageous and unafraid to follow his convictions" and by 55% to 33% that he was "an inspiration to a new generation in politics." In fact, there was ample evidence in March 1968 that Kennedy, much more than McCarthy, could attract the ultimate loyalties of the increasingly disenchanted young. Before LBJ's withdrawal at the end of March, among Democrats Kennedy was the choice of the young with 53%; Johnson trailed with 24% and McCarthy with 21%. When pitted against Nixon among all voters, Kennedy captured the vote of the young by 49% to 30% and McCarthy by a narrower 38% to 33%. Hubert Humphrey ran behind among the young by 34% to 30% in contrast to his anti-Vietnam opponents. The most dramatic evidence on just what Bobby Kennedy could do among the young emerged in April, after Johnson bowed out. Against Nelson Rockefeller, who had real appeal of his own among the young, in March Johnson had badly trailed with young voters by 59%

to 25%. But in April, against Rockefeller, Kennedy held a 54% to 26% lead.

That same month the crucial Indiana Democratic primary was held and we polled it for *Newsweek*. In a three-way race against McCarthy and Governor Roger Brannigan, a stand-in for Humphrey who did not enter the primaries, Kennedy won with 46% of the vote, a notable victory. Our firm felt particularly proud of having predicted that outcome correctly, since the other polls had come under attack for widely missing the mark in New Hampshire and Wisconsin, where McCarthy did so well. George Gallup was particularly gracious and called from California to say, "All of us were praying and are thankful you were so accurate." Kennedy won Indiana primarily because he was able to win a thumping 56% of the vote of those under 30. He was proving he could bring back the one group most disenchanted with the war and with the Johnson stewardship. Although he lost the Oregon primary to McCarthy, after Indiana, he won California in a close contest, and because he also would have controlled California and Illinois, probably would have given Humphrey a real battle for the nomination at the Chicago convention.

But Bobby Kennedy never made it to Chicago. Sirhan Sirhan's bullets cut him down on the night of the California primary. No one would ever know if Kennedy could have been nominated or elected. My own view many years later is that Kennedy probably would have defeated Humphrey for the nomination in Chicago (perhaps even with the help of Mayor Richard Daley of Chicago) and would have gone on to defeat Richard Nixon that November. The main reasons: He probably would have heavily cut the Wallace vote among trade union members, and he would have turned around the vote of the disenchanted young voters.

Humphrey's failure to win in 1968 could be directly traced to his inability to score with the under 30 vote. He lost the vote of the young to Richard Nixon by a 43% to 41% margin. Had Humphrey won the young by even a few points, he would probably still be president today. Humphrey was Johnson's hand-picked successor, had been put across at the 1968 Chicago con-

vention by the establishment of the Democratic party, had been
blackjacked into supporting Johnson war policies in the platform
in return for Southern votes, and quickly became the target of
youthful antiwar hecklers wherever he turned up to campaign.
In retrospect, there is little doubt now that the tactics of the
young so unnerved and untracked the Humphrey candidacy in
1968 that in the end they cost him the election, despite a late
surge that brought him to less than a point behind on election
day.

Much has been written and said about the shambles of a convention the Democrats staged in 1968. The course followed by
Mayor Daley of Chicago who was the host in that beleaguered
and besieged city of setting loose his police on the young demonstrators was later supported by a thumping 66% to 20% majority of the electorate, but by less than half the voters under 30.
Between the protesters in Grant Park and the helmeted police in
1968, the American people would opt strongly for law and
order. No more than 14% expressed sympathy for the street
demonstrators.

I had come to know Daley during the Kennedy days. That he
was pouring it on the demonstrators with some political fore-
thought was admitted to this writer by the mayor himself. The Illinois delegation was located front and center right below the
rostrum in that last convention ever to be held in Chicago's
stockyards. Daley could be seen on television giving cues to the
managers of the proceedings above him when to adjourn a session, when to extend it. The galleries were packed with the
Daley faithful and the mayor was in full command. The Illinois
delegation was surrounded by rugged plainclothesmen and the
mayor held forth in the center of the tight circle.

As I passed the delegation early Tuesday evening of the convention, I nodded at Mayor Daley and he beckoned me inside
the cordon. We had a most enlightening conversation. The first
of the bloody confrontations on the streets was taking place and
just had been shown on NBC television, which cut away from
the convention proceedings to show them. I asked the mayor if
he thought the street battles might not hurt the Democratic
chances in November. He replied, "Lou, they'll do us good. See

those people up there in the stands? They're from the Fiffie [5th Ward] and they're typical of Pucinski's supporters. [Representative Pucinski was a Chicago Democratic congressman known for his tough line on law and order.] I'm worried about Wallace gaining among them. If these kids out there were black, I wouldn't touch them. We'll need all their votes. But those kids are all white and most of them the sons and daughters of rich Republicans anyway. So I think what's happening will do us good in the Fiffie and places like that."

Daley, who was close to President Johnson, also indicated that Humphrey was not his candidate anyway, and he didn't seem too concerned with the Minnesota senator's fate. He strongly implied his real choice was Senator Edward Kennedy, the last surviving Kennedy brother. But he had just about given up on Kennedy, who was in Hyannisport during the convention. Daley told how he had tried to join forces with Kennedy and failed. "The brother-in-law is here in Chicago staying at that Jewish club," he said, referring to Steve Smith, married to Jean Kennedy, who was in town representing the Kennedy interests. "Well, I sent over my deputy mayor who had our count on what we could deliver. But when he got there, this young fellow had no count of his own at all. Why he isn't like his brothers Jack or Bobby at all, Lou. He hasn't learned how to read a map, and that can be fatal in politics. In Chicago, as a boy you learn quick how to read a map. If you don't, you know where you end up? Why right in Lake Michigan. So that young fellow has a lot to learn, Lou."

Humphrey was nominated amid raucous scenes of dissent both inside and outside the convention hall. Although the public sided with Daley directly, two criticisms to come out of the convention were to plague Humphrey right through election day. By 2 to 1, 46% to 22%, most voters felt "the Democrats at the convention did not let delegations have a fair say." The convention came across as boss-controlled. This led to the second major criticism, voiced by a lopsided 71% to 16%, that "Humphrey was picked by Democratic politicians not the people" and by a 51% to 41% margin that he was "too close to LBJ and his policies to be president." The youthful and radical protesters had lost the battle on the surface, but in the heavy-handed response of Daley and Johnson they had also taken away from Humphrey a most precious asset: Most voters henceforth doubted he was "his own man." If Humphrey could not control his own party, most reasoned, then how could he lead the country? This gnawing doubt about Humphrey would shadow him to the end; and, coupled with the opposition of the under 30 vote, deprived him of his lifelong ambition to win the presidency.

The events of 1968 were only a prelude to the storms that were to come up in the country in 1969 and in 1970; but by then the thrust of youthful outrage was directed against Humphrey's successful opponent of 1968, Richard Nixon, who had backed into victory by less than a 1% margin, as a less objectionable alternative to George Wallace, who appeared too racist, and Humphrey, who seemed too close to the prevailing establishment that had led the country into the morass most found it in.

The uproar from the Chicago Democratic Convention in August 1968 was hardly confined to presidential politics or even political issues as such. In the spring of 1969, CBS had cancelled the controversial weekly TV show, "The Smothers Brothers," two comedians prone to defend the new way-out tastes of the young and also to attack sacred cows in the establishment. The Smothers Brothers took their case to their young followers and then to the courts, where four years later they were to win a settlement for $750,000. In April 1969, the Smothers Brothers case became a cause célèbre for thousands of young people. A Harris Survey of that month showed that, by 55% to 32%, a majority of adult America expressed a dislike for the program, but, in contrast, most young people under 30 liked it. Further probing revealed that a majority of people over 30 thought " 'The Smothers Brothers' had too many off-color jokes on it." But by 48% to 32%, people under 30 disagreed. By a 3 to 2 margin, people over 30 thought the Smothers Brothers "were too much on the side of the hippies." But those under 30 thought the contrary. To older America, such programs as "The Smothers Brothers" were offensive and annoying on a "family type network," and should well be banned. But, to most of the young the Smothers Brothers were "saying it the way it is" and they were shocked that the comic team would be "censored off the air," as many put it.

Another essentially nonpolitical case in 1969 centered on Joe Namath, the controversial quarterback of the New York Jets football team, who ran into trouble in 1969 with Commissioner Pete Rozelle of the National Football League. Namath was accused of consorting with "undesirable types" in his nightclub, Bachelor's III, on Manhattan's East Side. "Undesirable types" in pro football parlance means hoods and underworld characters. The NFL keeps strict surveillance over all such possible connections, for the nightmare of America's most popular sport is the potential fix of a game by gamblers. Namath wore his hair long, on occasion had a walrus mustache, wore mod clothes, and cut quite an antiestablishment figure in his own unique way. By 60% to 26%, sports fans over 30 rallied to the side of Commissioner Rozelle. But by 58% to 32%, the under 30 group solidly supported Namath. By nearly 2 to 1, the over 30 group thought "Namath set a bad example for the young." Young people themselves disagreed by 2 to 1 and said they thoroughly liked the cut of "Broadway Joe" Namath's jib.

But the biggest nonpolitical event of 1969 was the rock festival at Woodstock, New York, which attracted an estimated four hundred thousand young people to the most celebrated rock music event of a generation. The whole question of rock music had long split the generations down the middle. No more than 5% of all people over 30 liked it, but a solid 73% of people under 30 did. When asked if they thought "rock music is a noisy, vulgar form of entertainment" in 1969, by 54% to 30%, people over 50 said they thought it was. By a resounding 79% to 15%, young people under 30 even more decisively said it was not. When asked if "rock music is one of the major cultural advances in this century," young people agreed that it was by 55% to 36%. People over 30 disagreed by a decisive 67% to 17%. The dividing line on rock music obviously was over and under 30 years of age, and the split was utter and complete, without any middle ground.

The overtones of Woodstock, however, were not simply a difference in taste in music. For those who attended Woodstock, the festival was a total experience, from the round-the-clock rock entertainment flown in by helicopter to the makeshift living in tents and other ad hoc accommodations to the drug-taking that was widespread. A highly successful record and tape album, a movie, and a special edition of *Life* magazine preserved the happening for posterity. After it was all over, the Harris Survey tested public reaction. Contrary to some who viewed the proceedings with total scorn, majorities of the public had some good things to say about Woodstock even though most still didn't like rock music: By 67% to 23%, they agreed that "young people showed they could enjoy themselves and their music in larger numbers and in ways never done before"; by 57% to 34%, that Woodstock proved "the rock music way of life has taken over with young people"; and, by 51% to 39%, that Woodstock was "remarkable since there was no violence and everyone there was so peaceful."

There were, however, other happenings at Woodstock. The festival was beset with rain and the entire location on the farm taken over for the event was awash with mud, mixed with the muck left behind by four hundred thousand occupants. Living conditions were less than tolerable, but many of the young people stayed the course in the muck. However, by 69% to 23%, including a majority of young people, most Americans reacted in agreement to the statement, "The way people there were able to live in such filth and dirt was disgusting." TV news programs widely reported young men and women swimming together in the nude, which was viewed as "shameful" to 68% of the public. The biggest negative reaction of all surfaced on the subject of drugs, with a 79% to 14% majority, including most young people, who thought "the drug-taking that went on should not have been allowed." The conclusion of the American people: By 62% to 23%, they denied that Woodstock was "a beautiful happening" (although those under 21 disagreed by 47% to 37%) and, by 52% to 29%, they felt the whole affair "did more harm than good" (although the under 21 group thought Woodstock did "more good than harm," by 50% to 29%). One interesting dimension split the generations into two warring camps. The charge that "Woodstock was just an excuse for young people to carry on in an immoral way" met with agreement among those over 30 by 55% to 28%. Among those under 30, there was a sharp 58% to 32% demur. To the young, Woodstock may have been full of excesses, but the music, the spirit, the nonviolence had deep appeal. Their elders wanted the young to enjoy themselves but were totally turned off by those freaked out on drugs and the apparent obliviousness of many to the subhuman living conditions they endured. It would be a serious mistake, however, to underestimate the symbolism of Woodstock to the young who grew up in the 1960s and early 1970s. It was a bold, if not entirely successful, attempt by the young to put a new cultural stamp on America. More important, it became a symbol of hope after a long depression of assassinations and negative experiences with the establishment. It would be a long time before rock music could command this kind of scene again.

The differences between the generations were not confined to music, styles, tastes, manners, and the perceived dangers of experimenting with drugs. The gulf was every bit as wide on some of the fundamental political and social issues that had ravaged the country in the violent sixties. One of these was race. In the summer of 1969, we polled the country on discrimination against blacks. The following table shows the wide disparity between the under 30 and 50 and over segments of America on the race issue:

Perceived Discrimination against Blacks (1969) [3]

	Under 30			50 and Over		
	ARE	ARE NOT	NOT SURE	ARE	ARE NOT	NOT SURE
Are Blacks Discriminated Against:	%	%	%	%	%	%
In getting decent housing	62	34	4	40	46	14
In achieving full equality	60	30	10	37	43	20
In obtaining white collar office jobs	54	39	7	33	49	18
In obtaining skilled labor jobs	52	41	7	31	55	14
In way treated as human beings	56	37	7	28	58	14

Across the board, in each key area, the young people under 30 saw blacks discriminated against, just as their elders 50 and over did not. On the general proposition "Are most blacks discriminated against?" the young answered they were by 65% to 26% and older people said they were not by 49% to 38%. A substantial 58% of the young favored "open housing laws," banning discrimination in housing, a view shared by no more than 44% of the older generation. When the U.S. Supreme Court ordered schools with dejure segregation to integrate immediately, the young supported the decision by 56% to 34%, but the 50 and over group opposed it by 45% to 41%. When Daniel Patrick Moynihan, the ex-Kennedy and ex-Johnson aide who joined Nixon's staff in 1969, advocated his controversial policy of "benign neglect" [4] for blacks, young people under 30 expressed disapproval by 48% to 29%, but people over 50 backed it by 40% to 27%.

There is little doubt that this new generation was deadly serious about race. A student at the University of Illinois put it for many when he said, "Look, we were preached at all our lives that all men are created equal. Only we believe it and our parents never did." An 18-year-old high school student in Keene, New Hampshire, added, "If you care about other people, then you don't care about the color of their skin." A 26-year-old white tool and lathe operator in St. Louis put it this way, "I work with colored guys here, have a beer with them, bowl with them. You judge them as people, just like anybody else. My daddy goes blind mad when I talk this way, but I know I'm right."

The range of issue differences between the generations was wide and deep. For example, the young opposed "preventive arrests" by 58% to 31%, while older people favored it by 42% to 36%. In 1968, when the U.S. finally landed a man on the moon, more surprisingly, the 18 to 29-year-old group said by 63% to 30% that "it was worth spending $4 billion to get to the moon," while people 50 and over said by 59% to 30% it was not. On labor's right to strike, 74% of the young stood in back of this right, although no more than 53% of the people who lived through the New Deal agreed. Early on, it was obvious that the environmental control issue would divide sharply along age lines. In early 1970, 63% of the young said they would be "willing to pay $15 more per person to control pollution," compared to no more than 45% of the older group who felt the same way.

But the issue that would ignite the young more than any other was the war. In the fall of 1969, moratorium marches were held across the country to protest the war. The young took to the streets in large numbers. Just after the marches, the Harris Survey polled the public and found a 45% to 39% plurality against the goals of the protest. The reasons given for the opposition were that "demonstrations lead to violence," "we can't just pull out like that so quickly," and "the protesters are a bunch of kids making a lot of noise." People over 50 opposed the marches by a thumping 55% to 28%. Young people under 30 supported them by 52% to 34%. The gap between the generations on the *methods* of the protest was even greater: The young were for them by 52% to 37%, compared with 64% to 23% opposition among older people. The young said, "We want the war over, we want peace," "we should not have been there in the first place," and "protesters are standing up for what they believe in."

President Nixon answered the moratorium marches in November 1969 with his pledge to withdraw U.S. troops on an unspecified phased timetable and to follow a policy of Vietnamization. At year's end, he appeared to have cooled the white heat of protest. He also announced a long-term plan to end the draft and to substitute a volunteer army, an idea that met with majority approval among the young. The proposition that "the military draft is wrong because it forces many young men to fight in a war they don't believe in" actually received 44% to 43% backing nationwide. The 57% to 35% agreement among the young outweighed the 46% to 40% disagreement among those 30 and over.

In late April of 1970, President Nixon ordered what came to be known as the Cambodian incursion, which was taken to clean out Communist sanctuaries across the border from South Vietnam, but which involved Cambodia in the war long after the ultimate cease-fire agreement in Vietnam. The antiwar protest movement exploded into a spate of demonstrations across the country. The immediate reaction of the public to the Cambodian incursion was a narrow decision to rally behind the president. By 56% to 32%,[5] a majority thought the president was "justified." However, on the "correctness" of his decision, Nixon received the backing of only 50% nationwide, with 43% expressing "serious doubts." Among the under 30 group, 51% were doubtful of the president's wisdom, while only 34% of the 50 and over segment shared these doubts.

The protests were particularly strident on the college campuses of the country. They continued well into May and clearly threatened to close down higher education in the country. In intensity and breadth, the post-Cambodian protests exceeded anything the country had previously seen. The fury on the campuses exploded into rage when four students at Kent State University were killed on campus in a confrontation with Ohio National Guard troops.

The public as a whole reacted sharply against the protests, with only 27% expressing sympathy with the students, 13% who said they didn't pay much attention to them, but a majority of 52% who condemned them. By 53% to 27%, a majority were opposed to outlawing student protests, with 70% of the young leading the way in reasserting this right. When President Nixon called the student demonstrators "bums," a close plurality of 47% to 43% disagreed with him. However, older people agreed with him by 49% to 38% while the young carried the day by disagreeing with Nixon by 60% to 36%. This support of student protests by the total under 30 group was significant, for no more than a third of the young nationwide were students. The results showed a majority of the nonstudents stood behind their peers on the campuses. Much nonsense has been written about the purported "fact" that most young people really reflected the view of their parents and that noncollege youth had little in common with those on college campuses. The response to the Cambodian incident merely bore out the consistent results of Harris Surveys throughout this period: Noncollege young people were highly sympathetic to college students in their protests and general orientation toward the major issues of the war, race, and environment; both were at almost complete loggerheads with their parents' generation in their 50s and 60s.

After the Cambodian incursion began, the eye of the hurricane of protest could be found on college campuses. The president appointed the distinguished chancellor of Vanderbilt University, Alexander Heard as a special adviser on campus unrest. Among other credentials, Heard was a board member of Time, Inc., and was a trustee of the Ford Foundation, of which he was later to become chairman. Through pure happenstance, our firm became involved in one of the most difficult and gratifying tasks ever assigned it. Chancellor Heard quickly assembled about thirty college presidents from every section of the country, under the auspices of the American Council on Education, the establishment in higher education, to discuss with this writer and two senior staff members, Bayard Hooper and Michael Edison, whether a cross-section of students could be polled under the chaotic conditions that obviously then prevailed. Fortunately, we had drawn a college sample in anticipation of a Peace Corps study which was never forthcoming, and we had staff to move with dispatch. Between May 16 and May 26, the survey was conceived, a comprehensive questionnaire constructed, revised, and then cleared by the American Council on Education, and the interviewing completed. We did have a problem with an estimated 21% of all the students who had left their campuses. However, when we asked the sample we reached about the political views of those who had left, fortunately we found that the representativeness was not affected. If anything, our final sample gave slightly more weight to students who were more conservative in their political views. Our task was to find out just what had happened to student opinion and behavior in this wild Cambodian period and how the federal government and university administrators might cope with the protests.

The results of the poll did not make big news, but they did trigger two pivotal reactions: a firm resolution by Alex Heard to stand by them and to defend the students, and an equally adamant refusal by President Nixon not only not to believe them, but to suspect their validity because the Harris firm had con-

ducted the study. How much the later Nixon resolve to make
student protesters the main target of his 1970 campaign effort
stemmed from his disbelief of our May survey is not known to
this writer. But in the fall of 1972, Heard told this writer that he
was convinced the survey had hardened instead of softened the
president's attitude toward the outbursts at the time.

The survey, taken at Mount Mary College as well as City College of New York, at LeMoyne College as well as Mount Holyoke, at Black Hills College for Teachers as well as the University of Wisconsin, at Calvin College as well as the University of
Texas, at Catawba College as well as San Francisco State, at
Western Washington College of Education as well as Stanford,
could not have told a clearer story.[6] Fully 80% of the colleges
reported that post-Cambodia protest had occurred on their campuses. Nearly 1 in every 2 students, 48%, said they had personally taken part in demonstrations. By 75% to 16%, they agreed
with the goals of the protest. At the outset, the students made it
abundantly clear they did not condone violence. When asked
who was responsible for the violence, they apportioned the
blame equally among the demonstrators and the authorites. By
70% to 21%, they agreed that "when students occupy buildings
and appear to threaten violence, school authorities are *right* to
ask for help from local and state police." However, after the
Kent State deaths, by 53% to 38%, they opposed calling in the
National Guard, although 48% credited the National Guard
with acting "responsibly" when called in.

In other ways, the student attitudes would appear reasonable
by many of their elders' standards. By 70% to 28%, they
thought ROTC groups ought to be permitted on campus; by
72% to 22%, that "companies doing defense business ought to
be allowed on campus"; and by 61% to 30% that individual
professors "should be allowed to undertake research projects for
the military."

What, then, had triggered the outpouring? By 76% to 22%,
they were critical of the president's handling of the war; by 66%
to 25%, they questioned Nixon's credibility on Vietnam; by 67%
to 30% they felt the "Nixon Administration was out of touch
with the mood of America." Their grievances went deeper and

broader than just the Cambodian decision and the war. By 52%
to 30%, they did not think "war protesters were being given fair
trials"; by 51% to 37% that "the Administration would not be
willing to clean up the environment," by a thumping 67% to
26%, they agreed with Yale President Kingman Brewster that
he was "skeptical that black militants could get a fair trial in
America." They expressed disagreement with one of their major
critics, Vice-President Agnew, on "major policy issues" by 87%
to 11%. By 57% to 23%, a majority said they "respected draft
resisters who refused to serve in the armed services more than
less." One in five said they would refuse to serve "if called up in
the draft." By 58% to 39%, they felt "America was becoming a
repressive society." And by 56% to 48%, they rejected the argument that "intellectual study on campus was too important to be
disrupted by protests and demonstrations."

The roots of the revolt were even more philosophically
embedded in the college campuses in 1970. By 65% to 32%, in
response to a projective question, a majority of students agreed
that "our troubles stem from making economic competition the
basis of our way of life." A higher 76% to 22% felt "the real
trouble with our society is that we are becoming a technology
where no one feels he counts for very much as an individual."
By 78% to 20%, they agreed that "the real trouble with U.S. society is that it lacks a sense of values—is conformist and materialistic." Closer to home, an 81% to 18% majority felt there was
"too much pressure on education and too much of it is irrele-
vant." Finally, by 81% to 17% they overwhelmingly agreed that
"until the older generation comes to understand the new priorities and life style of the young, serious conflict will continue."

Obviously, this student generation was deeply disenchanted
with the establishment. Cambodia had merely triggered a visible uprising. The targets of their wrath were those in power and
their causes were to end the war, enhance racial equality, improve the quality of life, and to persuade the country to allow
people to pursue pluralistic and nonconformist lives if they so
desired. However, when asked if the May 1970 protests had
been effective, only 57% could say they thought they were. And
when asked what they would do in the future, 47% said "con-

tinue the demonstrations," but an equal 47% looked to "other means." By far the most effective, in the eyes of the students, was to "work to elect better public officials," cited by 65% as "very effective," compared with no more than 22% who thought "demonstrating and protesting" would be as effective. Only a small 11% opted for "resorting to violent tactics if necessary, to bring about basic changes in the system." By a decisive 63% to 33% margin, the students agreed that "the democratic process is capable of keeping up with the pace of events and the need for action"; and by a massive 89% to 11% they also agreed that "change takes time but eventually governmental policy can be changed by public pressure."

By this evidence, as disenchanted as they might be with that state of affairs in the country, 89% of the students, at the height of their fury in that May of 1970, still were convinced they could change society from "within." Indeed, the young would have a real bearing on the 1970 off-year elections and on the congressional elections of 1972.

In 1970 the Republicans had their best chance to capture control of the U.S. Senate in two decades. They needed a shift of only five seats. Yet, when the final results were tallied, they gained no seats. As Charles Colson, aide to President Nixon, said afterward, "We blew the election, no doubt about it." The Nixon strategy for the 1970 election was to hone in on student unrest and to make youthful protesters whipping boys. The theory, articulated by Richard Scammon and Ben Wattenberg, in their book, *The Real Majority,* was that this aversion to youthful protesters, plus fear of crime and a desire to have law and order, constituted the social issue which supposedly won elections these days. On the surface, one could find evidence of public outrage at student demonstrators: In October 1970, 74% of the public thought "radical militant student groups" were a "major cause" of the unrest, 64% thought "irresponsible students who just want to cause trouble" were back of it all, 58% laid the blame for the unrest to "radical professors who encourage student unrest," and 53% to "college presidents who are too lenient and permissive." By contrast, no more than 26% traced the student unrest to a "lack of willingness on the part of the Nixon

Administration to listen to what students really think," and only 24% to "politicians such as Agnew who are trying to get votes by attacking student protesters."

According to the book and a quick, superficial glance at the polls, the attacks by Vice-President Agnew early in the campaign and by President Nixon in the last ten days—all centered on the irresponsible youthful protesters—should have brought in a harvest of Republican votes. But it did not work out that way. In February 1970, Agnew had a 47% to 42% positive rating on the job he was doing. By September, he had launched his attacks at student protesters and his rating was 45% to 39% negative. By the end of the campaign, in late October, he was given 50% to 40% negative marks. Among people over 50, he was doing fine: 48% to 43% positive. But, contrary to the Scammon-Wattenberg claim that the noncollege young held views similar to those of their parents, the noncollege young gave Agnew 63% to 27% negative marks on his performance, not as high as the 87% to 11% negative on the campuses, but highly negative all the same.

President Nixon was running into much the same kind of trouble. By 51% to 45%, a majority now said, "He was wrong to say he would not pay any attention to the anti-Vietnam protests." Only 44% of all those 30 and over agreed with the criticism. But the majority mark nationwide was reached with the help of the 66% of those under 30 who agreed with the charge. The oft-repeated Republican claim of that fall that "anti-Vietnam protesters are mostly young men who are trying to get out of the armed services" was denied by a narrow 46% to 44%. A majority of 53% of those 50 and over agreed with the draft-dodging charge; but no more than 37% of the under 30 group did. When asked to rate the president on his "approach to student protesters," the public came up 59% to 32% negative. The reasons for criticizing him were sharp and pointed: "He doesn't listen to the students," "He talks tough but doesn't do much," "He doesn't know how to handle it." Finally, when the public assessed "President Nixon's campaigning in the 1970 election," the decision was a 55% to 35% negative judgment.

A late Harris Survey in the vote for Congress in 1970 was revealing. Overall, it showed the Democrats with a 49% to 41% lead, approximating the actual election itself. People over 30 were voting Republican by 48% to 43%. If only they had voted, the Nixon campaign tactic of blasting youthful protesters would have worked. But the vote among the under 30 group was 50% to 30% for the Democrats, more than offsetting the GOP votes of the other age group. In the end, in 1970, the student minority was the target of attack, and the answer, in the form of ballots, came straight back from a turned-off, under 30 voting segment. The country did not "eat its young," but mainly because the young themselves would not let it happen. Almost all the foregoing information on the 1970 election was told to Nixon aides over two weeks before the election. Obviously, they didn't believe it. However, after 1970, the Nixon people not only became believers in Harris Survey results, but they carefully read the details and their implications as well.

By 1971 the campuses of the nation had cooled from the hot May of 1970 and there was much talk that the worst of student protests was over. President Nixon was withdrawing troops from Vietnam on schedule and the draft was not taking as many men. Many in the establishment felt the worst was over and that young people would begin to adopt a set of attitudes more in line with the presumably prevailing views of their elders. While many protests died aborning and students were going back to their books in earnest, the attitudes of the young did not change. In fact, with the granting of the vote to the 18 year olds, the voice of the young as citizens would be more important than ever before. For example, in 1971 extensive hearings turned up evidence of corruption in Army PXs and a less than superb record among military managers. People over 50 defended the men running the Army by 52% to 44%. The under 30 group was negative by 55% to 41%, enough to tip the national balance against the Army brass. On the key issue of admission of China to the United Nations, young people led the way by favoring such a move by a majority of 57% to 23%. No more than 45% of those over 30 favored the seating of China. On the prospects of a long-term accord between the U.S. and Russia, the young believed it could be done by 61% to 30%, while their elders over 50 believed it by a much lesser 46% to 38%. In laying down a mandate for business, the young were more critical of the corporate establishment than any other age group. A massive 72% of the young were critical of business for "not helping" to curb air and water pollution, compared with 54% of the older people who felt the same. An even higher 74% of the under 30 group charged business with "not really caring about the individual," compared with 55% of older people who shared that view. A high 67% of the young were critical of business for "not helping to wipe out poverty," a view shared by only 40% of those 50 and over. The young may not have taken to the streets over such issues, but the decisive thrust of their thinking was for change, much more than any other age group.

The young were even winning over public opinion on some of the major tenets of their protests during the turbulent years 1968–70: By 50% to 40%, the public now agreed it was "healthy for the young to want a greater voice in setting school policy"; by 63% to 29%, a majority also felt that on the subject of sex, young people were "more honest and frank" and were not merely "showing off"; by 75% to 22%, a big majority did not think "hippies were a real danger to society"; and by 55% to 26%, the public also did not feel that "rock music was an invitation to try drugs" as Art Linkletter had charged, but instead that it was "an expression of a point of view about life." When put to a test, by 52% to 30%, a majority of the public thought it more important for the president to "crack down on industrial pollutors" than "to crack down on youthful protesters."

Then came the 1972 election and another candidate emerged as a self-proclaimed champion of the cause of the young: George McGovern of South Dakota. Looking back on that election of 1972, many observers jumped to the conclusion that since McGovern lost the vote of the under 30 to Nixon by 51% to 46%, obviously there is not much generational difference and young people are not nearly as much for change as had been claimed. The fact is that McGovern lost the over 30 vote by 62% to 33% or by nearly six times the margin by which he lost the young. But the key finding of the 1972 election among the young is that George McGovern lost the young much more than

Nixon won it. To a degree, in miniature what happened to McGovern is what happened to him among nearly all groups.

It is true that, among the young, McGovern was believed to be more capable of "ending U.S. involvement in Vietnam sooner" by 50% to 35%, while the over 30 vote opted for Nixon on Vietnam by 50% to 30%. On the question of "putting in tax reforms," McGovern was trusted by the young over Nixon by 57% to 25%, compared with a 38% to 38% standoff among the rest of the electorate. On "keeping corruption out of government," the young also believed more in McGovern than Nixon by 40% to 30%, while the 30 and over group trusted Nixon more by 43% to 26%. All of these advantages going for McGovern kept the Nixon margin down to 5 points in their final vote.

But on a whole spate of other dimensions, McGovern struck out among the young as he did with the rest of the voters. On "keeping inflation in check," the young preferred Nixon by 46% to 37%, although their elders did the same by a more sizable 60% to 23%. On "negotiating with the Russians and Chinese," Nixon won hands down among the young by 69% to 15%, not very different from the 70% to 14% margin scored by the president among those 30 and over. On the pivotal issue of "more likely to move the world closer to peace," Nixon won among the young by 47% to 37%, lower than the 60% to 23% margin he held among older voters. And on the key dimension of "inspiring confidence in the White House," Nixon led among the under 30 group by 47% to 37%, although he won the older group on overall confidence by 60% to 23%.

The facts show that the 1972 election was a contest among the young and almost no other group. Nixon was able to make the peace issue through his visits to Peking and Moscow and the inflation issue through his wage-price freeze in August 1971. These advantages of Nixon among all age groups, including the young, served him in good stead. But on the pivotal issue of confidence among the young it was strictly a matter of the lesser of two evils. In October, the under 30 group was 57% to 37% negative on Nixon on "inspiring confidence in the White House." Yet when compared to McGovern on the confidence dimension, Nixon won by 10 points. The answer was that McGovern in-

spired even less confidence. There are some important clues as
to why this was so. First, in July and August, during the Eagleton affair, the only group not to show a majority in favor of
McGovern dropping Eagleton was the young. To the young,
central in the Eagleton case was whether a man should be dis-
qualified for high office because "he has had a background of
mental illness." By 60% to 30% the young did not think this
should be so, although people 30 and over disagreed with young
people by 49% to 39%. More than any other group, 71% of the
young said they had had periods of depression and 24% had reported having psychiatric treatment at some time in their lives.
To the young in the Eagleton matter, McGovern had turned his
back on an enlightened position on mental health and they did
not forgive him for it.

But there were other episodes in the McGovern campaign
that also turned off the young voters in 1972. Young people were
in favor of legalizing abortions by 64% to 31%, while the rest of
the public opposed it by 46% to 42%. McGovern's opposition to
legalizing abortions did not go down well with the young, as
was the case with his promising aid to parochial schools at an
assembly of Catholic school students in Chicago, or his endorsement of conservative congresswoman Louise Day Hicks in Bos-
ton. At the end of the campaign, by 59% to 30%, in a projective
test, a 2 to 1 majority of young people were to observe of
George McGovern, "he seemed to be a different type of political
leader, but lately he seems just another politician promising
each group of voters what it wants." McGovern turned out to be
a trimmer and to have feet of clay to most of the young in 1972.

However, as in 1970, the young did cast a decisive vote in
1972. Although Nixon won the presidency in a landslide, the
Democrats retained control of both houses of Congress by com-
fortable margins. In the race for the House, the final Harris Survey showed the Democrats ahead by a 46% to 41% margin. The
30 and over vote went Republican by a narrow 45% to 43%.
But the young voted Democratic by a lopsided 53% to 32%
count. The Democrats who control Congress today can thank
the under 30 voters for their margin of victory in 1972.

In their quest to change America, the young by 1973 had

come part way, but had still left in their wake much that raised the hackles of the rest of society. When asked if, with the war over, the young would continue to press for change, 87% of adult America said they thought they would. The widespread use of marijuana among people under 30 still deeply disturbed their elders. In 1971, when asked if they would "turn in to the authorities a son or daughter who had a supply of marijuana in their room," by 52% to 34%, a majority said they would report their own offspring. Only the under 30 group would not. By 1973, the answers to an identical question produced a 43% to 43% standoff among the entire adult population. By 2 to 1 the under 30 group reported they would not turn in a son or daughter possessing grass in the house. But by 49% to 36%, most 30 and over would do it, or at least said they would. In 1971, when asked if they were "bothered or not by young people's styles, tastes, dress, and language," by 52% to 48%, adult America said it was uptight about them. Two years later, the division was no better than 50% to 50%. The young obviously were not troubled, by a 70% to 30% margin, but those 50 and over still were bothered, by 61% to 39%. There was still a long way to go before older Americans could afford the luxury of abiding the tastes and ways of the young. A big majority of 69% to 24% still clung to the view that "when the young pass the age of 30 they will change and become more like other adults in their styles, manners, and tastes." To the older generation, it was apparent now that they fully expected adolescence in an affluent society to last to the age of 30.

The likelihood of such still-hoped-for changes remained to be seen as the 1970s unfolded. A much better bet was that the young would not soon change their views about society. For in the broader social area, they were hitting pay dirt. The rest of the country was slowly but surely coming around to their broader views on a whole host of subjects. And, much as they were the balance of power in the congressional elections, young people were becoming the marginal difference in many areas. On establishing diplomatic relations with Cuba, favored by 51% to 33% nationwide, the under 30 group led the way in 1973 by supporting such a move by 56% to 29%. On further

U.S. bombings of Hanoi, even if the peace terms were violated, with their 50% to 38% opposition young people turned the national balance in 1973 into a narrow 44% to 40% opposed plurality. On a key philosophic issue of whether income in the U.S. should be dependent "only on skill and merit" or partly on "what it costs to live decently," the young again led the way by opting by 63% to 31% on some form of guaranteed floor for decent living, resulting in a 54% to 38% majority for their point of view. Nor were the young turning out to be isolationists. On the use of U.S. troops to defend England in case of attack, by 56% to 32% the under 30 generation would send troops, thus carrying the day nationally by 52% to 35%, even though the 50 and over group favored full military support of our most traditional ally by no more than 45% to 43%. Young people were considerably less restrictionist in their foreign trade policy views than the older generation. On eliminating the Office of Economic Opportunity, although the 30 and over group favored doing away with it by 46% to 42%, the young outnumbered them by opposing such a move by 50% to 38%. On a choice between a "stricter crackdown on permissiveness" or "building greater safeguards for the privacy of the individual," the young again led the way by opting for more privacy by a 71% to 20% margin, much higher than the national average of 56% to 34% who agreed with them. In June 1973, people over 30 were opposed, by 43% to 42%, to "President Nixon resigning if it is proven he ordered the cover-up of White House involvement in Watergate." But young people under 30 favored a Nixon resignation by 54% to 35%, thus creating a national plurality of 46% to 40% who favored resignation.

The major impact of young people was being felt with increasing weight in the areas of their greatest social concerns: on the race issue, on environmental controls and the quality of life, and on the responsible use of U.S. power around the world. But their causes to a large measure were still viewed with horror and dismay for daring to look, speak, act, and think differently in more radical ways than their elders ever did. As they approached adulthood, young people were still vastly unpopular in America and the prize of youth was not sought after as it had been in the brief Kennedy era. But out of the welter of confrontation and the crucible of agonized dissent, the long marches and the bitterness of the 1968–70 period, change in public opinion was measurably taking place, and a major impetus for it could be directly traced to the persistence of youth. In the rhetoric of their black predecessors of a decade before, it looked very much as though the young would "overcome."

XIII

BLACKS
A Time of
Benign Neglect

The main trouble with the racial problem in the United States is that most blacks and most whites as groups don't like each other. Both are prone to make generalizations about the other, as races not as people. Yet, at the very same time, both blacks and whites know that the laws of the land made it indelibly clear in the 1960s that it was illegal and wrong to discriminate against blacks in jobs, housing, voting, education, and in the use of public accommodations. Congress wrote the laws, the president signed them, the U.S. Supreme Court upheld them and even insisted they be lived up to. Beyond the law, most knew it was morally indefensible to treat blacks or other racial minorities in an inferior way to whites. Their ministers told them, their public media told them, their schools told them.

Yet as the mid-1970s approached, no summer could be contemplated in the urban centers of the North or South without members of the establishment, white or black, asking each other, "Do you think the blacks will blow up this summer or not?" In the spring of 1972, Alabama's George Wallace won the Michigan Democratic primary, almost exclusively because he whipped up the white working districts with tirades against "forced busing of white children to black ghetto schools"—a "message" was what he called it. Unquestionably, of all the changes being wrought in America in the latter half of the twentieth century, the efforts to integrate the races, to achieve equality for colored minorities were the most agonizing for both whites and blacks.

Ironically, the issue among most of the country was not in doubt. Majorities of both races expected integration to take place. The nation's schools were far from desegregated, yet around Christmas 1972, 88% [1] of all blacks and 71% of all whites said "one of my fondest hopes is that the public schools all over the country be desegregated." When asked if they thought desegregation in education would take place "in their lifetime," by 58% to 29% a majority of blacks and by 55% to 33% a majority of whites said they thought it would. As rough as the struggle has been to achieve integration in the schools, the problem of making desegregation in housing a reality was even tougher. The growing pattern of urban America was a central city filling up with blacks with a ring of almost lily-white suburbs around the outside. Yet in late 1972, the same electorate which gave Richard Nixon a landslide win could say by 71% to 22% that "one of my fondest hopes is that housing be desegregated in America." A nearly unanimous 91% of the blacks and 68% of the whites said they felt that way. When asked if racially integrated housing would take place "in their lifetime," by 53% to 31% a majority of blacks thought they would live to see it and, by 51% to 36%, a majority of whites had the same expectation.

However, if a majority of both blacks and whites was in agreement about the inevitability of racial integration in America, each race reached its conclusion by quite different reasoning. By the 1970s blacks had reached the point of possessing pitifully little faith in the white establishment. A massive 72% [2] had said that under Kennedy and Johnson they felt they "depended on the federal government a great deal for black prog-

ress." Under Nixon, no more than 3% of all blacks were prepared to stake their lot on what the federal government would
do for them. Instead, the prevailing view among blacks was that
they would achieve desegregation of education and housing,
better jobs, and, hopefully, equality by extracting their own progress out of the hide of the dominant white society. Persuading,
pleading, begging, asking were all words that had ceased to be
common currency among many blacks. As a black college student at Greensboro's A&T College put it for many blacks,
"We're entitled to it under the law and it's right, so we don't
need to ask for it. We'll push and we'll grab and we'll work and
one day, not later but sooner, we're going to get it, all of it.
Whitey better know that."

The depths of black suspicion and hostility toward whites
emerged in an in-depth and comprehensive Harris Survey of 1,-
191 black households nationwide in mid-1971, with all the interviewing conducted by black interviewers. A massive 81% to
11% majority of all blacks believed that "whites feel that blacks
are inferior." This is an extremely touchy point, for one of the
real struggles within black people, especially black men, has
been to develop a sense of self-confidence to assume any challenge in holding a job, doing well in school, or in running a
family or holding it together. By 48% to 41% nationally most
blacks feel that "white society has treated blacks so badly that it
is hard for black men to have any real authority, even in their
own homes." Among those on welfare, this feeling of insecurity
existed by a 56% to 33% margin. Tied closely to this worry of
not being able to get one's head above water to perform in society is the view of 65% that "with some black families, in order
to get on welfare, the man in the family has to disappear." The
cruel end result is the conviction that "because white society has
tried to cut down black men, the burden of holding the family
together has fallen on the shoulders of black women," agreed to
by a 69% to 18% majority among all blacks. The boiling point
for blacks on the charge that they are "inferior" had been dan-
gerously lowered in recent years. It was widely viewed as a
challenge to the basic manhood of black males.

By 52% to 28%, blacks also felt that "white people need to
have somebody like blacks to lord it over." Coupled with this

was the belief among blacks that "whites have a mean and self-ish streak in them," a view held by a 68% to 18% margin nationwide. Out of this obviously deep suspicion and even hostility emerged the central conviction that "whites give blacks a break only when forced to," a proposition agreed to by an overwhelming 79% to 13% black majority. At the same time, there was a remarkable strain of commitment among most blacks to a course of nonviolence, much in line with the preachings of the martyred Martin Luther King. By 75% to 6% blacks professed to favor nonviolence over violence.

The depth of black hostility toward whites could be seen in the following table from 1970 and 1971 Harris Surveys among national cross-sections of blacks:

Black Stereotypes of Whites

	1 9 7 1			1 9 7 0		
	AGREE	DIS-AGREE	NOT SURE	AGREE	DIS-AGREE	NOT SURE
	%	%	%	%	%	%
Whites feel that blacks are inferior	81	11	8	81	11	8
Whites give blacks a break only when forced to	79	13	8	77	15	8
White men secretly want black women	76	7	17	74	7	17
Whites are really sorry slavery for blacks was abolished	70	14	6	63	18	19
Whites have a mean and selfish streak in them	68	18	14	65	20	15
Whites are physically weaker than blacks	65	15	20	55	21	24
Whites are scared that blacks are better people than they are	62	23	15	66	21	13
Whites are less honest than blacks	58	19	23	50	23	27
White people need to have somebody like blacks to lord it over	52	28	20	49	31	20
Whites are more apt to catch diseases	49	18	33	44	21	35

Fundamentally, by the 1970s, most blacks had reached the point where they felt nearly all major parts of the establishment touching their lives "really didn't care" about blacks achieving full equality. The roster of "don't care" institutions was long: local real estate companies ("don't care" by 59% to 14%); white churches ("don't care" by 60% to 16%); small local companies (by 57% to 17%); the Nixon Administration (by 60% to 20%); state government (by 57% to 20%); local police (by 63% to 21%); large corporations (by 50% to 22%); local government (by 57% to 23%); newspapers (by 50% to 27%); and the U.S. Congress (by 42% to 30%). Only the U.S. Supreme Court (thought to "care" by 39% to 35%) and television (thought to "care" by 47% to 39%) seemed to have credibility among blacks.

The point seemed clear: Blacks thought they would achieve desegregation in housing and education and their other objectives not so much out of white largesse, but by pressing and pushing for gains to be won from the white power structure. They thought the leadership to do the job would come from black elected officials, such as congressmen, U.S. senators, judges, and mayors.

The important point is that, even though blacks had "confidence" that equality *would* be granted to them, none saw this coming easily, without a struggle every inch of the way. The measure of their self-confidence could be found in the majority who in late 1972 thought both education and housing would be desegregated "in their own lifetimes."

Among whites, the problem was quite different. A substantial 89% [3] nationwide said as 1973 dawned that they earnestly wanted to see "equality for blacks." No more than 6% remained die-hards, at least willing to acknowledge out loud that they thought blacks were not entitled to be equal. By 52% to 37%, a majority of whites believed that blacks indeed would achieve "equality," and not too far off in the future. Among most whites there was a sense of inevitability about it. Well over 3 in every 4 whites had long felt discrimination against blacks was "morally wrong," that "after three hundred years of mistreatment," black people in a democracy such as ours deserved no less than full equality.

At the same time, by 57% to 35%, a majority of whites

thought "blacks were asking for more than they were ready for." And 52% added that "blacks were trying to move too fast in their push for equality." Although this number who believed blacks were ahead of their time and trying to demand more than they should had declined substantially from the 70% of all whites who felt that way in 1966, nonetheless, it still meant that at least half the whites were saying "yes—but" to black demands for equality. Whites could agree in principle but not in reality. They wanted to see blacks achieve equality but they didn't want particularly to give it personally.

Part of the white rationale in claiming blacks were "not ready" was rooted in the feeling that, if offered equality, blacks couldn't take full advantage of it. This white sense of black inadequacy came out in a number of different ways. No more than 22% of all whites claimed in the 1970s that "most blacks were inferior to whites," down from 31% who had felt that way in 1963 when the civil rights movement was marching peacefully on Washington. A somewhat higher 37% viewed blacks as having "less native intelligence," not appreciably lower than the 39% who said the same nearly a decade earlier. A still higher 39% of all whites cast doubt on black willingness to really take advantage of an opportunity for equality when they expressed the view that "blacks want to live off the hand-out," again down no more than 2 points from what it was in 1963. In the same vein, a much more substantial 52% of all whites felt that "most blacks were less ambitious than most whites," implying that it was useless to offer blacks equality since they didn't have the get-up-and-go to take advantage of it. So the white noose of rationalization was closed: Blacks were asking for more than they were ready, because blacks themselves really didn't have the native capacity or the will to deliver if offered equality.

Nonetheless, most whites were resigned to the fact that black equality in America was inevitable. The moral code dictated that it had to be that way, the laws now all said that was the way it had to go, and to fight it might delay it, but would not alter the ultimate course that history seemed bent on taking.

The racial conflict in America in the 1970s had fuel heaped on the already blazing fire by a whole host of other emotional stereotypes each race held of the other, none of which could possibly help convert the country into an embodiment of the brotherhood of man. For example, among whites, 26% held the view that "most blacks care less for their families," down only slightly in nearly a decade from 31% who felt that way in 1963. Closely tied to this was the more sizable 35% of whites who also felt "blacks keep untidy homes," a notion that had declined from the 46% who felt that way in 1963. In addition, 40% of all whites felt "most blacks have lower morals than whites," again down from 55% who said that nearly ten years before. All of those stereotypes cut to the quick, for they hit the already sensitive black nerves about family instability and the view in the black community that the white power structure was out to emasculate black men. Two other white stereotypes were pure white mythology: "Most blacks laugh a lot," was still believed by 48% of all whites; though down from 68% who believed it in 1963; it showed how long the memory of Stepin Fetchit could linger on; and "most blacks smell different," was also believed by 48% of all whites, down from 60%. In a country where over 8 in 10 whites now used underarm deodorants, it was a wonder that more whites could not imagine that blacks had responded no less to the TV commercials that promised to ban undesirable odors.

These white prejudices against blacks are illustrated in the following table drawn from surveys of national cross-sections of white opinion. On most items, white stereotypes of blacks have diminished, although they are still substantial:

White Stereotypes of Blacks

Whites Who Agree That:	1971 %	1963 %
Blacks are less ambitious than whites	52	66
Blacks laugh a lot	48	68
Blacks smell different	48	60
Blacks have lower morals than whites	40	55
Blacks want to live off the hand-out	39	41
Blacks have less native intelligence	37	39
Blacks keep untidy homes	35	46

Whites Who Agree That:	1971 %	1963 %
Blacks breed crime	27	35
Blacks care less for their families	26	31
Blacks are inferior to whites	22	31

But blacks were not without their own myopia on the subjects of whites. By 49% to 18%, most blacks believed that "most whites are more apt to catch disease." For many years apparently blacks had been raised to think that whites were not only more susceptible to disease, but that close contact with whites could mean being in greater danger of catching a communicable disease. By a substantial majority of 58% to 19% blacks felt that "most whites are less honest than blacks." This belief undoubtedly stemmed from long-standing black experience of being charged more for food in white grocery stores, paying higher interest rates on loans, higher premiums on life insurance, and generally paying more in many other areas of their dealings with whites. By 62% to 23%, most blacks also held the view that "most whites are scared that blacks are better people than they are." This belief, of course, is a black rationalization for why whites seem so reluctant to yield to the equality demands put upon them by the law and black pressures alike. It ties in closely with the 65% to 15% majority among blacks that "most whites are physically weaker than blacks." Back in the early part of 1963, when our firm first broke ground in major studies on the race issue for *Newsweek,* a majority of black men had expressed the view that "in a showdown, even though outnumbered 10 to 1, blacks could take whites." Blacks have always had a disproportionately high share of athletes in most major sports in America, since the color line was broken, and black pride in black heavyweight boxing champions usually runs very high. Two other stereotypes of whites showed the depth of black bitterness toward whites. By 70% to 14%, most blacks feel that "most whites are really sorry slavery for blacks was abolished." The other was that "most white men secretly want black women," believed by a 76% to 7% black majority, a throwback to the slavery days when white plantation owners were widely believed to have had black mistresses. The last two beliefs, obviously widespread in the black community, certainly could not contribute to amicable relations between the races.

The blacks wanted "equality now" in 1973 every bit as much as they did when they optimistically carried banners with identical slogans in 1963, ten years past. Whites tended to say that black were not ready for "equality now," and wished the pressures for integration would go away. But the blacks in America were not going away and, most important, even whites themselves knew down deep that blacks would persistently be around, pushing to win equality.

One reason the blacks would not go away was that there were twenty-four million if them, over 11% of the population. And, despite claims that their lot had improved measurably, there was still much misery in the way they were faring in America. When asked about major sources of "a great deal of discouragement" over the past several years, 51% of all blacks singled out "white stubbornness in giving blacks equality." An even higher 53% cited "lack of real change in the way blacks live."

As blacks entered the decade of the 1970s, the roll call of their miseries was a depressing litany: 42% said someone in their family or a close friend was a high school dropout (10.5 million blacks reported it in their own families); an unwed mother in the family was reported by 35% (8.7 million); a family in which the father had left home was a condition admitted to in 32% of the families (8 million); 38% reported cockroaches in their homes (9.5 million); 26% said there were too many people living together in their residence (6.5 million); 29% reported having rats in their homes or apartments (7.2 million); 32% reported faulty plumbing where they lived (8 million); 25% had holes in the ceilings of the rooms they lived in (6.2 million); 15% said that they had members of their family who did not get enough to eat (3.9 million); 19% had teenagers in the home who often stayed out all night (4.7 million); and 11% reported a teenager in the family who was on hard drugs (2.8 million). Being black in America as the latter third of the twentieth century began was to put up with miseries in living conditions that stood in stark contrast to the brimming affluence of most of white society. Yet, despite their state of existence, by a massive 90% to 5%, blacks also said that, "in spite of all our problems, there is still a great deal of warmth and love in most black families."

In fact, an incredible mark of every Harris Survey conducted among blacks since 1963 is the amount of optimism and "progress" reported by blacks themselves. In 1971, for example, 52% of all blacks reported progress for blacks compared with five years before was "better." When asked for specific illustrations of progress, 65% saw improvement in education for black children, 59% mentioned better job opportunities, and 52% reported better chances "to live where you want to." As a 51-year-old black woman who worked on piecework in the Watts area of Los Angeles put it, "When you started with nothing, anything you get has to be looked on as something better. But that don't mean it's so good, either."

Blacks felt some progress had been made, but most also believed they had a long way to go to achieve even a modicum of "full equality to whites." By 47% to 44%, a plurality thought "education for white children was better than that for blacks." On "living where you want to live," by 63% to 31%, a majority thought whites had much the better of it. On "job opportunities," a 70% to 25% majority thought whites had much the better of it.

A growing area of felt inequality could be found among blacks in the realm of crime and the administration of justice. Consistently in every survey we have conducted on the subject, 68% of blacks worried more about their own safety on the streets compared with 50% of all whites; and blacks reported a higher incidence of crime in their neighborhoods. If ever any group in society ought to look to the police for protection, the blacks should lead all others. But this simply has not been the case. By 67% to 18%, a sizable majority of blacks complained in the early 1970s, "Too many policemen here are more interested in cracking the heads of blacks than in stopping crime." Their cynicism about the police was heightened by the charge on the part of 76% that "many policemen around here are just as dishonest as the numbers runners and petty thieves." Thus, many blacks could defend their behavior in the riots of the 1960s by saying, "When people do some looting in a riot, they are just releasing some of the tension and bitterness built up through years of discrimination," a view held by a 49% to 37% plurality. This experience over a lifetime of observing the white-dominated system of justice at work had led to nearly a total breakdown in confidence in law enforcement on the part of blacks. When asked if law enforcement were being applied equally for blacks and for whites," by 56% to 19%, a majority said it was not by "courts around here"; by 60% to 21%, that it was not by "local police"; and, by 56% to 20%, that it was not by "the Justice Department under the Nixon Administration." An identical question about the FBI produced a 39% to 39% stand-off on its "evenhanded enforcement of the law," sharply down from an affirmative 50% to 27% only the year before. The U.S. Supreme Court alone was still seen as a sanctuary for justice for blacks by 52% to 26%; but confidence in the high court had dropped a full 10 points among blacks in one year. Much of the despondence of blacks on the subject of law enforcement could be traced to the profound grief most still felt over the assassinations of Martin Luther King and John and Robert Kennedy, believed by better than 3 in every 4 blacks to have been "deeply discouraging experiences." As a black minister in the Hough district of Cleveland put it, "the best were wiped out and just for standing for the best."

This backdrop of sad and tragic violence and the lack of any real confidence that white society can be any longer counted on to deliver on the promises of "full equality" led the vast majority of blacks to take a more militant attitude in the 1970s. There could be little doubt about where violence could erupt on some hot summer evening in the seventies nor from where the spark to ignite could emanate.

Scarcely more than 1 in 5 blacks still felt that "until blacks give up violence altogether and rely on peaceful means of pressing their demands, they will not achieve real equality." A much larger 6 in 10 went along with an alternative course: "Blacks should continue to push peacefully for equality, using violence only when nothing else works." This did not mean that blacks had finally come to advocate a path of violence. But neither did it mean they would rule it out. A sizable majority was saying that if it came down to a choice between not surviving as a last resort or using violence, they would prefer to go out fighting. No more than 11% of all blacks went along with the extreme proposition that "only revolution and readiness to use violence will ever get blacks real equality." This 1 in 9, of course, constituted the radical core of the black community in America. The number who had been radicalized among black teen-agers was a much higher 19%; among those aged 21 to 29 the number stood at 17%. It was perfectly apparent that in the large metropolitan ghettoes of the North, where unemployment among young blacks ran highest, radicalism also ran highest. With the pending cutbacks in federal money for summer jobs, major flare-ups of violence in the black inner cities, a brutal and tragic phenomenon of the 1960s, could strike again in the 1970s.

In their sharply diminished expectations from white society, blacks were turning increasingly to depend on a growing black pride to fortify their push for equality. But blacks were selective about what indeed did enhance pride in being black and what did not. For example, "wearing African clothes" was rejected as an important and permanent sign of black identity by 61% to 31%. "The setting up of black militant organizations" ended in a standoff of 44% to 43%, just on the side of "an important sign," although to a clear majority of 57% of all black teen-agers, militant groups had become a permanent and vital part of the scene. "Wearing Afro haircuts" did slightly better, believed by a 45% to 40% margin to be a lasting mark of black identity. They were particularly important to urban blacks and to those in professional and managerial positions, a kind of notice to white employers they should not be taken as Uncle Toms because they now had joined "the management team" and had found a place in affluent society. "Interest in Swahili and African culture" was viewed as permanently important by 46% to 41%, again scoring high with a majority of the most privileged blacks in the professions and ranks of business executives. But the area believed to have the most lasting effect on perpetuating black pride was "black study programs in high schools and colleges," seen as

highly important by 84% of all blacks. The reasoning was direct
and to the point. Blacks had a cultural history which generations of blacks had never known about. By learning about a
black legacy from the past, blacks could both find out about
their roots and take some pride in their own self-identity. Education in the 1970s had become a more sacred cow for blacks
than even for whites, who for many generations had seen a college education as the key to material success and status. Now
blacks saw much the same reward for their young; but they also
saw education as a way to teach black culture, to instill a sense
that "black was beautiful," and with it establish a self-identity
so long missing in the aftermath of freedom from bondage a century before. The deep interest in "being black and liking it"
could well prove to be the psychological foundation upon which
blacks could fight the widely believed notion that whites
thought "blacks were inferior to whites."

In 1970 a private memorandum from Daniel Patrick Moynihan, at that time chief domestic aide to President Nixon, surfaced and caused much controversy over his use of the words,
"benign neglect." [4] The thrust of Moynihan's thesis was that, if
both blacks and whites cooled it, let the rhetoric de-escalate,
enough assistance to blacks was in the government and private
sector pipeline to achieve quiet but significant progress. Literally, "benign neglect" meant putting new steps of progress for
blacks on the back burner but not to the point where the situation for blacks became "malignant neglect," where black society
would actually deteriorate and ultimately blow up again. The
Moynihan thesis and other later expositions such as one by Ben
Wattenberg put forth in 1973 said to blacks in effect: You have
to admit you have made progress, you never had it so good, so
don't knock a good thing. Implicit in their reasoning was that
white society had found the way to improve the lot of blacks,
and, if blacks were only patient, one day they would achieve
their promised land of full equality. The trouble was that blacks
were convinced not that the white establishment would "be-
nignly" work for their betterment, but instead that only their
own efforts to *make* white society yield progress would produce
results.

Indeed, by 1973, blacks did begin to report declines in discrimination against them in many areas, compared to their lot in 1969. The number who felt discriminated against in "getting hotel and motel accommodations" had dropped 24 points from 68% to 44% [5] in four years; perceived discrimination in "providing a quality education for black children" fell 19 points from 72% to 53%; discrimination in "obtaining skilled labor jobs" was believed to have declined from 83% to 66%; discrimination in "getting white collar jobs" was seen by blacks as falling off from 82% to 68%; discrimination "in getting into labor unions was perceived as dropping from 64% to 47%; and discrimination in "getting decent housing" was believed to have fallen from 83% to 66%. Out of twelve areas of possible discrimination tested, blacks themselves were less inclined on the average to feel discriminated against by a full 15 percentage points compared to the way they felt in 1969. Overall, on all twelve areas, 57% of the blacks felt discriminated against in 1973, compared with 72% who felt that way in 1969. At the same time, among whites there was a gnawing awareness of discrimination against blacks in housing, in obtaining skilled labor and white collar jobs, in the way they were treated by the police, in the quality of public school education their children received, in the prices they paid in grocery stores, and in the way they were treated as human beings. In the same twelve areas, whites by 1973 believed blacks were discriminated against on an average of 32%, up from 30% in 1969. While a 2-point greater perception of antiblack discrimination was not sizable, and while the 32% white figure paled before the 57% black level of believed discrimination, nonetheless the *gap* between black and white perception of discrimination against blacks had declined from 42 to 25 percentage points in four years. One might assume that if ever whites and blacks agreed on the amount of discrimination that existed against blacks, then that discrimination might be ended more quickly.

These results on the sharp decline in the gap between white and black perception of antiblack discrimination were used by some to prove indeed that a policy of "benign neglect" was paying off. Another argument was that the black vote for Nixon in

1972 jumped to 19% up sharply from 6% in the 1968 presidential election, thereby proving that blacks were not so unhappy with the way things were going. The argument was also made that after blacks had seen the massive white reaction in both North and South in 1972 to the federal court orders to bus children to schools to achieve racial balance, surely blacks would receive the message that further efforts to push too hard for "equality now" would badly backfire and damage their hopes for progress.

The school busing issue first needed to be put into proper focus. When asked directly if they "favored or opposed busing school children to achieve racial balance," 82% of all whites answered resoundingly that they were opposed. The reasons for the opposition were twofold: (1) White parents were worried that their children would be shipped considerable distances and with a loss of time to inner city areas where their physical safety might be in jeopardy; (2) whites were also worried their children would end up going to inferior black schools. And no more than 50% of blacks favored busing to achieve desegregation. They, in turn, worried about the safety of their children as a token minority in hitherto all white schools. Governor George Wallace exploited these fears expertly in Maryland, Indiana, Michigan, and other states in the 1972 Democratic primaries.

The fears over school busing in 1972 were real. But they did not reveal two other sides of the question and two significant consequences of the school busing fracas. When the very same cross-section that could yield 76% to 18% opposition to school busing was also asked if they "would be willing or unwilling to have children of a different race bused to school into your neighborhood to achieve racial balance," a 47% to 46% plurality expressing "willingness to bus" resulted. And when the same people were asked if they favored or opposed desegregating the public schools" an even higher 55% to 35% majority in favor resulted. How could the same people wobble so widely all over the lot on essentially the same subject? The answer is that clearly the American people in the 1970s did not like the busing route as the way to solve the problem of desegregating schools. Yet, when put in its least obnoxious terms, shipping children of other races to *your* school, busing remained objectionable to less than a majority. And when the principle of desegregation of public schools as a national objective was put to the test, a clear majority opted for it. Was this last result showing majority support for desegregation mere lip service, something to be adhered to as a generality but certainly not to be abided by when it came to *your* child being bused to achieve racial balance? If that were so, then was the finding at the end of 1972 that an even higher 71% of all whites actually *hoped* school desegregation would take place an even greater mark of hypocritical piety? The one result that could not be challenged on these grounds was the 55% to 33% majority among whites in late 1972 who said they actually thought the public schools *would* be desegregated in their lifetimes. That was not likely to be lip service. That was more likely to be reality, albeit one that would be tomorrow if not today. The net conclusion that this public opinion analyst has reached is that this matter of school desegregation is enormously aggravating to most whites, not only because they find it upsets much of their all-white living patterns, but also because it fills most whites with pangs of massive guilt feelings. They can't stand the integration, but they also can't stand their guilt.

The two consequences of the 1972 outburst against the school busing edict that have been largely ignored were that by early 1973, a year later, whites were taking more cognizance of discrimination against black children in education (up from 23% to 29%). There were signs that having vented their concerns against busing in 1972, whites were feeling their guilt and were making attempts to be more charitable in their racial views in 1973. The other consequence was that federal court orders to desegregate were still the law of the land, and in most communities where they were enforced somehow whites and blacks were abiding by the law; desegregation, slowly and agonizingly, was taking place in many schools. But these consequences were far from the result of "benign neglect." Given President Nixon's own predilection to fan the flames of antibusing sentiment repeatedly in 1972 in hardly a benign way, it seemed patently apparent by 1973 that the two forces which had moved school desegregation along toward at least some progress had been the dogged determination of blacks not to yield on their demands for equality and the repeated determination of the federal courts to stick by their basic decisions. It is significant to note that the only law enforcement body a majority of blacks still had confidence in was the U.S. Supreme Court.

The remaining claim that "benign neglect" was paying off was the increase of the black vote for Nixon by 13 percentage points between 1968 and 1972. The answer to this is that the overall Nixon vote among whites increased by an estimated 17 points between the two elections, more than the movement among blacks. George McGovern was no hero among blacks any more than he was among whites. Blacks never felt he connected with them or their needs in the election. Their final vote of 71% to 19% Democratic for president was far more a measure of their distrust of Nixon and the Republicans than an outpouring of affection for McGovern. In 1972, in presidential politics, blacks were alone and swimming against the tide. But in their vote for Congress, blacks played as key a role in returning the House to Democratic rule as did the young. Nationwide, whites voted an estimated 51% to 49% Republican for Congress, but blacks voted an estimated 88% to 12% Democratic, thus enabling the Democrats to win a clear margin nationwide.

Another sign that blacks had not grown used to "benign neglect" and were not in a state of euphoria about their future prospects could be found in late 1972 results that showed 100% of all blacks wanted to see "full equality for blacks" attained. Yet by 49% to 37%,[6] a plurality of blacks also said they did not expect to see this goal attained "in their lifetime." A majority of blacks did expect desegregation of schools and of housing to take place, but not "full equality." The reason could be found in still another question that asked about "a decline in prejudice," a desired goal on the part of 100% of blacks and 95% of all whites. Neither whites nor blacks expected this to happen. But blacks were more skeptical than whites that prejudice would decline in their lifetimes. Therefore, most blacks concluded, they could only achieve progress by standing their ground and pushing steadily for further gains, not by begging but by demanding, by electing, by working harder to mobilize more power and more support, and by extracting more concessions from the white establishment. They had few illusions that their struggle ahead would be easier than it had been over the previous ten years after the euphoric beginnings in 1963. To their by now traditional hymn "We Shall Overcome," they had added, "We shall not be overcome" by "benign neglect," by the "messages" of George Wallace, nor by those who told them they "never had it so good." As George Foreman, by 1973 the new heavyweight champion of the world, told this writer in 1969, when we both were testifying at a House Job Corps hearing, "I don't know the fancy words. I couldn't afford to skip the 1968 Olympics like some other blacks who had a college education. But I know if you're black, you have to work harder, hope harder, and not let the Man put you off. I'm going to make it as heavyweight champ and we're going to make it. But like I can only depend on my fists and my strength, we've got to depend on what we do ourselves for ourselves." Self-pride, self-confidence, and rugged determination probably were going to make it for blacks in America. Even a majority of whites had become anguished believers.

XIV

POLITICS
Choosing Leaders in a Time of Real Change

After Lyndon Johnson won election in 1964 by a record 61% of the vote, there were dire predictions that the Republican party was finished. Yet, only eight years later Richard Nixon, a Republican, thought to be politically extinct in 1963, won re-election with 60.7% of the vote, failing by a whisker to break Johnson's record.

Just after the voting in November 1972, on the surface, at least, a pleased as punch President Nixon seemed to have it all figured out. He had talked about creating "a new majority" in the 1972 campaign and then he went out and did it. What some might have supposed was mere campaign rhetoric in talk about a new political era, apparently the president took seriously. An analogous case was made by some White House political theorists that in 1964 Johnson had received a massive mandate and had rammed through Congress in 1965 and 1966 more programs of social reform than the country had seen since the New Deal days of the 1930s. Johnson not only had felt such social welfare extension was right, but also that this was precisely what the voters had in mind when they elected him over Barry Goldwater. Goldwater was a right-wing conservative and Johnson a liberal. The liberal had won in a landslide and acted accordingly.

Thus, in 1973, the case could be made that 1972 saw another classic confrontation between a left-wing liberal, George McGovern, and a conservative, Richard Nixon. The country, this reasoning went, had swung much more conservative in the eight years since 1964 and it was only fitting and proper now that things be "balanced up," as Justice Powell had said in 1971 and Spiro Agnew seemed to say at every GOP banquet in 1973. Therefore, it was wholly proper to interpret the Nixon mandate in 1972 as a desire to swing to the right on domestic affairs in the United States. Early in his second term, Nixon called for massive budget trimming; the prime targets were the Great Society social programs of Johnson, which were now called a "total failure" by White House spokesmen. The conservative had won in a landslide and was acting accordingly.

A look below the surface of American politics would produce quite a different set of facts. Despite the instability of the electorate in veering from 61% Democratic to 61% Republican in eight years, the vote for Congress, also a national mandate, had remained remarkably stable: in 1964, the Democrats won by 57% to 43%, up only 2 points from the 55% to 45% margin they had in 1960. In 1972, the Democrats also won by a comparable 54% to 46%. If LBJ had had such a massive mandate for social reform in 1964, then why didn't the House vote go to over 60% to 40% Democratic, as it had in 1934, when indeed there was demand for just such reform? And if Nixon had received such a massive conservative mandate in 1972, then why hadn't the House vote gone Republican, as it had when the country did go more conservative at the height of the Cold War in 1950? Such pat and easy ideological mandate readings had been wrong in 1964 and again in 1972. In 1964, the Harris Survey showed that 36% of all voters viewed themselves as conservative, 44% as middle of the road, and 20% as liberals. By 1972, 37% classified themselves as conservative, 37% as middle of the road, and 24% as liberals. The middle was slipping away some and the extremes had gained marginally. A much more significant political truth was that such ideological imputations to the American people are largely figments of the thinking of ideologues. We have always been a highly pragmatic, notably un-ideological people and indeed still were as we approached the last quarter of the twentieth century.

Part of the reason both Johnson and Nixon were prone to read their mandates as containing deeper messages rather than massive outpourings of personal adulation was that both were keenly aware of their own lack of charismatic appeal. In private, in 1968, LBJ would readily admit that he had never found the way to "whip up the crowds as those Kennedys could." In 1971, Richard Nixon was skeptical in private just how important personality really was for him to be able to govern the country well. On the eve of his greatest victory in 1964, by 52% to 29% a majority of the voters viewed Johnson as a "wheeler-dealer politician," compared to a 61% to 18% majority who thought Barry Goldwater was a "nice guy." Early in 1972, by 46% to 43%, most Americans felt Nixon was "lacking in personal color and warmth," while by 46% to 26% most thought George McGovern had a "sincere, appealing personality." Obviously, neither Johnson nor Nixon won their landslide victories on personality.

If neither ideology nor personal appeal lie in back of the remarkable swing in presidential elections in the last decade, what then were the cutting edges? The answer lies in understanding the phenomena at work politically in this country in the 1960s and 1970s and their implications both for the system and for the future.

Back in those now distant days of the 1964 election between Johnson and Goldwater, the facts showed that foreign policy rather than domestic issues actually dominated the concerns of the electorate. A substantial 60% late in the campaign in October said the most important issues for the next president to handle were international: foreign aid, Cuba, the Cold War with

Russia, and Vietnam. It may seem ironic in retrospect, but the biggest areas of Johnson superiority to Goldwater could be found in his "ability to keep the U.S. out of war" (70% to 30%), to "handle a sudden world crisis" (68% to 32%), to "work for peace in the world" (68% to 32%), to "give leadership to the free world" (66% to 34%), and to "handle Khrushchev" (63% to 37%). Goldwater had frightened the voters by his talk about using atomic weapons to defoliate the jungles of Vietnam. The most effective Johnson TV commercial that fall, banned after one showing, simply showed a little girl picking petals of a flower to a countdown in the background, and when it reached zero, an atom bomb mushroom cloud went up behind her. A better than 2 to 1 majority of the voters felt Goldwater "would act before thinking things through." The issue that shadowed the 1964 campaign was which candidate the voters trusted to have his finger on the button that could set off the bomb.

During the 1964 campaign in October the back-to-back news that Chairman Khrushchev had been ousted in Russia and that China had exploded the nuclear bomb made people even more aware of foreign policy. Overnight, the number of people who wanted to "negotiate with Russia and China" rather than "to get tougher" went up from 32% to 46%. Given the world developments, the electorate said it preferred Johnson to handle relations with the Communist world by 2 to 1. LBJ's highest personal rating was in "working for peace," which stood at 68% positive. In 1964, peace became the dominant issue, and, as the man whom people trusted on foreign policy, Lyndon Johnson won going away on election day by 61% to 39%. Peace and a desire not to have three presidents in a year basically determined the outcome.

Despite growing American absorption in the war in Vietnam, the desire on the part of the public for a thaw in the Cold War was growing. Although admission of China to the UN was opposed in 1965 by 61% to 21%, this was a softening from the 73% to 10% [1] margin of opposition just a year earlier. A year later, the public would oppose admission for China by only 51% to 30%. Diplomatic recognition of China was opposed by 44% to 35%; but when asked if we should recognize China if she were admitted by the UN, public opinion reversed itself to favor recognition by 45% to 39%. The major, impelling reason for the softening of traditional hard-line views toward China could be found in the 49% to 35% plurality who wanted to see the U.S. and China negotiate a nuclear test-ban treaty. As for Russia, with the change in heads of state, 40% of the public now thought the Soviets were more disposed "to want peace." A lop-sided 74% to 17% favored "exchanging cultural missions" with Russia, 70% to 21% supported "student exchanges," 56% to 34% were for "selling U.S. wheat and other goods" to the Soviets, 52% to 39% favored "selling U.S. autos" to Russia. Three other areas of possible cooperation were ruled out: by 72% to 20%, the public opposed "selling surplus jets for commercial aviation use" to the Russians; by 61% to 29%, a majority opposed "the sale of machine tools and computers"; and by 51% to 37%, the public opposed "exchanging engineers, physicists, and scientists" with the Soviet Union. A narrow plurality of 45% to 41% also opposed joint cooperation "in sending a man to the moon." However, a plurality of 44% to 32% favored trade with Iron Curtain countries.

A desire for a thaw in the Cold War had started in the minds of the American people. This trend of public opinion was to continue throughout the rest of the decade of the sixties and well into the seventies. By mid-1966, a 43% to 33% [2] plurality favored official U.S. recognition of China, and by 78% to 7% opposed U.S. withdrawal from the UN if China were seated in that body. By 1968, the desire for "an end to wars" had reached the point where 96% said it was "one of their deepest desires," although with Vietnam then a raging reality, 55% thought it "just would not happen in my lifetime." In the 1968 election, of course, Vietnam took over as the major issue and the Nixon 6-point margin on the eve of the election that he would "handle the war better" than Humphrey proved decisive in the end. In addition, in October of that year, Nixon led Humphrey on "working for peace" by a comparable 6-point margin. Certainly the pivotal role of the Vietnam and peace issues in 1968 had been well documented. By 70% to 18%, Nixon was credited with being "widely experienced in foreign affairs," easily his strongest appeal in that election. In 1968, as in 1964, the yearning for peace was a powerful motivator at the polls on election day, and it mostly worked for Nixon, despite the last minute flutterings for a Vietnam truce that died aborning and that might have elected Humphrey. The inescapable fact, however, is that by election time, it was evident both major contenders' fates would be settled by whom the voters trusted most on bringing peace. In his first term, the most urgent part of Richard Nixon's public mandate was that he move the world measurably closer to peace.

In the 1972 election, for the third presidential election in a row, peace was to become the dominant issue again. Early on, George McGovern had staked out a position as the leading Democratic opponent of the war, for which he was praised in the spring by 54% to 21% of the voters for "being against Vietnam before others." Right up until late in the campaign, Vietnam remained the trigger issue that might elect McGovern. In the end, he helped sour voters on his appeal on the issue by a series of bizarre happenings, ranging from sending Pierre Salinger to see the North Vietnamese in Paris, to becoming associated with Ramsey Clark's visit to Hanoi, to Sargent Shriver's claim that peace could have been obtained back in 1969, to his own prediction that Thieu would flee Saigon if he were elected, to his saying he would go to Hanoi to "beg for the release of U.S. prisoners of war," and to his charge that Henry Kissinger's travels to Paris and Saigon were just "publicity stunts," all of which met with substantial public disapproval. With Nixon's rating on "negotiating a final Vietnam settlement" given 58% to 37% negative marks by the voters as late as early October, McGovern could well have had the war working in his behalf as an issue. But, due to his own ineptitude, when the public was asked "which candidate would be more likely to end U.S. involvement in Vietnam quicker," McGovern trailed Nixon by 48% to 35%.[3]

For Nixon, Vietnam was his potential Achilles heel, along with public disenchantment with the trend of rising prices and unemployment at home. He took some of the bite out of the economic issue in August 1971 with his freeze on prices and wages.

On Vietnam, McGovern helped him, although not nearly as much as the North Vietnamese announcement of the tentatively agreed peace terms of October 8 and Kissinger's late October statement that "peace was at hand."

But it was neither Vietnam nor the economy which gave Richard Nixon his landslide victory in 1972. Instead, Nixon's most powerful weapon in the campaign was his ability to convince the American people that he had moved the world closer to peace. His promise of "a generation of peace" may have sounded like political rhetoric, but he had a potent record of specifics to back it up, in the judgment of most Americans. By 1971, the mood of America had reached the point where wide-ranging agreements between the U.S. and the USSR were no longer even controversial. "Joint exploration of outer space," opposed five years earlier, now was favored by 64% to 25%. "Taking joint action if another nation threatens to use nuclear weapons" met with 68% to 15% approval. Agreement "to reduce the number of American and Russian troops in Europe" was favored by an even higher 71% to 17%. "Joint explorations of the oceans" was supported by 71% to 14%. The key issue of arms control, "limiting antimissile (ABM) systems" met with favor by a massive 72% to 14%. "Expanded trade between the two countries" was backed by 76% to 14%. By 56% to 33%, a majority of the public now believed that the "U.S. and Russia can come to long-term agreement." Significantly, the idea of a major thaw in the Cold War appealed to 61% of the young voters and to 65% of the college educated. The issue of peace between the major superpowers was to make a profound impression on the "pro-change" groups in politics: the young, the educated, the high income, suburban dwellers, and independent voters.

The most dramatic evidence of the deep appeal of the peace issue could be found in the May 1971 response to the visit of the U.S. table tennis team to Peking. By 55% to 26%,[4] a majority felt the visit would improve relations between the U.S. and China. A sizable 70% to 14% majority expressed a desire for "friendlier relations" between the two nations. Majorities favored "increased trade in nonstrategic goods," "a lot of travel by U.S. citizens to China and by Chinese citizens to the U.S.," and "more exchange of sports teams between the two countries." A massive 76% to 11% favored "an agreement between the U.S. and China on control of nuclear weapons." The key immediate issues, of course, were admission of China to the UN and diplomatic recognition of China by the U.S. On recognition, by 55% to 20%, a majority favored an exchange of diplomatic missions. A UN seat for Peking was favored by 48% to 27%, a complete reversal from the 73% to 10% opposition in 1964. This was the prevailing mood before any word was known publicly that Kissinger was in Peking working out a presidential visit to the Chinese capital.

Significantly, 61% of suburban voters, 65% of the under 30 group, 66% of independent voters, 68% of the $15,000 and over group, and 70% of the college educated favored recognition. These were the groups where Nixon could have been most vulnerable in 1972 and where he turned the election around on the peace issue. In the same survey which showed these striking shifts in American attitudes toward seeking accord with China, Nixon trailed Senator Edmund Muskie by 48% to 45% among suburban voters, by 54% to 39% among voters under 30, by 48% to 47% among voters $15,000 and over, and by 50% to 42% among independents. He led among the college educated by a narrow 50% to 46%. It was obvious that Nixon was in trouble, as he trailed Muskie by 50% to 46% nationally in a two-way race. Clearly, he had to turn around the "pro-change" groups or be in deep trouble in 1972.

In July of 1971, the president made the electrifying announcement that he would visit Peking. Later that year, he announced an upcoming summit meeting with Chairman Leonid Brehznev of the Soviet Union in Moscow. Coupled with his price-wage freeze of August, these bold foreign policy strokes had moved Nixon from no worse than a 50–50 bet that he would be a one-term president to a heavy favorite to win re-election. In the end, by November 1972, he won the vote of the young by 53% to 47%, suburban residents by 64% to 36%, the college educated by 62% to 38%, the $15,000 and over group by 69% to 31%, and the independents by 67% to 32%. The issue he won their votes on was that of peace.

The singular and overwhelming vote that the peace issue played in President Nixon's 1972 victory can best be seen in the following table of the ratings accorded him on his handling of key issues in mid-October:

Nixon Ratings by Voters
Mid-October 1972 [5]

	POSITIVE %	NEGATIVE %	NOT SURE %
Overall Rating	59	40	1
His trip to China	75	20	5
His handling of relations with Russia	73	22	5
His Russian summit trip	72	22	6
Working for peace in the world	67	31	2
Handling relations with China	66	26	8
Inspiring confidence personally	48	44	8
Handling war in Vietnam	46	52	2
Stand on busing for racial balance	42	45	13
Handling race problems	43	52	5
Helping curb drug abuse	43	49	8
Handling air and water pollution	39	49	12
Negotiating final Vietnam settlement	39	53	8
Helping keep economy healthy	38	57	5
Handling crime, law and order	38	57	5
Keeping unemployment down	34	61	5
Keeping effective controls on wages and prices	33	63	4
Handling taxes and spending	32	63	5
Handling corruption in government	32	55	13
Keeping down cost of living	22	76	2

On every single key issue below the line in the table, ranging from Vietnam to school busing, from curbing drug abuse to environmental control, from handling crime and law and order to keeping effective controls on wages and prices, from handling corruption in government to keeping unemployment down, Richard Nixon, two weeks away from a landslide victory, received negative marks from the American people. Had he been running on the issue of his own personal confidence alone, he would have held no more than a slim 48% to 44% lead. But it was obvious that the Nixon magic lay in his ability to say in nearly every speech and point up in nearly every TV commercial that he had moved the world closer to peace by his dramatic trips to Peking and Moscow. When the people were asked who could "best negotiate with the Russians and Chinese," Nixon swamped McGovern by a 70% to 14% margin. Nixon gained his basic credibility as a candidate on the peace issue, and that was the main reason, by 56% to 26%, most Americans in the fall of 1972 felt that he, rather than McGovern, could best "inspire confidence in the White House." In turn, this was reflected in the massive 61% to 37% victory margin of the president on election day.

The dramatic breakthroughs in Peking and Moscow, along with the miserably frustrating Vietnam experience itself, had gone a long way toward finally severing the hold of straight economic self-interest as the determinant of presidential elections. The Nixon election in 1972 and the Johnson sweep in 1964 were both rooted in dominantly foreign policy contests. Both were powerful testaments to the force the peace issue would play in national politics for some years to come.

It is still popular among politicians and an unfortunately large number of political analysts to claim that voters are little affected by matters beyond the water's edge. They still think that most people vote their pocketbooks and, if they are hurting, they will turn out the "ins" and put in the "outs." But in 1972, they were hurting economically, they did criticize Nixon on his handling of the economy and nearly every other economic issue, and he still won by a massive 24 points. The abject failure of McGovern to convince voters on any issue contributed to the size of the Nixon sweep, but, in the end, all the evidence points to the peace issue as the decisive cutting edge. As President Kennedy had discovered at the Mormon Tabernacle as early as 1963 on the nuclear test-ban issue, peace was a most popular idea; demonstrably by 1972 it had more political potency than any other issue.

In the future, in 1976 and in 1980, the peace issue will continue to be important. If President Nixon proves to be successful in putting an indelible stamp of peace on the Republican party during the rest of his term, he could measurably improve the chances of having a Republican successor in the White House in 1976. By the same token, it would be absolutely essential for any Democratic nominee in 1976 and 1980 to have a proven record and an identification with foreign policy matters. Certainly any vulnerability in the Republican Administration's record on peace would be fair game for Democratic exploitation in a major way.

In supplanting economic concerns as the top issue now determining the outcome of our presidential elections, the peace issue also was likely to spring loose a whole host of other noneconomic issues which would count heavily in the years ahead. The question of environmental control had never really been made an issue in a presidential contest. Given the association of pollution with business operations, and the vulnerability of the Republican party (believed by 59% [6] in 1972 to be "too close to big business"), an aspiring Democratic challenger could make much of the environment issue. Strangely, no candidate for president has made a major issue of consumerism, Ralph Nader's cause, nor embraced Nader as a political ally. Again, however, it was a made-to-order issue for the Democrats, since consumerism was tied closely to anti-big business inclinations. While both pollution and consumerism have economic implications, neither fit in any way the old New Deal formula of promising a direct improvement in people's incomes or pocketbooks. Another prime issue that had much potential is the tax reform issue, which could imply ultimately lower taxes for moderate income people at the expense of the rich. McGovern ended up with the public 7 to 1 opposed to his tax reform income redistribution proposal in 1972. The reason soon became perfectly apparent: Instead of promising moderate income people that they would be the beneficiaries of tax reform, McGovern seemed to go right past the mass of working people and to promise to give all the benefits to those on welfare. Significantly, tax reform had real appeal, not only to lower income people, but also to affluent, professional types, who did not behave according to the traditional laws of economic self-interest by any means.

All of these issues—peace, environmental control, consumerism, and tax reform—promised to form the basis for the kind of issue appeal that a candidate for president in 1976 or 1980 can ride to victory. The mark of all of them, with the possible exception of tax reform, is that they have far greater intensity of appeal to the "pro-change" groups in America than any others. As the electorate grows younger, better educated, more affluent, more suburban, and more independent in numbers, these issues will take greater hold. They are likely by 1976 to replace the old economic issues of the past in importance, and, indeed, already have done so.

Yet all of these issues must be viewed as being essentially positive in nature. One negative issue has emerged in 1973 that will remain a stain on the Republican party for many years to come: the Watergate affair. Watergate has placed a mark of corruption and deceit on the GOP that goes well beyond the normal bounds of political behavior. For instance, political spying did not shock the American people in the early 1970s as such, for politics had achieved such a low status that indictments of public officials were more or less expected. As many as 1 in 3 people felt the Mafia had "a great deal of influence in Washington" in 1973.

The shocking part of Watergate was the arrogance of topmost officials in the Nixon Administration to use the very law enforcement apparatus of the federal establishment to violate the rights of political opposition and to subordinate the nonpartisan agencies of the FBI and the CIA to a role of political pawns. The use of law enforcement to gain political power is a chilling and even foreign concept to most Americans. The president of one of the largest manufacturing companies, observed in May 1973, "Thank goodness for all of these Watergate exposures. If we had three more years of undiscovered bugging and harassment of organizations and individuals, we all would have been put out of business, individually and as organizations."

Although during the period of the Watergate exposures the Democrats had maintained an essentially nonpolitical stance, it was a safe bet that in the 1974 off-year elections and again in 1976 they would exploit Watergate to the hilt. They might turn a negative issue into a positive one. Certainly there would be high moral cries from the Democrats that the basic freedom of the country had been placed in jeopardy for partisan political advantage. Republican candidates in turn would be scurrying to disassociate themselves from involvement or support for a president tainted by Watergate. Pledges of support for the freedom of the press, ringing defenses of the inviolable right to dissent would all be forthcoming as prime campaign rhetoric.

A high priority campaign issue for the Democrats in 1976 was sure to be a clarion call to restore confidence in a federal government which operated entirely out in the open, which allowed the citizens of the republic to know how decisions were arrived at, without secrecy and with candor. Integrity in government and respect for the rights of individuals had become issues, perhaps more than at any time since the founding of the country.

The groups who felt most deeply about the Watergate scandals were precisely the same who felt most strongly about almost all the new issues of change: the upper income, affluent, better educated, and younger parts of the public. Watergate underscored for them the necessity of leadership which was attuned to the changing needs rather than to seeking to gain and to consolidate power simply for the sake of power itself. The long-term impact of Watergate politically is likely to be both greater cynicism about politics and politicians, on the one hand, and a demand that leaders in the future engage in far franker dialogues on key and even sensitive issues that face the country.

Watergate seems inevitably to improve the chances for Democratic gains in 1974 and in 1976. However, there is one important caveat the Democrats had best pay heed to: easy promises and easy rhetoric, in which the Democrats picture themselves as all moral, all good, and all of the side of the angels likely would be greeted with high skepticism. It is far more likely that Democratic credibility in making hay over Watergate will only wash if Democratic candidates were prepared to admit that all politics, including their own, had been tainted by moral corruption and that it is time to begin a new slate and a new style in conducting political campaigns and in running government once in power. If the Democrats protest too much, large segments of the electorate will become tempted to look for nonpolitical people to provide the new leadership, so deep does the cynicism about politics-as-usual run.

Of course, in the 1974 off-year elections and in 1976, the Republicans will also be judged by their stewardship of the economy. If there is another recession, with widespread unemployment, this could bring back many of the now straying union, Catholic, and lower-middle-income voters to the Democratic line. However, even the economic issue has changed its character rather decisively. The public has been badly burned by inflation and is playing for keeps on this issue, as the widespread consumer boycotts of meat, which involved 63% of the families of the country indicated in the spring of 1973. When asked if they would rather forego pay increases if they could be assured prices could be kept in line, or whether they would like to have no controls on prices and be able to obtain unrestricted pay increases, in April 1973, the public nationally opted for fewer pay increases and control of prices by 83% to 7%. The inflation issue of curbing both prices and pay seems likely to take over from the old "more pay and more social benefits in the pocket" appeal so traditional in American politics. Economists have been slow to see the political implications of inflation and the demand by the public for some form of controls for many years to come. If the Nixon Administration were to pursue an essentially laissez-faire approach to economic controls over inflation, as its performance in the early days of 1973 indicates, it may well be handing a powerful issue over to the Democrats in 1976. On the other hand, if inflation is kept under control in a reasonably prosperous economy, the Democrats could find themselves on the short end of the economic issue for the first time in many years.

Another whole roster of issues centered around the problems of welfare, crime, race, the poor, and the young. The so-called social issue, put forth by Richard Scammon and Ben Watten-

berg,[7] was assumed to be the trigger that brought political cohe-
sion to "Middle America." The basic thesis was that the country
was "unpoor, unblack, and unyoung" and that politicians who
claimed primarily to be fighting for the causes of the poor, the
blacks, and the young, were going to find themselves roundly
trounced at the polls. The reasons given were usually a series
of snappy, although highly superficial, references to polling results: after all, it was said, was it not true that, by 88% to 6%,
nearly everybody wanted to "make people on welfare go to
work" (unpoor); that by 81% to 14% nearly everybody was opposed to "school busing to achieve racial balance" (unblack);
and that by 77% to 16% nearly everybody was against "legalizing the sale and use of marijuana" (unyoung). As though this
were not enough, the analysts who leaned heavily on the social
issue also pulled out another result that read, "give stiffer penalties to hard drug users," favored by 68% to 25%.

There were two answers to this argument. The first can be
found in a counterset of results, indeed almost all drawn from
the same Harris Survey in 1972 from which the previous results
were taken: A majority of 57% to 32% also wanted to "increase
federal aid to the poor," a majority of 53% to 36% favored "desegregation of the public schools," a majority of 66% to 23%
wanted to "spend more money to rehabilitate criminals back to
a normal life," and a majority of 72% to 20% praised young
people for "being more honest and frank about sex." The trouble
with both sets of results was that they committed the cardinal
sin in analysis by taking the results to a single question and
based a whole series of ad hoc generalizations on them. When
people said that those on welfare "ought to be made to work,"
they were not necessarily favoring cutting off the poor from government assistance, nor were they writng off their concern for
the poor. Instead, they believed that many on welfare might be
induced to work, and they would like to see efforts made iu reduce the welfare rolls this way. Ample testimony to this explanation can be found in the result out of the same survey where,
by 87% to 8%, almost exactly the same number of people who
advocated "putting welfare people to work" also came down in
favor of "a federal program to give productive jobs to the unem-

ployed." Obviously, the area of government help for the poor was fraught with ambivalence as well as compassion.

The same was true of the problems surrounding blacks and other racial minorities. Majorities of over 9 to 1 among whites expressed real alarm in 1971 when it was widely believed police killings were part of a plot by the Black Panthers to immerse America in guerrilla warfare. At the same time, almost as large a majority could be found who agreed that "it is a disgrace the way blacks have been treated in America for the past three hundred years." As was pointed out in Chapter XIII, both blacks and whites harbored many hostile antagonisms toward each other in this country; but, in the end, by and large both races agreed that desegregation must happen, because it was morally right and it was the law of the land, which was nearly irreversible so long as our system was not overturned by a racist autocracy.

On the subject of youth, there was little doubt that people 50 and over were upset by what they viewed as their life style and their penchant to conduct deeply troubling protests that could spill over into violence. The problem of drugs had driven the older generation close to despair. Yet, for all of these difficulties, the country was gradually becoming less uptight about its young, and there were signs the drug problem was being sorted out as professionals from medicine, psychiatry, education, and law enforcement attacked the issue.

Underlying it all was the fact that the American people are not immature, emotional automatons waiting for a demagogic politician to push the right buttons and obtain a flood of votes which would add up to a majority on election day. Just before he was shot, George Wallace was run in the Harris Survey as the Democratic nominee for president against Nixon and Eugene McCarthy on a third-party, independent ticket. Even with the presumed prestige of the Democratic nomination, Wallace received no more than 21% of vote, behind McCarthy's 22% and a much higher 47% for Nixon. The "social issue" faddists implicitly suggested that the Nixon and Wallace votes were both affected by the law and order, social unrest, outrage at youth, and people on welfare syndrome. Therefore, they concluded there was a big social issue vote out there that automatically spelled a "Middle American" majority. They even suggested that the proof of the pudding was that in 1968, the Wallace vote would have gone 70% to 30% for Nixon, and, indeed in 1972, with Wallace out, the Wallace vote did go to Nixon 68% to 32%. Again, the only trouble with such analysis was that this happened to be the case with George McGovern as Nixon's opponent. When Senator Edward Kennedy, who in 1972 had few major substantive differences on the issues, was substituted for McGovern, the Wallace vote went just about 50–50 to Nixon and Kennedy. In fact, in May 1972, before McGovern blew his chances, with Wallace out, his vote went no more than 4 to 3 for Nixon. The reason was apparent with only a little digging: The Wallace voters (59%) were deeply alienated from the establishment. Only blacks were more alienated and felt more powerless. In 1972, the center of the establishment was the White House, then occupied by Richard Nixon. The McGovern people expected the Wallace vote to come to their column automatically because they were the "outs." But McGovern made such a singular mess of his campaign, veering from way-out radical on the left to more regular than Mayor Daley's troops in Representative Pucinski's district, that Wallace backers, along with most of the rest of the electorate, gave up on him. Some have claimed the Wallace vote went to Nixon because the president talked racist code language to them on the busing issue. However, the facts show that on his busing stand and his handling of race matters, not only was Richard Nixon rated negatively by the entire electorate, but Wallace supporters rated him an even lower 71% to 22% and 69% to 24% negative on both issues affecting race.

The point is that the Nixon vote and the Wallace vote in 1968 and in 1970 were not the same. More important, there was solid evidence in the relatively poor ratings he received on drugs, crime, and youth that had Nixon run on these issues, he could well have lost the election, as indeed the 1970 election amply demonstrated. In fact, had Nixon not stood for "change that works," a phrase this writer used early in connection with the Nixon moves to freeze prices and wages and his peace initiatives in Peking and Moscow and later picked up by the president himself, he would have been in deep trouble. In 1972, and even more so in 1976 and in 1980, any candidate who thinks he can win the White House by riding a status quo majority whose main concern in life is to resist the forces of change represented by the poor, the blacks, or the youth will find his demagogic cacophony falling on deaf ears and his army of voters no bigger than the 21% recorded for George Wallace as the Democratic nominee in May 1972, just before a near-fatal assassin's bullet took him out of the race.

Parts of the so-called social issue must be sorted out, for some have political potential although most do not in politics in America for the rest of the 1970s. The crime and law and order issue, except perhaps in some local municipal elections, has lost its political bite if in fact it ever had it. Few candidates are going to say they are against strict enforcement of the law and are willing to mollycoddle hardened criminals. Certainly any candidate found with Mafia connections (some of whom shout loudest about law and order and who deny there even is a Mafia) will be resoundingly rejected by the voters. On the other hand, a candidate who can say he is not going down the easy road of wrapping himself in a cloak of law and order but is going to demand that the people themselves participate in a program to stop the monstrous rate of recidivism that bred the soldiers for the army of crime could find a responsive electorate. Similarly, a prosecutor who fearlessly goes after the really big pins in the Mafia and their "legitimate" front men could quickly find himself heavily in demand for higher office. What will not wash with voters any more are such mouthings as, "I will make the streets safe for every man, woman, and child"; "I'll really get tough with the street punks"; or "I'll drive the addicts and the pushers out of your community." For people have become too knowledgeable and have lived with the problem of crime too long to believe such emotional appeals. And after the Watergate scandal, it will be hard for Republicans to be anything but defensive on the issue of law enforcement. Similarly, with the drug issue, most people have finally realized that political promises in this area were cheap, that no candidate wanted to be "soft on heroin," and that only a sober public and high professionalism, plus some sound education of the young will ultimately solve the problem. Quick political promises on drugs seem sure to backfire increasingly in the 1970s.

As for political campaigns on the promise of a crackdown on "youth who have gotten out of hand" or even broad and sweeping condemnations of a "permissive society," such as those invoked by Vice-President Agnew in 1970, the outlook is dim at best. First, with Vietnam gone, the chances of sustained protest marches are likely to subside. Second, the young people themselves, as the 1970 study we did for Chancellor Alexander Heard indicated, are more inclined to want to be effective politically and will be heard from more and more in political activity at the local level. Contrary to the observations of some political reporters, the 1972 Democratic party reforms were well received by the public: "Greater representation of women" was received with favor by 81% to 13% of the public; "greater representation of black and Spanish-speaking groups" appealed to a 76% to 17% majority; "greater representation of youth as delegates" was approved by 76% to 19%; "the behavior of the new delegates" was viewed favorably by 67% to 26%; "the appointment of a woman head of the Democratic party" was approved by 74% to 17%. The fact was that party reform was popular with the public, and the chances are that the Republicans will have to follow suit in 1976 or before in adopting reforms to "open up the conventions," an idea that was attractive to a 73% to 19% majority. The young people are likely to find mainstream politics more open than closed to them for the rest of the decade. In turn, as more young people hold party positions and participate in the political process, the chances are good that their turnout at the polls on election day, estimated to be 20% below that of their elders in 1972, will increase. So the actual political muscle of the young should rise in 1976 and 1980.

On the interlocked issues of the poor and the racial minorities, it was well to remember that the black vote can be as volatile as any part of the electorate. When Nixon increased his black vote from 6% to 19% in 1972, he increased his spread over McGovern by as much as 3 full percentage points. In a close election, as Harry Truman in 1948 and John Kennedy in 1960 learned, a high black vote can spell the difference. Although the blacks were largely going against the tide in the 1968 and 1972 elections, their normal 80% to 20% Democratic party inclination gave any Democratic nominee a 6-point beginning advantage nationwide. Balanced against this, of course, was a die-hard white vote, mainly from the Deep South, that is 4% of the vote nationally. But it would be dangerous for any politician to count the white racially affected vote nationwide beyond the 10% mark. In 1968, Wallace received 13.5% of the vote and, by the time of the election, he had coralled about the maximum that could be dredged out of the extreme white side of the race issue. But the price he paid for this was the 45% of the voters who believed him to be "racist, whom I couldn't vote for."

The advantage a candidate could obtain in being at least a moderate on the race question is that he has a chance of winning part of the black vote and he could make a strong appeal to the underlying moral conscience of white America. The chances are that by 1976 the school busing issue will give way to the much tougher issue of housing desegregation, now the most pressing demand of blacks. While open housing, nondiscrimination against racial minorities, is the law of the land, thanks to Lyndon Johnson, there have been few court orders demanding massive housing desegregation. It is entirely possible that Governor Wallace, if he were well enough physically, or another candidate, might take to the stump in 1976 and pledge to preserve "the God-given right to live in a neighborhood of your own choice" or "every man's home is his castle" as did the Democrat who unsuccessfully tried to defeat Spiro Agnew for governor of Maryland in 1966. While such rhetoric would have some appeal, the chances are even better that people would suspect by then that such promises are rather empty in the light of the prevailing law of the land. The risks of provoking racial confrontation by such talk will become more apparent, even though sizable numbers of whites will not be happy at all at the prospect of desegregating their neighborhoods. The racial issue bends back and forth and it would now appear that the zenith of antiblack feeling may well have been reached in the 1967–72 period. Ironically, as blacks achieve more integration, the heat surrounding the issue is declining instead of rising. The contempt from familiarity will not be as great as the realization that the clock of history just cannot be turned back.

The issue of the poor will depend to a large degree on the outcome of the battle between the Republican White House and the Democratic Congress on spending for programs for the disadvantaged. If Congress prevails and the proposed cuts are less than Nixon has asked for, then aid to the poor is unlikely to be a major issue in 1976 and in 1980. But if the White House wins, then there is every likelihood that the Democrats will make an issue of it by spelling out a long litany of poignant examples of neglect for the most wretched and miserable in our midst. Such an issue would likely touch the guilty consciences of affluent America and win the Democratic votes.

One of the most interesting issues that will be operating for the rest of the decade is which problems should be primarily handled by state and local government or the private sector and which should be federally oriented. There is no doubt that from 1968 to 1972, public confidence in federal government solutions on nearly anything had hit perhaps an all-time low. There is likely to be a slow but steady restoration of dependence on the federal government in a second Nixon Administration, but not necessarily related to specific Nixon acts or pronouncements. As people become more knowledgeable on subjects of pressing concern, such as environment and consumerism, they will realize that only strongly enforced federal standards are going to clean up air and water and insure quality and safety in products and services. Ironically, if business is smart about it, it could initiate many of the ground rules which the federal government must establish to get the job done. If business displays a foot-dragging attitude, however, there is every prospect that individual corporations, entire industries, and business as a whole could become real whipping boys in the 1976 and 1980 elections.

There is another reason why the much-touted shift to state and local control of many programs might not be as readily accepted by these local governing bodies as might have been thought a few years ago. On the surface in 1973, it looked as

though the time for a vast expansion of state responsibilities had
come. The reason could be found in the fact that, while the federal government was running a deficit of $25.3 billion a year,
more and more states, which had raised their tax bases in the
late 1960s and early 1970s, were actually producing surpluses,
thus making them eligible to spend more on previously federally
financed programs. This dramatic turn-around made state government and governors' chairs much more attractive than they
had been in many years. Back in the middle 1950s, this writer
had observed that for the immediate future, the next few presidents were much more likely to come out of the U.S. Senate
than the state houses for the simple reason that senators had a
national visibility and were exposed to the key foreign policy issues that governors rarely could find. However, governors were
much more apt to learn how to be successful administrators and
in many ways received more direct training for the White
House than did U.S. senators. And if governors could report surpluses in their budgets, while the federal establishment was run-
ing deficits, governors could become highly attractive candidates for the presidency again. However, any ambitious
governor who has national aspirations is far more likely to want
to harbor and to hoard his surplus rather than to bail out the
federal government. Thus, there is every likelihood that an increasing number of governors would resist taking over federal
programs, even if there are promises of federal monies to go
with them, for their fear would likely be that the federal support
would not be enough and their own surpluses would have to be
used to make up the difference. Far more attractive to many
ambitious governors would be to give back part of their surpluses to the taxpayers in the form of tax cuts, especially in
years when they were up for re-election or their parties were
choosing their candidates for president and vice-president. The
likelihood of this political reality of self-interest on the part of
governors outweighing the public's antipathy for more massive
federal programs is high in the remaining years of the decade.

There is another reason why the federal establishment would
in all probability come back to assume more rather than less
responsibility. New crises are just now shaping up which are

going to require a strong federal hand, much as is the case with environment and consumerism as well as inflation problems. If a problem is national in scope and it reached crisis proportions, no matter how inclined a president might be toward giving the power to act and the money to do the job to the states, the pressures would be great to come up with a federal solution. One such issue that is just aborning is the much-talked about energy crisis. The fact of the matter is that there already is a world-wide shortage of energy resources to satisfy the exploding demands of growing industry and agriculture as well as the rapidly rising demands of consumers. The United States by 1973 had no more than a two-day reserve of oil and its power supply was in scarcely better shape. With 42% of the country already owning air conditioners and with another 40% who said they wanted and expected they would have them in the foreseeable future, the potential demands for energy frightened nearly every knowledgeable scholar of the subject as the mid-1970s approached. The irony of the situation is that it might be worse in the short run, over the next 10 to 15 years, than in the long run. For by 1985–90, it is anticipated that new sources of energy, mainly nuclear but not discounting solar, could be developed to satisfy demand. But from 1973, when the shortages began to surface in massive cases, for at least another 5 to 10 years, there is every likelihood that America and its people will be faced with a rather steady diet of fuel shortages, brown-outs, possible periods of gas rationing, mandatory periods when heating or air conditioning cannot be used, cancellation of bus and airline schedules due to fuel shortages, and even times of prohibition of the use of the automobile for many pleasure purposes. Above all, the one absolute certainty was that the American consumer was going to pay perhaps as much as two or three times more for his energy for all purposes. Little of this was recognized in America as 1973 dawned. Few previously had experienced energy crisis pains; over 8 in 10 people said they had never known a power shortage where they lived.

Yet the problem clearly was national and even international in scope and had to end up essentially in the lap of the federal government. It would probably become a hot political issue in the 1976 campaign. First, there would be the howls of the consuming public who had been raised for many years on a diet of "power is cheap" and "gasoline is a good buy," both of which implied an abundant supply. The public would be expected to generate a retributive fury over why the crisis had been allowed to come about, which could be quickly followed by the anguish of paying higher energy bills. Finally, if and when their own personal comforts had to be restricted, there would be all the makings of a consumer revolt and a demand to "throw the rascals out" in the best American tradition. Compounding the problem even more would be a head-on collision between those who were worried about clean air and water and those who wanted their heating and air conditioning kept intact no matter what. The issue promised to be mean and ugly.

Nor was it the only one. Despite the lull in the population boom in the U.S., the world-wide problem of population was rapidly reaching crisis proportions with the promise of widespread food shortages unless the population growth was aborted. The crisis in transportation had not been reached full-blown, but America was largely unprepared for wholesale shifts from rubber tires to rails and mass transit. All could have major political impact in the next two presidential elections.

As the 1976 run for the White House began to take shape, the roster of make or break issues would have made John F. Kennedy or even Lyndon Johnson blink with amazement. Even though peace was a dominant issue in 1964, that same year, by 3 to 1, the public was convinced that the way to avoid war was to have a strong American defense and a willingness on the part of this country to come to the armed assistance of countries who were the victims of aggression. Such a policy of "peace through strength," of being so strong that the Communists would not dare aggression, stemmed directly from our World War II experience. The reason Barry Goldwater frightened voters in 1964 was that he seemed "trigger happy," an advocate of a preventive war, which 86% [8] of the people rejected in the case of China. Peace, essentially having come to mean coexistence between the U.S. and Communist superpowers and successive agreements to defuse tensions and to increase interdependence, was the most powerful issue of the time. Consumerism, ranging from the quality of products and services to bitter protests over the high price of meat or the shortage of energy, had become a mark of the new affluent society. Environmental control was just reaching its peak as an issue with real bite to it. The race issue would cause ongoing anguish as in the 1960s. The plight of the poor amid unparalleled affluence would prick the consciences of the country as it did in the 1960s. Federal government could no longer view inflation as an upswing phenomenon that presaged the arrival of a boom, but rather it was a permanent crisis that required continuing federal treatment in the form of controls. Although still a crisis among the poor, and with a national health insurance plan still to go as the unfinished business of the New Deal and Great Society, health would not be a major political issue, for somehow the growing affluent felt they could meet their health needs in the private sector, essentially without federal help. Despite a chronic housing shortage, this traditional New Deal issue was likely not to have the spark it once had, for the poor had shrunk in numbers and the growing affluent were not likely to look to government in a massive way to solve the housing problem. Such measures as the minimum wage and unemployment compensation would be extended to account for the impact of inflation, but the days when they were major issues of controversy seemed by and large over. Even some of the pressures for aid to education would taper off as the last of the generation of the population boom passed school age.

The issues were changing partly because the needs of affluent America were changing. But an even greater moving force would be the shifts in political power, dictated by where the votes were. Even by 1976, the electorate would bear like resemblance to that of 1968. The following statistical judgments, based on projections of the Harris staff, show where the new center of political gravity likely would be:

Changes in the Electorate
1968–1976 [9]

	1976	1968	CHANGE
Shrinking in Power	%	%	%
Under $5,000 income	19	25	− 6
Small-town voters	11	22	11
Union members	15	23	− 8

	1976	1968	CHANGE
Shrinking in Power	%	%	%
Education not beyond 8th grade	11	19	− 8
Democrats	41	51	−11
$5,000–9,999 income	23	43	−20
Increasing in Power			
College educated	40	29	+11
$15,000 and over income	25	12	+13
Independents	28	18	+10
Suburban residents	34	26	+ 8
Under 30 voters	27	18	+ 9
Professionals in occupation	20	9	+11

Both the heartland of the old New Deal and the Middle America majorities will have shrunk to minority status. The literacy of the electorate will have leaped ahead. By 1976 it would be wrong to think of voters as having a 12-year-old or even 21-year-old mentality. A better description would be of someone with some college exposure, and, if not, a high school graduate with interests akin to the college educated of a generation before. By any previous standards in the history of the world, it would be an elitist country in quality, but for the first time it would be on a mass basis. More important, these voters would be a society capable of thinking in larger terms about the world and about the quality of life around them at home. They would be highly mobile, both in having the money to travel extensively and in having the background and motivation to move quickly mentally across a whole world of events and ideas.

But, above all, this would be a pluralistic, highly selective American electorate. It would quickly turn aside the easy rhetoric of politicians who promised them easy panaceas for their troubles. Soothing syrup from men in high places would be viewed as pure cant. Such a voting constituency would be wed increasingly to the proposition that presidential candidates had better mean business on peace, consumerism, ecology, the energy crisis, tax reform, and other basically noneconomic issues. There would be a Middle America vote and it would resist many of the changes wrought by the emerging majority for change. But essentially, the porkchop vote of the past would be changing places with the educated, affluent vote, and Middle Americans would become a minority.

These changes in the center of voting power promised to wreak havoc with the existing political parties as we have known them. Split-ticket voting would accelerate even more than its rapid rate of increase since 1960. The following table dramatically illustrates where the phenomenon of ticket splitting has gone since 1960. It is based on the difference in the aggregate between the major party vote for president and the House of Representatives:

Ticket Splitting Trends
for President and Congressman [10]

	NUMBER SPLITTING TICKETS %	VOTE SPREAD RESULTING FROM TICKET SPLITTING %
1972	16	32
1968	11	22
1964	6	12
1960	3	6

The number of voters who split their tickets between 1960 and 1972 had increased by more than 400%. This trend could be expected to increase rather than decrease in 1976 and in 1980. In 1972, President Nixon was quoted by aides as believing that the more he campaigned for fellow Republicans running for the House and U.S. Senate, the lower his own ultimate majority would be. By and large, this was the case, as the election results showed. In the contests for the House, he ran 32 percentage points ahead of his fellow GOP candidates. However, the earlier point about the lack of any conservative mandate in 1972 was underscored in striking fashion by a comparison of the president's vote with that of liberal and moderate Republicans running for the U.S. Senate. When the votes for moderate candidates such as Charles Percy of Illinois, Clifford Case of New Jersey, Mark Hatfield of Oregon, Edward Brooke of Massachussetts, John Chafee of Rhode Island, and Mrs. Margaret Chase

Smith of Maine (the latter two lost) were all added up, as a group they ran 4 percentage points *ahead* of President Nixon. But fifteen other GOP nominees for the U.S. Senate, all clearly conservatives, ran 16 points *behind* Nixon. So in 1972, President Nixon would have cut his margin of victory had he campaigned for more conservatives. But he might have helped his cause by taking the stump for more moderate and liberal Republicans.

The future of the political parties for the rest of the 1970s would likely depend on how well they read the rapidly changing priorities and make-up of the American electorate. There would be little safe middle ground left. Yesterday's center would constantly be found in the recent dust of the past. It would be a time demanding political skill in selecting candidates and in mounting campaigns. But it would probably take an equal amount of courage on the part of political leadership in both parties. For, as with so many of their counterparts in business, labor, and other fields, they had spent much of their lives clawing their way to the top and, once there, it would be hard to learn new tricks and to learn new lessons about a new electorate. The safety valve would be growing party reform. As 1976 approached, the chances were that, just as the face of the electorate had changed, so the faces of political leadership would change. Such portents might not be pleasant for such men as Governor Rockefeller and Governor Reagan in the GOP, nor even for Vice-President Agnew. Nor would they augur well for men such as Senators Jackson and Muskie and Governor Wallace or even Senator McGovern in the Democratic party. The times demanded new men and it appeared that only new men, sensitive and alert to the changes but even more a part of them, would read this electorate successfully.

XV

SEEDS OF JOY
AND SHADOWS
OF DESPAIR

Whenever he was faced with a situation that was acute but lacking in an immediate solution, President Kennedy took some solace in one of his favorite expressions: "Things have to get worse before they get better." During the period of the 1960s and the early 1970s, most people thought things in America indeed had grown worse. As the decade of the seventies began, by 56% to 31%,[1] a majority of the country agreed that "polarization was taking place." By 49% to 42%, most people also thought there were "forces preventing people from doing what they had a right to do." The public was evenly divided in laying the cause of infringement of rights to government, on the one hand, and to divisive antigovernment "radicals" on the other. The status quo clearly was under attack by a wide-ranging assortment of youthful antiwar protesters, militant black activists, newly founded environmentalist groups, marching women's lib advocates, homosexual gay liberationists, among others. Some were irresponsible and destructive as the panty-raiders had been in the 1950s. But many others felt there was "something deeply wrong in America," as 64% of the public agreed (though not for all the same reasons), and they felt change was urgent and pressing.

Basically, the period could be viewed as an assault on the heart of the establishment itself. The most fundamental challenge was to the traditional idea that if enough American know-how could be brought to bear on any problem or any situation, American know-how would prevail. Vietnam pitted American military know-how, albeit stripped of the nuclear capability, against Asian guerrilla power; somehow it didn't work. In a period when many were predicting unprecedented rises in material acquisition by people who finally had the money to gorge themselves in gadgetry, somehow instead those same people recoiled in horror at the dangers of products and damned the industrial machine for fouling the air and water to boot. Nearly everyone found fault with something, and, sadly, most of all with each other. It could truly be said in the early 1970s that the time had come to stop attacking each other individually and as groups, and to begin to attack our common problems.

There were those who admitted to no flaws in the system, who viewed all the criticism as a tearing down of all that was good and right in the country. By the same token, there were those who could see no foundation upon which to build a better America. Both groups were pitifully small minorities. The "status quo at any price" people were no more than 1 in 10. The "overturn the system because it is rotten to the core" people came to no more than 1 in 20. But the worst mistake that could be made was to assume that the remaining 85% were bland and apathetic, with no strong views on where the country ought to be headed, and who made up the amorphous center.

To the contrary, the shape of the future deeply concerned and would be shaped mainly by that 85% who wanted desperately to find orderly change. The changes they wanted were not always clearly spelled out. It was always easier to say what was wrong than how to right it. People were convinced, however, that change could be found. By nearly 3 to 2, the public felt, if it had to make a choice, it would sympathize "more with young people who favor change" than with "older people who oppose change." Nonetheless, by 1973 the mood was visibly shifting. Instead of choosing sides, people were beginning to want to find solutions—not in talk alone, not in retreats to by-gone nostrums, but by substantive improvement in the quality of life.

Anyone who had lived with the diverse strands that layer this country knew both the enormous strength in that diversity as well as the dangers inherent in such a pluralistic society. If confrontation were the only method that worked, then we might be headed for national suicide. However, much of the change, such as in racial or environmental progress, would not be accomplished without tough governmental action based on laws which must be enforced at all costs. The challenge obviously was how to find a way for reasonable and orderly change, which would hurt and be painful to some, but which would make for a healthier state of life for the vast majority. All of the changes would not take place at once, nor would they even be uniform among all sectors of the pluralistic society. There would be prototypes of advanced change and there would be pockets of cultural lag. The secret to successful change was to bring about the reality of change, but in a style and manner that allowed a broad bridge with the past people have known. The more acute the need for change, such as in the case of racial minorities, the more painful the process of change and the less its ties with the past could be left intact.

To accomplish this kind of change in a pluralistic America requires a far better understanding of the rights of others than now exists in the country. A Harris Survey conducted early into the decade of the 1970s showed some enormous gaps between the protestations of freedom in principle among our people, and their patent willingness to scrap freedom in specific instances. Out of eighteen basic guarantees laid down in the Bill of Rights, the public would willingly violate a majority of eleven in the test we conducted. Although by 91% to 5%, almost all Americans believed "every citizen has the right to express any opinion he wants to," a majority of 67% to 22% also favored outlawing "organizations which preach the violent overthrow of the government." Although, by 86% to 7%, most people believed in the right of the accused "to question witnesses against him," by 50% to 32%, the public also supported allowing "FBI agents to testify in criminal cases without cross-examination." Although, by 79% to 11%, a sizable majority believed in the right to "reasonable and not excessive bail," by 57% to 31%, a majority favored that "criminals rearrested a second time, be held without bail." By 66% to 23%, a majority believed in the right to "hold a meeting on any subject a citizen pleases," but, by 48% to 37%, the public also believed that "attendance at campus protest meetings ought to be grounds for an expulsion of a college student" and, by a larger 53% to 34%, that "protest meetings ought to be reviewed in advance to make sure they are not going to preach the overthrow of the government." Obviously, the statement in the Declaration of Independence that, "when a government abuses the rights of its citizens, they have the right to overthrow it" would have trouble mounting widespread support two hundred years after the republic was founded. In fact, when precisely that proposition was tested, by 48% to 37% a plurality disagreed with it. The right "not to be sentenced to cruel punishment" was supported by a relatively narrow 46% to 35%, but, by 47% to 43%, most people also believed that "torture is not too strong punishment for a drug pusher who gives heroin to a 12 year old." Two other "basic rights" did not meet with outright rejection in practice, but had close calls. By an overwhelming 97% to 2%, most Americans believed "a citizen should never have his property taken away from him without being fairly paid for it," but the public was evenly divided 40% to 40% on simply "taking away wealth from rich exploiters." The right to "a speedy trial if accused of a crime" was supported by a 71% to 23% majority, but, by only a close 47% to 42%, a plurality rejected the proposition of "locking up sex offenders for a long time before trial to keep them out of circulation."

During the Nixon era, a major controversy surrounded the right of a citizen to "print any point of view he wants," agreed to in principle by a lopsided 73% to 19% majority. A 52% to 35% majority, however, in 1970 favored "banning newspapers which preach revolution." By 63% to 29%, a majority also wanted to give "authorities the right to censor films, TV shows, and the theater for obscenity." By 57% to 32%, a majority also favored giving authorities the right to "censor TV, radio, newspaper, and the theater for unpatriotic or revolutionary content." When coupled with the 52% to 39% who expressed agreement that "Vice-President Agnew is right to criticize the unfair reporting of news about President Nixon and Vietnam," a case could be made that traditional freedom of the media in the U.S. could be in considerable trouble in the 1970s. Indeed, respected commentators such as Walter Cronkite, a household name, face, and voice on his nightly telecasts of the news on CBS, expressed real concern that the basic right of reporters to probe the facts of a story and to report it were being threatened by federal pressures and threats, some subtle but others rather bold and crude. Part of the problem was inherent in the build-in struggle between any White House and the media that cover it. Any president tends to feel trapped in the Oval Office, surrounded by suspicious newsmen who are ready to print the worst they can dig up. Most presidents worry about communicating their own views on programs and on important events to the people of the country. Yet they tend to feel the threshold through which they must go —the newspapers, television, radio, and news magazines—is "out to get them." Therefore, all administrations in modern times have tried to manage the news out of the White House.

For their part, Washington reporters are a tough and somewhat jaundiced lot who often have to balance maintaining good contacts with high officials to obtain the facts on hardbreaking news with avoiding being used as tools of administration propaganda. Things were widely viewed by working reporters as having gotten out of hand in the Nixon years in three ways: (1) President Nixon had been more inaccessible than his recent predecessors, so that much of the news about the president came from Administration "spokesmen" instead of from the man himself; (2) far too much of what went on in high Administration circles was felt to be deliberately kept from the working press, leading many old hands to grumble about a "closed White House;" and (3) traditional presidential carping at unfriendly pieces escalated to frontal assaults by Vice-President

Agnew against the media establishment, charging that a small group of leftist-inclined news editors controlled the mass media. The courts were sending reporters to jail for refusing to disclose their sources of information. Public television was being stripped of public affairs shows which seemed to advocate too much change. The Washington *Post* which, along with the New York *Times* was a favorite target of Agnew as the heart of the liberal establishment, was being challenged over license renewals of two of its television stations. The difference between the Nixon years and those of Kennedy and Johnson in the eyes of many working newsmen was that the Nixon people seemed more retributive, to be more thorough and, in the aggregate, to threaten the basic freedom to "print any point of view." Much of the pressure was in the name of achieving "balance" in the media, the approach Justice Powell had recommended in his 1971 memorandum.

A serious question was whether basic freedom of inquiry was in jeopardy. This question of just how secure freedom was in America could be a sobering one, for, as survey results indicated, there was in fact little actual tradition of respect of the rights of others among the people themselves. The founding fathers themselves had carefully conceived the system of checks and balances by insuring the independence of the judiciary, distinct and apart from the executive and legislative branches. It became apparent that the great protector of individual freedom through the years had been the courts, not public opinion. The reason, upon reflection, was apparent: The test of freedom was not the ability of people to hold views or to advocate measures which a majority agreed with, but rather freedom could only be measured by the tolerance by society of full expression by the most unpopular, most outlandish points of view, including those who might preach overthrow of the system itself. Defense of such extreme views turned out to be very much in the tradition of the American court system, but very little ingrained in the patience, experience, or instincts of the people. Over 90% of the people had been raised to give lip service to freedom in the abstract, but few unfortunately seemed consistently to be willing to back up in their own lives Voltaire's timeless words, "I disagree with all you say, but I will fight to the death for your right to say it."

For a country that prided itself on its tough, pioneering spirit, which still loved cowboy films long after its people had become citizens of stone, glass, and chrome cities, the romance of freedom had a good sound, but freedom in reality was a fragile commodity. This fact was important, for it pointed up a new challenge to the survival of the pluralism so basic to tolerating change in the 1970s. If most Americans were going to allow basic rights to perish, then the hope for new ideas, for changing one's mind, for adapting to new approaches could be in peril. Perhaps most of all, the fear of such abridgement of liberty, the central trigger of our own American Revolution nearly two hundred years ago, could stifle the ascendancy of the new leadership so critical to produce the men to match the challenge of the times.

The risks in the 1970s would be those born of despair. The roots of discouragement were plain to see: the scars and even the still open wounds from the shock that the United States had become a violent country where a popular young president or the most obscure citizen could be in equal jeopardy of their physical safety on the nation's streets; that vaunted American know-how could turn out products that could contaminate, pollute, injure, or even kill people who bought and used them; that "the better life" had to be found in urban America, often through a dense cloud of smog and air pollution; that the dreams of "making it" according to 1950 standards of how many gadgets, cars, and other material possessions were now suddenly believed to be sadly out of date to the new generation of young people and to the growing professional, affluent segment of society; that raising children was no longer a test of instilling in them enough drive to achieve good grades in school to later qualify for college, in turn to become a material success in life, but even more whether young children could be kept from experimenting with drugs. All of these shocks were the fertile ground from which potential repression could grow. When compared with the fragile state of commitment to tolerance of the freedom of others, both as individuals and as people acting in concert, it was not hard to be pessimistic about the chances of liberty and an open society surviving in America in the 1970s.

Yet there were also signs that the rugged individualism that had been so much a stamp of the American people since the Revolution would win out in the end. The fact that there was so little hero worship left for politicians, businessmen, labor leaders, scientists, military leaders, those most visible in the media, even among performers in the pop arts, all could be read just as much as a healthy skepticism as turned off cynicism.

When asked to choose between "a stricter crackdown on permissiveness" or "greater safeguards of the privacy and freedom of the individual," by 56% to 34% [2] a majority in 1973 rejected the "crackdown" and opted for "greater safeguards" for liberty. When asked if the newspapers which leaked the Pentagon Papers in 1971 acted properly in printing their contents, by 46% to 36%, the public said they were "more right than wrong." In the case of the Watergate bugging of Democratic headquarters in Washington in 1972, 84% had said it was a "basic violation of individual freedom." Irrespective of the impact of that scandal on the political fortunes of President Nixon and the Republican party, there was little doubt that in the aftermath of Watergate any White House in the future would have to operate far more openly than this one had and that efforts to invade the rights of others through illegal wire tapping or other surveillance that abridged individual privacy would be extremely unpopular and viewed as contrary to the traditionally open American way. The Watergate episode would also heighten public skepticism of those who preached the rhetoric of moral indignation over protests against the establishment, but who themselves violated the law.

In many ways, the Watergate scandal marked the end of an era. It certainly could be counted on to bring to new depths the already low estimate the American people had for the federal government. In April 1973, a majority of 52% of the public said that "corruption in the federal government was very serious." The federal establishment now was viewed as the "most corrupt" of any level of government. The news that the head of the FBI, the chief lawman, had destroyed possibly incriminating papers in the Watergate case and that the attorney general himself had initiated unlawful entry would make a mockery of all the pious claims about restoration of law and order, an old campaign cry of this Administration.

The Watergate trauma also produced a remarkable new appreciation of the role of a free press in a democratic society. By a 5 to 1 majority, the public felt that "in exposing the facts about Watergate, the Washington *Post* and other newspapers were an example of a free press at its best." By 3 to 1, a majority also agreed that "if it had not been for the press exposés, the whole Watergate mess never would have been found out." By the same token, by 61% to 17%, the public rejected the oft-repeated charge that "the press was just out to get President Nixon on Watergate." Finally, Watergate radically altered Spiro Agnew's credibility in attacking "the liberal Eastern press." The 2 to 1 majority who supported the Agnew attacks turned into a growing view that Agnew was wrong to "try to stifle a free press."

Also out of the ashes of Watergate, there would be a new urgency to restore confidence in the federal government. Almost as though one final and complete purge of the period had to take place, so Watergate would become the symbol of a time when America moved from the use of violence and the waves of fear it generated to earnest efforts on the part of the people and a new leadership to attack the business of orderly change. Emerging from the Watergate aftermath as well would be a new demand upon government at all levels to operate in the open, to find convenants for governing America openly arrived at. It would be a long time before top governmental officials would believe that they could engage in shadowy activities which could be kept from an inquiring media.

The instinctive refuge of the American people probably would be found in the long-ingrained practice of "live and let live." The very skepticism about politicians that had led to disillusionment with the leadership of the country in both the public and private sectors would probably keep the country from following any leader who promised to keep order, but at the price of freedom. People had reached the point where any sweeping promises to restore law and order, to bring tax relief, to come up with categorical solutions to the frustrating problems of the day would be openly scoffed at. For example, in 1973, by 87% to 8%, the public overwhelmingly agreed that "politicians promise tax relief before election and then do nothing about it when elected."

However, if the deep skepticism about political leadership and government at all levels would act as a break against incursions on freedom, then the problem remained of how to restore confidence in leadership which the people would follow in order to solve the new set of ills which beset the country in the 1970s. It could well be that the very safety valve that would serve to preserve an open society could also prevent the country from finding the resolve to act decisively.

The answer to this dilemma would not be easy. But as the middle 1970s approached, the prospects were beginning to brighten. The people were saying that although "rich, natural resources" had contributed in a major way "making the country great," in the next ten years they would depend on them less. The people also were saying that no matter how much the country had been built by strong backs and diligence in the past, "a hard working people" could be depended on far less in the future, despite exhortations of the president to the contrary. "U.S. success in fighting wars" was also a stock which was rapidly declining. The old formula of rich natural resources, hard-working people to exploit them, and a strong military to keep the peace was fading as the national mission of destiny. In its place, there was rising sentiment for a country which "extended a full, unlimited education to all qualified," which possessed "an ability to get along with other nations" (particularly Communist superpowers), which "gave every race and creed a chance to get ahead," which produced a government that "looked after the less fortunate," and which "better regulated business abuses." All of these elements had been viewed as less important in the country's past, but would be more important in the future. Clearly, the American people were beginning to find the will to strike out in new and more humane directions.

The challenge of the 1970s was to close the gaps of powerlessness and frustrations and of confidence in the institutions which made up American society. But how to do it was the core of the problem. In an age of proliferation of information and communication, the need was to find a new literacy and selectivity. In an age of mass society with vast overcrowding, the need was how to find individual identity. In an age of high mobility and fluidity, the need was how to find orderly personal growth. In an age of boundless treasure, the need was how to share that treasure with the blacks, the Spanish-speaking, the poor whites, and countless billions around the world on the edges of starvation. In an age of total nuclear destruction, the need was how to achieve control of the mass murder known as war. In an age of unparalleled technological know-how, the need was to learn how to use that know-how to enhance the quality of existence. In an age of political cynicism, the need was how to convince the people that politics could be dedicated to serving the people and their freedom, not to take power from them in the name of national security. In a time of secrecy in high places, the need was to open up the workings in high places to full public scrutiny.

As a nation, we had raised the question of whether the pain, sacrifice, and troubles involved in achieving these aims were worth it. Then we had to ask if they were capable of attainment. These were not easy questions. For beneath them was the challenge to commitment. The 1960s had begun with high dudgeon exhortations to commitment. By the 1970s, that commitment was beginning to take shape, but had not yet been attained.

The facts in this book have pointed up perhaps more clearly than anything else just how badly the leadership of the country has read the temper, mood, and serious intent of the American people. Taken together, the record is a serious indictment of the political, social, and economic leadership of this country over the past decade. There is little doubt in this writer's mind that the public, although far from correct in many areas, nonetheless is far more sophisticated, far more concerned, and far more advanced than the leadership believed. It can be said with certainty that the people by and large have been well ahead of their leaders.

The leaders have been floundering partly because they have

read the signs from the people wrong, but also partly because we have yet to produce leaders willing to demonstrate a commitment themselves. As a nation, we have a terrible, gnawing, hungry need for leadership which can genuinely care equally about the sense of powerlessness among those who backed George Wallace and the blacks who felt even more passed by. Above all, it must be leadership which is committed to change, not for its own sake, but for the sake of humanity's survival. We must find leadership which will squarely face the risks involved in ending the Cold War and will make coexistence a reality. We must have leadership which will insist on cleaning up the environment, even at the risk of radically altering such traditional means of heating with oil and coal and of traveling in gas burning vehicles. We must have leadership with the skill to bring about tax reform and a redistribution of the nation's larder to the poor of all colors, even at the risk of shaking up the economic well-being of some of the nation's most powerful and affluent people. We must produce leadership which is willing to restore law and order by taking on organized crime and rehabilitating criminals, even at the risk of demanding that the people themselves treat ex-convicts with compassion and respect. We must find leadership that will face down violence firmly and resolutely, but not snuff out the brief light of nonconformity in the process, and will face the risk of defending the rights of the unpopular and off-beat to exist. We must find leadership which will find ways to solve the energy crisis, while not adding to pollution in the process, at the risk of outmoding many established and conventional ways of obtaining energy. After Watergate, we must find leadership which can act resolutely in a crisis, but not leadership which will subtract the basic liberties of the country to consolidate its power.

The great irony of America as it approaches its two hundreth year is that leadership which advocates almost all of these objectives would meet with overwhelming approval from the people themselves. This leadership would have to be more than political, for in the future political leaders are likely to have to share their power and authority with much of the private sector. Restoring confidence in government will be a major task, and a sorely needed one. But the days of either noblesse oblige, where the rich would allow a few crumbs to trickle down to the rest, or of "father knows best," where big and massive governmental programs can solve any social problem with money and bureaucrats, has simply run out. Now the people themselves have reached a point of literacy and knowledge, where they are insisting on sharing in their destiny, not simply in the benefits, but in deciding the means to achieve it. And the surest fact of the 1970s is that, if the current crop of leaders do not wake up to the drastically changed national priorities and the desire for commitment, then the people will not rest easy until they throw them out and put a new generation at the helm. The time for change, full of anguish and pain, nonetheless is joyfully at hand.

Notes

Wherever possible, only those figures of major importance have been cited specifically. Source information for all other items is available at Louis Harris and Associates.

I JOY IS DEAD

1. In the official count, Richard Nixon received 60.8% of the popular vote in 1972.
2. Blue Cross Survey, May 1968, conducted by Louis Harris and Associates.
3. U.S. Public Health Service, 1968 estimate.
4. U.S. Census, 1970.
5. *Life* Magazine Year-End Poll, January 1970.
6. Harris Survey, December 1972.
7. Harris Sports Survey, February 1973.
8. Harris Survey, January 1971.
9. Harris Survey, November 1972.

II THREE VIEWS FROM THE TOP

1. Private conversation with President John F. Kennedy in the Cabinet Room of the White House, August 27, 1963.
2. Harris Survey, May 1971.
3. Private survey conducted for Senator John F. Kennedy of West Virginia Democratic primary prospects, December 1959.
4. Harris Survey, July 1963.
5. The final official results for the 1968 election were: Nixon 43.4%; Humphrey 42.7%.
6. The final official results for the 1972 election were: Nixon 60.7%; McGovern 37.5%.
7. Harris Survey, September 1972.
8. Statement of Whitney Young, president of the Urban League, 1967.
9. *America Was Promises* by Archibald MacLeish (New York: Duell, Sloan, & Pearce, 1939).

III KARL MARX UPSIDE DOWN

1. Conference Board Report, 1968.
2. Harris Survey, December 1972.
3. Department of Commerce, Bureau of Census, Current Population Reports, July 1972.
4. Harris Survey estimates 1960–80.
5. Harris Survey, March 1973.
6. Harris Survey estimates, 1960–80.
7. U.S. Census, 1970.
8. "Meritocracy and Equality" by David Bell, *Public Interest,* Fall 1972.
9. *Is There a Republican Majority?* by Louis Harris (New York: Harper, 1954).
10. The official 1964 vote: Johnson 61.1% ; Goldwater 38.9%.

IV VIETNAM
Out Damned Spot

1. Harris Survey, July 1963.
2. Harris Survey, September 1963.
3. Harris Survey, April 1964.
4. Harris Survey, August 1964.
5. Harris Survey column, August 10, 1964.
6. Harris Survey, December 1964.
7. Harris Survey, February 1965.
8. Harris Survey, December 1966.
9. Harris Survey, July 1968.
10. Harris Survey, October 1967.

V VIETNAM
The Nixon Light at the End of the Tunnel

1. *Time*-Louis Harris Poll, January 1970.
2. Harris Survey, September 1970.
3. Harris Survey, May 1971.
4. Harris Survey, November 1971.
5. Harris Survey, July 1971.

VI WOMEN
The Struggle To Be "More Equal"

1. *The Animal Farm* by George Orwell (New York: Harcourt Brace, 1954).

2. U.S. Census, 1970.
3. Virginia Slims Women's Opinion Poll, conducted by Louis Harris and Associates, 1972.
4. Virginia Slims Women's Opinion Poll, conducted by Louis Harris and Associates, 1971.
5. Estimates of U.S. Census, 1970.
6. Decision of Equal Economic Opportunity Commission (EEOC), February 1973.
7. Harris Survey, September 1972.
8. Harris Survey, June 1972.

vii WHERE HAS ALL THE QUALITY GONE?

1. Harris Survey, November 1972.
2. *Life* Consumerism Survey, conducted by Louis Harris and Associates, 1971.
3. Harris Survey, November 1972.
4. *Life* Consumerism Survey, conducted by Louis Harris and Associates, 1972.
5. Federal Trade Commission findings, February 1973.
6. Harris Survey, December 1972.
7. Harris Survey, April 1971.
8. Ibid.
9. Survey for Pacific Northwest Bell Company, "Environmental Concerns in the State of Washington," conducted by Louis Harris and Associates, 1970.
10. *Life* Consumerism Survey, conducted by Louis Harris and Associates, 1971.

viii THE POOR
"The Living Sick"

1. Bureau of the Census, Current Population Reports, July 1972.
2. Harris Survey, June 1972.
3. Report of National Center for Health Statistics, 1967.
4. Blue Cross Survey, conducted by Louis Harris and Associates, 1968.
5. Ibid.
6. Harris Survey, May 1972.
7. Ibid.
8. Bureau of the Census, Current Population Reports, July 1972.

IX ORGANIZED LABOR
New Defender of the Status Quo?

1. AFL-CIO COPE meeting, Washington, D.C., September 17, 1963.
2. Harris Survey estimates, drawn from cross-sectional studies.
3. Harris Survey, July 1970.
4. Harris Survey, August 1972.

X BUSINESS
Public Expectations Up But Social Performance Down

1. Estimate of Edison Electric Institute, 1972.
2. U.S. Chamber of Commerce, "The Powell Memorandum," issued in 1973, written August 23, 1971.
3. Harris Survey, November 1971.
4. Harris Survey, December 1972.
5. Foundation for Full Service Banks survey of Public and Leaders on Banking, conducted by Louis Harris and Associates, June 1972.
6. Conference Board Senior Executives Council, New York, January 17, 1973.
7. David Rockefeller, "The Essential Quest for the Middle Way," New York *Times,* Op-Ed page, March 23, 1973.

XI FEAR AND VIOLENCE
A New Way of Life

1. Harris Survey, June 1971.
2. Harris Survey, June 1968.
3. Ibid.
4. Harris Survey, September 1968.
5. Joint Commission on Correctional Manpower and Training Survey, conducted by Louis Harris and Associates, 1967.
6. "National Polling Day," ABC Television, survey conducted by Louis Harris and Associates, January 1971.
7. Joint Commission on Correctional Manpower and Training.
8. "National Polling Day."
9. National Commission on Marijuana and Drug Abuse, final report, March 22, 1973.
10. Veterans Administration study of Veterans and U.S. Public, conducted by Louis Harris and Associates, September 1971.
11. Harris Survey, September 1969.

12. "National Polling Day"; Harris Surveys, May 1964, June 1965, March 1968, April 1970, December 1972.
13. *Time* survey on morality, conducted by Louis Harris and Associates, April 1971.

xii YOUTH
When Will We Ever Learn?

1. Harris Survey, August 1967.
2. Harris Survey, November 1967.
3. Harris Survey, July 1969.
4. Memorandum from Daniel P. Moynihan to President Richard Nixon, January 16, 1970; published by the New York *Times*, March 1, 1970.
5. Harris Survey, May 1970.
6. "A Survey of the Attitudes of College Students," conducted by Louis Harris and Associates for the American Council on Education, June 1970.

xiii BLACKS
A Time of Benign Neglect

1. Harris Survey, November 1972.
2. Harris Survey, June 1971.
3. Harris Survey, November 1972.
4. Memorandum from Daniel P. Moynihan to President Richard Nixon, January 16, 1970; published by the New York *Times*, March 1, 1970.
5. Harris Survey, November 1972.
6. Ibid.

xiv POLITICS
Choosing Leaders in a Time of Real Change

1. Harris Survey, November 1964.
2. Harris Survey, June 1966.
3. Harris Survey, October 1972.
4. Harris Survey, May 1971.
5. Harris Survey, October 1972.
6. Harris Survey, November 1972.
7. *The Real Majority,* by Richard M. Scammon and Ben J. Wattenberg (New York: Berkley Publishing Corp., 1970).
8. Harris Survey, October 1964.

9. Based on projections by Louis Harris and Associates.
10. From Harris Surveys: 1960–72.

xv SEEDS OF JOY AND SHADOWS OF DESPAIR

1. Survey for *Time* on repression, conducted by Louis Harris and Associates, September 1970.
2. Harris Survey, February 1973.

INDEX